D1827168

Dynamics of Asian Development

The series situates contemporary development processes and outcomes in Asia in a global context. State intervention as well as neoliberal policies have created unusual economic and social development opportunities. There are also serious setbacks for marginalized communities, workers, the environment, and social justice. The rise of China, India, and new dynamism of South Korea, Indonesia, and Vietnam in East and South East Asia have given a new meaning to Asian development dynamics. Japan's energetic ties with India and Vietnam, Korea joining the OECD's Development Assistance Committee, and China and India's investments and foreign aid in Africa and Latin America are some of the new processes of development whose impact transcends the vast Asian region. Globalization compounds uneven development, affecting macroeconomic stability, internal and international migration, class and caste dynamics, gender relations, regional parity, education and health, agriculture and rural employment, informal sector, innovation possibilities, and equity. Thus the series views development studies as an unfinished agenda of economic, social, political, cultural interactions, and possible transformations in a fluid policy and global contexts. The editor, with the assistance of a distinguished group of development scholars from Asia and elsewhere specializing in a variety of disciplinary and thematic areas, welcomes proposals that critically assess the above-mentioned wide-ranging developing issues facing Asian societies. With Asia's contemporary transformation, the series promotes the understanding of Asia's influence on the prospects of development elsewhere. The editor encourages interdisciplinary, heterodox approaches within the social sciences, and comparative work with solid theoretically informed empirical research. Critical development policy debates in Asia and regional governance issues that have a bearing on development outcomes are also sought.

More information about this series at https://link.springer.com/bookseries/13342

Reena Marwah · Lê Thị Hằng Nga

India–Vietnam Relations

Development Dynamics and Strategic
Alignment

 Springer

Reena Marwah
Jesus and Mary College
University of Delhi
New Delhi, Delhi, India

Lê Thị Hằng Nga
Institute for Indian and Southwest Asian
Studies
Vietnam Academy of Social Sciences
Hanoi, Vietnam

ISSN 2198-9923   ISSN 2198-9931 (electronic)
Dynamics of Asian Development
ISBN 978-981-16-7824-0   ISBN 978-981-16-7822-6 (eBook)
https://doi.org/10.1007/978-981-16-7822-6

This Springer imprint is published by the registered company Springer Nature Singapore Pte Ltd.
The registered company address is: 152 Beach Road, #21-01/04 Gateway East, Singapore 189721,
Singapore

Foreword by the Ambassador of India to Vietnam

Nearly two millennia back, Buddhist monks from India reached Vietnam following the maritime and land routes linking India with Southeast Asia. They were one of the earliest messengers of Buddhism as Lord Buddha's message spread across the region in successive centuries, connecting India philosophically and culturally with these lands. Vietnam's unique geographical location also brought Indian traders and craftsmen who adapted their customs and traditions to the local sociocultural milieu and formed enduring imprints of Indian civilization in the form of Champa or Cham traditions in Central Vietnam.

India–Vietnam exchanges continued ever since over the centuries. They reached a new high again during our freedom struggles and our common endeavors of national rejuvenation in the twentieth century. Exchanges of ideas and shared empathy between the founding fathers of the two nations created a lasting bond of friendship that continues to nurture the ties between our two countries even to this day.

As India and Vietnam celebrate the 50 years of their diplomatic relations in January 2022, this has been a remarkable journey of togetherness as both countries have overcome adversities to pursue nation-building and socioeconomic transformation. The depth of our ties has been affirmed frequently in our relations, most recently when we elevated our relations to a "Comprehensive Strategic Partnership" during the visit of Prime Minister Shri Narendra Modi to Vietnam in September 2016.

This partnership today spans across wide-ranging collaborative pursuits—from political engagement to trade and investment ties, energy cooperation, development partnership, defense and security cooperation, and people-to-people relations. We are building new partnerships in emerging sectors such as information and communication technology, renewable energy, and innovation. The depth of our relations is also reflected in our commitment to take a long-term and strategic view of our relationship based on converging visions and common interest in the peace, stability, and prosperity of our shared Indo-Pacific region.

This book is a joint endeavor by two well-known experts on India–Vietnam relations to trace our common linkages and to explore the path for the future. I hope the book will contribute to a more comprehensive understanding of India–Vietnam ties in the twenty-first century.

Hanoi, Vietnam   H. E. Mr. Pranay Verma
August 2021   Ambassador of India to Vietnam

Foreword by the Ambassador of Vietnam to India

At the outset, I congratulate Prof. Reena Marwah and Dr. Lê Thị Hằng Nga for the thoughtful efforts and valuable insights they have put into Vietnam–India relations, which have been deeply immersed in the book *India–Vietnam Relations: Development Dynamics and Strategic Alignment*. It stands as an excellent scholarship on the topic based on rigorous academic inquiry and in-depth research.

India and Vietnam have interacted with each other amicably throughout the course of history. Civilizational contacts date back to ancient times, and Hinduism has been part of Vietnam over the last 2000 years. Historically speaking, Vietnam and India have never stood against each other and have never had significant enmity. We supported each other mostly. Such a relationship has been cultivated by Ho Chi Minh and Jawaharlal Nehru and generations of leaders in both countries. Vietnamese Prime Minister Pham Van Dong once reckoned the relationship between India and Vietnam "as clear as a blue sky without a single cloud."

Currently, the two countries consider each other as important partners. Cooperation has steadily expanded over the past years, especially since the two countries upgraded their ties to a Comprehensive Strategic Partnership in 2016. India is now one of Vietnam's only three comprehensive strategic partners. Prime Minister Narendra Modi asserted that Vietnam is an important pillar of India's Act East Policy and is an important partner in India's Indo-Pacific Vision.

Mutual political trust has continuously been strengthened with regular exchanges at all levels. Even amidst the COVID-19 pandemic, the two countries have managed a range of dialogues and cooperative programs within the framework of strategic comprehensive partnership. During the summit held on December 21, 2020, Prime Minister Nguyen Xuan Phuc and Prime Minister Narendra Modi adopted the Joint Vision for Peace, Prosperity and People, opening up space for the enhancement of bilateral relations. At the same time, two countries' foreign ministers endorsed a plan of action to implement the partnership.

In terms of defense and security, the two sides have achieved significant progress in implementing the credit line of US $100 million and have been close to the finalization of negotiation of the US $500 credit line, which will be an important element for maritime capacity building cooperation between the two countries. Cooperation is also expanding in joint activities, defense industry, military and language trainings, and peacekeeping operations.

Economically speaking, India is an increasingly important development partner of Vietnam. Our bilateral trade has grown quickly over the last decades, from just US \$200 million in 2000 to US \$12.34 billion in 2019–2020. India has extended aid and loans to several infrastructural projects in Vietnam through its quick-impact scheme. In terms of energy, India's biggest oil corporation, ONGC Videsh, is working productively in offshore oil fields in Vietnam. India is a new leader in the renewable energy, and Vietnam is catching up quickly. The two countries are relatively closer since the launch of the direct flights in 2019.

People-to-people ties are also growing. Both sides have also strengthened institutional linkages such as parliamentary friendship groups, relations between localities, political party exchanges, as well as cultural exchanges and people-to-people contacts. I saw greater number of Indian students interested in going to Vietnam and more Vietnamese students enrolled in Indian universities. Most notably, both sides are in the final stage of installing the bust of Mahatma Gandhi in Ho Chi Minh City and the bust of President Ho Chi Minh in New Delhi. It serves as an important indication of our appreciation of each other's histories and cultures.

Most of these developments are captured in the book very nicely. Throughout the chapters, readers will explore the historical length and depth of Vietnam–India relations in various aspects, from political and diplomatic bonds, defense and economic ties to science, technology, and innovation cooperation, cultural connectivity, and mutual support at multilateral forums. More importantly, they will understand how Vietnam and India have become friends and strategic partners, and how they cooperate with each other to defend the rules-based order. The convergence of strategic interests is discussed. Above all, it is also the shared mindedness for a peaceful and just world.

The book represents truly an important contribution the authors made to mark the 50th anniversary of the establishment of diplomatic ties between Vietnam and India. It is highly recommended for diplomats, policymakers, academics, and those interested in Vietnam–India relations. I once again express my sincere thanks and congratulations to the authors for their pioneering academic endeavor.

New Delhi, India   Ambassador Pham Sanh Chau
July 2021

Preface

Nothing is more precious than independence and liberty.
President Ho Chi Minh

Strength does not come from physical capacity. It comes from an indomitable will.
Mahatma Gandhi

The parallelism between the writings, speeches, and attitudes of the leaders of Vietnam and India manifests in several arenas. From the peasant movements in both countries to an innate love for their nations and a longing for peace, it was the spirit of patriotism and nationalism that their struggles yielded to independence for their peoples in the 1940s.

This book is dedicated to the reminisces of the past as it recognizes that the bilateral relationship has been fortified by fifty years of a diplomatic relationship that has very few equivalents. The present times have witnessed the two countries move into higher echelons of understanding, bulwarked by the strength of their friendship. The edifice of this friendship is ring-fenced with the Buddhist ideals of "the Four Noble Truths," the "Eight Noble Paths," and the Hindu traditions of the Cham people. When culture, religion, and history are embedded within the civilizational intercourse, it is impossible that these deep-rooted connections will not present opportunities in commerce, connectivity, and a shared vision for humanity.

Even as the two countries navigated the turbulent tidal currents set in motion by the superpowers, over the last decade, India seized the opportunity to invigorate its neglected Eastern neighbors through its Act East Policy, while Vietnam sought greater defense and strategic partnership with India. This culminated in the "Comprehensive Strategic Partnership" of 2016. This convergence of interests and inclination to engage bilaterally and within the multilateral forums, with greater resilience, has seen the two countries emerge as natural partners for middle and major powers. The pandemic has unleashed a new narrative on the global order, especially in terms of the threat to multilateral institutions, de-globalization as well as the nosediving relations between USA and China. Given the shared interests of both countries in keeping peace in Asia and the world, the authors have delineated areas of mutual interest which could be strengthened through cooperative endeavors and initiatives.

The book is comprised of eight chapters. Chapter 1 titled, *Histories, Affinities, and Leaders: Vietnam–India Political and Diplomatic Ties*, delineates the struggles of the peoples and articulates their shared past, given that both India and Vietnam have historical roots in the common struggle for liberation from colonial rule and the national struggle for independence. Mahatma Gandhi and Ho Chi Minh, regarded as the Father of Nation in India and Vietnam, respectively, led people in their heroic struggle against colonialism in the two countries. Jawaharlal Nehru forged ties with Ho Chi Minh even before India's independence. India was the chairman of the International Commission for Supervision and Control (ICSC), which was formed pursuant to the Geneva Accord of 1954 to facilitate the peace process in Vietnam. Among the people, there was mutual support for each other. India has also supported Vietnam in several wars in the past. India initially maintained consulate-level relations with the then North and South Vietnams and later established full diplomatic relations with unified Vietnam on January 7, 1972. Relations between the two countries were elevated to the level of "strategic partnership" during the visit of Vietnam's Prime Minister Nguyen Tan Dung to India in July 2007. In 2016, during Prime Minister Modi's visit to Vietnam, bilateral relations were further elevated to a "Comprehensive Strategic Partnership."

The relations have been cemented through our cultural linkages, manifested in architectural sites, religious sentiments, and civilizational treasures. *India–Vietnam Cultural Linkages*, comprising Chap. 2, underlines that the process of indigenization underpins cross-cultural borrowings, further reinforced by cross-cultural contacts. It is to the credit of the mariners, before the coming of the European colonizers, that cultural intercourse took place. As extensive contacts were established by traders, goods travelled along with artifacts of culture including literature, philosophy, belief systems, as well as art and sculpture. India and Vietnam share close cultural affinities through the Champa civilization, also known as the Cham civilization, in Vietnam. Architecture, agriculture, language, religion including Buddhism, and traders provide varied aspects of the Cham civilization. The influence of India in the Cham civilization from archaeology to language underpins an important component of the relations between the two countries. Da Nang, which is well known for its World Heritage Site My Son, is the origin and home of the Hindu Cham civilization which is at least 2000 years old. The kings of Champa constructed temples during the fourth and thirteenth centuries AD; these temples also have Buddhist connections. The scope to further enhance these civilizational and cultural linkages is elucidated in this chapter.

Foreign Policies of Vietnam and India: Articulating Convergences is detailed in Chap. 3. Here, the authors highlight the bilateral engagement with a focus on their strategies to manage big power relations. While India's engagement increased with countries in Southeast Asia post the "Look East" Policy (LEP), there are few countries with which India upgraded its relations within a short span of time. India's relationship with Vietnam developed to a strategic partnership in 2007 and a Comprehensive Strategic Partnership in 2016, soon after India's LEP advanced to the Act

East Policy in 2014. India also seeks the cooperation of Vietnam in groupings as Quad Plus and the Indo-Pacific. India's strategic partnership with Vietnam reflects its high appreciation of the Indian factor in its foreign policy since the Southeast Asian country promoted multilateralism and diversification in its international relations. This chapter analyzes the salience of India in Vietnam's foreign policy since its reform by examining its relations with India in fields of strategic politics, security, and defense which were specified in the important political documents of Communist Party of Vietnam (CPV).

Chapter 4 titled, *India–Vietnam Economic Relations and Development Dynamics* discusses the bilateral economic relations in terms of trade and investment. Despite the historical and cultural linkages, the economic engagement has been rather limited. A detailed analysis of trade flows, investment flows as well as the economic interdependence with China, provides the reader with a holistic view of the challenges which continue to keep this arena in shackles. While navigating the contours of intra-country and inter-country development dynamics, the authors not only assess the scope for deepening the economic engagement but also list specific areas where the complementarity aspects can be leveraged. The decoupling debate within the milieu of the US–China trade war is not neglected.

Chapter 5 discusses the shared vision for partnership in science, technology, and beyond. *India–Vietnam Partnership in Science, Technology, and Innovation* reiterates that scope for synergy between India and Vietnam in the fields of education, science, technology, and innovation is immense, given the imperative for both countries to improve these capabilities. Both countries per capita incomes are almost similar, being just over US $2000 in 2019–2020. While India's English-speaking skills are well known, Vietnam encourages teaching in both English and Chinese. India's digital sector's growth and innovation in information technology have been leveraged by several countries in Southeast Asia, especially Vietnam. The fact that both countries need to invest in new technologies and in the areas of research and development assumes even greater priority given the possibilities emerging from the USA–China trade war and the decoupling from China in the post-pandemic phase.

Chapter 6, *Multilateral Engagement: Envisioning a Peaceful, Cooperative Multilateral Architecture*, posits a disorderly world, marked by a near stalling of the global economy unleashed by the COVID-19 pandemic, with concomitant distress being visible within all economies. Vietnam has demonstrated (by controlling the spread of COVID-19) that if nations are agile and quick to respond, even intractable challenges can be surmounted. Moreover, there is a need for the revival of multilateralism, and countries must work with each other and through the existing multilateral institutions to deal with global challenges. India and Vietnam, as countries with shared interests in the domains of international trade, climate change, cybersecurity, and public health, can work together for the revival of growth in a sustainable way (that also reduces the inequalities among and within nations). This chapter delineates the contribution of India and Vietnam to the multilateral system and projects the pathways for greater cooperation through the different mechanisms in the region and the world.

The power projection of China has incontrovertibly made China the elephant in the room in Asia and beyond. Chapter 7 brings this discussion to the reader through **The China Challenge: Strategic and Security Cooperation.** China has had difficult historical relations with both India and Vietnam.With India, the 1962 war altered the discourse of the "*Bhai Bhai*" narrative that had preceded it. With Vietnam, China has fought several wars, the last one being in 1979.The questions of boundary continue to dominate India and Vietnam's respective bilateral relationships with China. In Southeast Asia, China has held sway over all Southeast Asian countries, despite conflicting territorial claims over the South China Sea as well as support of Communist insurgency. These positive perceptions of China were reinforced in the wake of the Asian financial crisis of 1997/98 and after China's economic rise became more perceptible. Since the turn of this century, and with China in WTO since 2001, its relationship with Southeast Asia is undergoing a significant shift. In the present times, China's "charm offensive" and economic diplomacy as well as its proximity to authoritarian regimes has downplayed territorial disputes while focusing on economic relations with Southeast Asia, through both trade and investment in BRI projects. While this chapter brings in aspects of bilateral cooperation between China and India as well as China and Vietnam, it focuses on overlapping claims. In 2020, an overtly aggressive China has brought in the military and navy, in the Himalayas, to alter the status quo border with India and with Vietnam in the South China Sea, respectively. Given the China challenge, India and Vietnam, as also other like-minded countries in Asia, seek to cooperate for the realization of a peaceful global order. New Delhi was quick to remind China that it stands for the freedom of navigation and overflight, and unimpeded lawful commerce in the international waters in accordance with international law. These contemporary and current issues have been discussed.

Vietnam and India: A Futuristic Perspective is comprised within Chap. 8. Given that the world order is in a state of flux, the United States is declining "relatively," and China is not yet in a position to emerge as the leader, multipolarity will prevail. Hence, in the near to medium term, the international situation will be characterized by the chaos of "no polarity," "Warring States," and "transition," with cooperation between major countries becoming more difficult. This presents an opportunity for countries as India and Vietnam, to come together through trilaterals or minilaterals, to engage through cultural, economic, educational, technological, and strategic pursuits.

At the bilateral level, opportunities and specific areas for joint cooperation have been addressed in this chapter. India has had several achievements in the S&T sector, such as in space and IT. Cooperation in these fields would help capacity building in Vietnam. Moreover, bilateral investment and trade present significant opportunities. Vietnam must be embedded in India's Act East Policy as a strategic partner in the bilateral and multilateral spheres; enhancing people-to-people exchanges through joint research, military cooperation, and joint initiatives for capacity building. These would result in a more enhanced Indian presence in the region.

A futuristic perspective has been embedded in the narrative, seeking to answer questions as:

a. Given the historical and cultural affinities and repositories of shared values between India and Vietnam, how can this partnership be further strengthened? Can the relationship be upgraded within the parameters of India's Act East Policy and beyond?
b. How are India and Vietnam re-assessing their economic and strategic partnership in the context of the transforming world order?
c. What are the pathways in which multilateralism and regional institutional frameworks will embrace both these countries?
d. Could India and Vietnam afford to rethink their economic relations with China, given that there is a potential wariness of China's growing economic footprint and possession of their key resources on land and on sea?

Ultimately, it is the indomitable will of the leadership that the bilateral relationship has been nurtured through five decades and will further mature in the succeeding decades. Independence and liberty, values taught by forefathers, will ensure that the sailing is smooth.

New Delhi, India   Reena Marwah
Hà Nội, Vietnam   Lê Thị Hằng Nga

Acknowledgements

This volume titled, *India–Vietnam Relations: Development Dynamics and Strategic Alignment*, seeks to commemorate fifty years of India–Vietnam diplomatic relations. Our endeavor to document the past and present and project the future trajectory of this relationship could not have been accomplished without the unflinching support of our governments, especially the diplomatic missions in both countries. Despite the limitation of conducting face-to-face interviews due to the pandemic, we have been fortunate to have received kind guidance, mentoring, and knowledge from several senior experts, policymakers, officials, members of the Indian diaspora, and friends in Vietnam and India. We are particularly thankful to the Indian Embassy in Vietnam and Vietnamese Embassy in India for their magnanimous cooperation. Discussions and candid sharing of views helped to enrich our understanding of the subject. We are grateful to each one mentioned in the book.

We are particularly grateful to Ambassador Pranay Verma, Indian Ambassador in Hanoi, for his continued guidance and for encouraging us by writing the foreword for our book. We are also truly grateful to Ambassador Pham Sanh Chau, for his kind indulgence and valuable insights on several issues of significance. By penning the forewords for our book, the two ambassadors have lent the volume unequivocal support, veracity, and commitment in taking this bilateral relationship to greater heights. Vietnam's former ambassador to India, Dr. Ton Sinh Thanh's candid sharing of ideas from his experiences has been invaluable for our study. Our sincere thanks are also due to Prof. Ngo Xuan Bình, Prof. G. Jayachandra Reddy, Assoc. Prof. Do Thu Ha, Dr. Satoru Nagao, Dr. Tillotama Mukherjee, Mr. Amit Saxena, Mrs. Sadhna Saxena, and Mr. Nguyen Van Nien for enriching the contents of our book, with their learned views. Our gratitude is also due to Mr. Sushil Prasad at the Embassy of India to Vietnam, Dr. Do Thanh Hai, Deputy Chief of Mission, Embassy of Vietnam, New Delhi; and Mr. Trieu Hong Quang, Ph.D. student at Eötvös Loránd University (ELTE), Budapest, Hungary.

We are also grateful to the Institute for Indian and Southwest Asian Studies, Vietnam Academy of Social Sciences, and Swami Vivekananda Cultural Centre, Hanoi, for the various academic seminars and cultural activities that provided valuable inputs to the book. We are blessed to have been in the midst of people who have keen interests in India–Vietnam relations and cultural linkages. Much of the materials used in writing this book have been presented at conferences or seminars at Hanoi, Ho Chi Minh City, New Delhi, Bangkok, Manila, Chiang Mai, Perth, Erfurt, by the authors. We must also express our thanks to the participants at the discussions of various online seminars in recent years of COVID-19 pandemic who have significantly helped in enriching our understanding and keeping us updated on the developments of India–Vietnam relations over the years.

Our families have been our constant strength and have encouraged us in every way to complete this seminal work. This volume also acknowledges the pivotal contribution of several authors, who have contributed to augmenting our knowledge of the subject.

This book would not have been possible without the kind cooperation of the production and editorial team of Springer. Each one deserves our sincere appreciation.

Prof. Reena Marwah
Dr. Lê Thị Hằng Nga

List of Interviewees

1. H.E. Ambassador Pham Sanh Chau, Ambassador of Vietnam in India.
2. Mr. Amit Saxena, Former Chairman of the Indian Chamber of Commerce in Ho Chi Minh City. Lives with his family in Ho Chi Minh City since 1987. Interview to authors on August 10, 2021.
3. Mr. Nguyen Van Nien, Director of Vina Tan A Joint Stock Company, Hanoi, on August 11, 2021.
4. Ms. Sadhna Saxena, Hindi Lecturer, Department of Indian Studies, Faculty of Oriental Studies, Ho Chi Minh City University of Social Sciences and Humanities. She shared her views with the authors on August 10, 2021.
5. Prof. Do Thu Ha, Head of Department of Indian Studies, Faculty of Oriental Studies, Hanoi University of Social Sciences and Humanities, Vietnam National University. Interview to authors on August 13, 2021.
6. Prof. Ngo Xuan Bình, Former Director-General of Institute for Indian and Southwest Asian Studies, Vietnam Academy of Social Sciences. Interview to authors on April 15, 2021.
7. Ambassador Dr. Ton Sinh Thanh, Former Ambassador of Vietnam to India, Nepal, Bhutan, and Sri Lanka. He is currently senior lecturer at Vietnam Academy of Diplomacy, Ministry of Foreign Affairs of Vietnam. Interview to authors on April 15, 2021.
8. Dr. Satoru Nagao, Visiting Fellow at Hudson Institute. His research area is US–Japan–India security cooperation, interview on May 8, 2021.
9. Prof. G. Jayachandra Reddy, Director and Chairman, Board of Studies, UGC Centre for Southeast Asian and Pacific Studies, Sri Venkateswara University, Tirupati, India. Interview to authors on April 15 and 20, 2021 15/04/2021 and 20/04/21.
10. Dr. Tillotama Mukherjee, Assistant Professor and Head of Department of Political Science, Syamaprasad College, Calcutta University. Interview to authors on April 15, 2021.

Contents

About the Authors

Reena Marwah (M.Phil., Delhi University; Ph.D., India, International Business) is Professor at Jesus and Mary College, Delhi University. Among her research interests are international relations issues of China, South East Asia, and India. In addition to several chapters and articles published in books/journals, she is Author/Co-author/Co-editor of 15 books and monographs including *On China by India: From a Civilization to a Nation State, 2012*, (Cambria Press, USA); *Transforming South Asia :Imperatives for Action* , (Knowledge World, India) 2014; *The Global Rise of Asian Transformation*, (Palgrave Macmillan) 2014. Her latest co-edited book is *China Studies in South and Southeast Asia: Pro-China, Objectivism, and Balance*, (2018) Editors: Chih-yu Shih, Prapin Manomaiviboo, and Reena Marwah; (World Scientific Publishing Company, Singapore). Her most recent books are *Re-imagining India Thailand Relations: A multilateral and bilateral perspective (2020) and China's Economic Footprint in South and Southeast Asia (2021).* Both books are published by World Scientific Publishers, Singapore. She is Founding Editor of Millennial Asia, a tri-annual journal on Asian Studies of the Association of Asia Scholars, published by Sage.

Dr. Lê Thị Hằng Nga is Deputy Editor-in-chief, in charge of Journal for Indian and Asian Studies, Institute for Indian and Southwest Asian Studies (VIISAS), Vietnam Academy of Social Sciences (VASS). Her research areas include Indian history, foreign policy and relations, Indian thought and philosophy, Vietnam-India relations. She has been coordinator and presenter at many international conferences in Vietnam, India, Thailand, Australia, Philippines, Germany, Japan, Hong Kong, Taiwan. She has published many articles in domestic and international peer-reviewed journals. Some of her recent published books include: "India's Relations with some Regional Countries and Implications for Vietnam" (Editor, Social Science Publishing House, Hanoi, 2020); "Indo-US Relations (1947–1991)" (Author, Political and Truth Publishing House, Hanoi, 2018); "Buddhist Women with Journalism" (Co-editors, Social Science Publishing House, 2021); "Hind Swaraj—Indian Home Rule" in Vietnamese (Translator, Social Science Publishing House, 2021).

Abbreviations

AAGC	Asia-Africa Growth Corridor
ADB	Asian Development Bank
ADIZ	Air Defense Identification Zone
ADMM	ASEAN Defence Ministers' Meeting
AEP	Act East Policy
AERB	Atomic Energy Regulatory Board
AI	Artificial Intelligence
AIFTA	ASEAN-India Free Trade Area
AIIB	Asian Infrastructure Investment Bank
APEC	Asia-Pacific Economic Cooperation
ARC-ICT	Advanced Resource Centre in Information and Communications Technology
ASEAN	Association of Southeast Asian Nations
ASEM	Asia–Europe Meeting
BBIN	Bangladesh, Bhutan, India, Nepal (Motor Vehicles Agreement)
BDN	Broadband Data Network
BECA	Basic Exchange and Cooperation
BOT	Build–Operate–Transfer
BRI	Belt and Road Initiative
BT	Build–Transfer
BTO	Build–Transfer–Operate
CAGR	Compound Annual Growth Rate
CDAC	Centre for Development of Advanced Computing
CDRI	Coalition for Disaster Resilient Infrastructure
CENTO	Central Treaty Organization
CMLV	Cambodia, Myanmar, Laos and Vietnam
CoC	Code of Conduct
COMCASA	Communications Compatibility and Security Agreement
CPEC	China–Pakistan Economic Corridor
CPI	Communist Party of India

CPTPP	Comprehensive and Progressive Agreement for Trans-Pacific Partnership
CPV	Communist Party of Vietnam
DBT	Department of Biotechnology
DoC	Declaration on the Conduct of Parties
DPIIT	Department of Promotion of Industry and Internal Trade
DRTTS	Data Reception and Tracking and Telemetry Station
DRVN	Democratic Republic of Vietnam
DTF	Distance to Frontier (Score)
EAMF	Expanded ASEAN Maritime Forum
EAS	East Asia Summit
EEP	Educational Exchange Programme
EEZ	Exclusive Economic Zone
EPC	Engineering Procurement and Construction (Contract)
EPQI	Expanded Partnership for Quality Infrastructure (Initiative)
EPZs	Export Processing Zones
EU	European Union
EVFTA	EU-Vietnam Free Trade Agreement
EWEC	East–West Economic Corridor
FDI	Foreign Direct Investment
FOIP	Free and Open Indo-Pacific
FTA	Free Trade Agreement
FY	Finance Year
GCSS	General Cultural Scholarship Scheme
GDP	Gross Domestic Product
GIS	Geographic Information System
GOI	Government of India
HAUFO	Hanoi Union of Friendship Organization
HDI	Human Development Index
HEPZA	Ho Chi Minh City Export Processing and Industrial Zones Authority
I.Z.s	Industrial Zones
ICC	Indian Cultural Centre
ICC	International Control Commission
ICCR	Indian Council for Cultural Relations
ICJ	International Court of Justice
ICS	Institute of Chinese Studies
ICWA	Indian Council of World Affairs
IGHCL	Indira Gandhi High-tech Crime Lab
IMF	International Monetary Fund
IORA	Indian Ocean Rim Association
I-P	Indo-Pacific
IPOI	Indo-Pacific Oceans Initiative
ISEAS	Yusof Ishak Institute (Institute for Southeast Asian Studies)
ISRO	Indian Space Research Organisation
IT	Information Technology

ITEC	Indian Technical and Economic Cooperation
JBIC	Japan Bank for International Cooperation
JICA	Japan International Cooperation Agency
JVI	Japan–Vietnam–India (Trilateral Cooperation)
LAC	Line of Actual Control
LEFASO	(Vietnam) Leather, Footwear and Handbag Association
LEMOA	Logistics Exchange Memorandum of Agreement
LEP	Look East Policy
LMC	Lancang–Mekong Cooperation
M&A	Mergers and Acquisitions
MEA	Ministry of External Affairs
MFN	Most Favoured Nation
MGC	Mekong–Ganga Cooperation
MGCSS	Mekong–Ganga Cooperation Scholarship Scheme
MNCs	Multinational Corporations or Companies
MNRE	Ministry of New and Renewable Energy
MOU	Memorandum of Understanding
MRC	Mekong River Commission
NATO	North Atlantic Treaty Organization
NBDS	National Biotechnology Development Strategy
NE	Northeast (Region)
NIIT	National Institute of Information Technology
NTT	Nippon Telegraph and Telephone
ODA	Official Development Assistance
OECD	Organisation for Economic Co-operation and Development
ONGC	Oil and Natural Gas Corporation
ORF	Observer Research Foundation
PCA	Permanent Court of Arbitration
PLA	People's Liberation Army
PLI	Production-Linked Incentive
PQI	Partnership for Quality
PRC	People's Republic of China
PRG	Provisional Revolutionary Government
PSC	Production Sharing Contract
PSU	Power Supply Unit
PVN	Vietnam Oil and Gas Group
QIPs	Quick-Impact Projects
QSD	Quadrilateral Security Dialogue
R&D	Research and Development
RCEP	Regional Comprehensive Economic Partnership
RVN	Republic of Vietnam
S&T	Science and Technology
SAARC	South Asian Association for Regional Cooperation
SAGAR	Security and Growth for All
SCRI	Supply Chain Resilience Initiative

SCS	South China Sea
SDNT	Single Draft Negotiating Text
SEA	Southeast Asia
SEANWFZ	Southeast Asia Nuclear-Weapon-Free Zone Treaty
SEATO	Southeast Asia Treaty Organization
SHTP	Saigon Hi-Tech Park
SIPRI	Stockholm International Peace Research Institute
SMEs	Small and Medium Enterprises
SVCC	Swami Vivekananda Cultural Centre
TPP	Trans-Pacific Partnership
TPSA	(America) Tibetan Policy and Support Act
UK	United Kingdom
UN	United Nations
UNCLOS	United Nations Convention on the Law of the Sea
UNCTAD	United Nations Conference on Trade and Development
UNESCO	United Nations Educational Scientific and Cultural Organization
UNO	United Nations Organization
UNSC	United Nations Security Council
US	United States
USA	United States of America
USD	US Dollar
USSR	Union of Soviet Socialist Republics
VAFIE	Vietnam Association of Foreign Investment Enterprises
VARANS	Vietnam Agency for Radiation and Nuclear Safety
VASS	Vietnam Academy of Social Sciences
VBS	Vietnam Buddhist Sangha
VCOSA	Vietnam Cotton and Spinning Association
VIFA	Vietnam–India Friendship Association
VIISAS	Vietnam Institute for Indian and Southwest Asian Studies
WEF	World Economic Forum
WHO	World Health Organization
WTO	World Trade Organization

List of Figures

List of Images

List of Tables

Chapter 1
Histories, Affinities, and Leaders: Vietnam–India Political and Diplomatic Ties

1.1 Historical Background of India–Vietnam Relations

India and Vietnam both have unique historiographies, marked by struggles for independence. Both countries have had visionary leaders who believed in the strength of their peoples to stand up to the forces which sought to divide and rule. This chapter provides insights into contemporary relations undergirded in history, with sterling contributions of leaders also documented.

1.1.1 Early Contacts

It has been emphasized repeatedly by leaders, peoples, and scholars of both India and Vietnam that the two countries have had lively cultural and civilizational contacts in early history through Buddhism and Hinduism. This will be the focus of chapter two. It is sufficient to mention here that these early cultural and civilization linkages did have some political implications. The political meaning of the early contacts between the two countries can be seen through the formation of several well-known kingdoms such as the Funan and Champa Kingdoms in South Central Vietnam. The idea of kingship, the form of the government (Mandala system) from India, was adopted by the early kings in Vietnam.

During the medieval period, there was some disruption of direct communication due to the invasion of Islam. However, the flow of ideas of Buddhism and Hinduism continues its task of sustaining the bonds of friendship between the two countries.

© The Author(s), under exclusive license to Springer Nature Singapore Pte Ltd. 2021
R. Marwah and L. T. Hằng Nga, *India–Vietnam Relations*, Dynamics of Asian Development, https://doi.org/10.1007/978-981-16-7822-6_1

1.1.2 Colonial Period

The bilateral interaction was revived in the nineteenth century when the two countries shared common interests and supported each other in their struggles for independence. In India, the 1857 Revolt brought about new changes in the British domination, and the national movement in India started its new phase. In 1858, the French arrived in Vietnam and began the process of colonization. At this time, India was already under British domination. The foreign domination in both countries generated the national spirit to fight against the exploitation of outsiders, which culminated in the national movements in India and Vietnam. The Indian National Movement impacted the national movement of Vietnam to some extent. The nationalist leaders of both countries perceived that the movements of both countries were intertwined. Nehru believed that the future of India was closely linked with that of Asia, especially Southeast Asia (Reddy, 2009, p. 5).

In the early decades of the twentieth century, the popular mass movement of Mahatma Gandhi inspired the nationalist movement of Vietnam. Ho Chi Minh wrote an article in French newspapers describing the nationalist activities in India. He wrote on *Le Paria* (a French newspaper) No. 33, April–May 1925 article titled "Rule Britania" (Minh, 2011, pp. 350–352; Toan et al., 2019, p. 43 and p. 519):

> …Earlier this year, the official capital of India suddenly felt obliged to apply the "Defence of India Act" in 1918, an extraordinary act that imposed further curfew. Under the regime, all the British officials and policemen, from the inspector level upwards, have the right to arrest and detain suspended Indians, irrespective of any procedures or judging. Within only one morning, high schools and students' dormitories and some 100 buildings were examined. Hundreds of arrests occurred. The army and police occupied offices of Indian companies. The British rulers in Bengal intended to deal with all political difficulties by violence.

In another article published in the *Inprekorr* (French) No. 28 dated March 17, 1928, Ho Chi Minh (using nickname *Wang*) wrote about the Hartal (to boycott the Simon Commission) in India (Minh, 2011, pp. 350–352; Le Van Toan et al. 2019, p. 45 and p. 521):

> …Despite principals' threats, ten thousand students attended the rally. The police did their jobs. More than 80 people were injured, including several who were seriously wounded, while around a hundred protesters were arrested.
>
> In Bombay, Madras, Ahmedabad, etc., all the office buildings were closed, everything was stopped. In large centers, there were rallies of up to 50,000 people. Many armed soldiers and police officers were sent to guard strategic locations in cities; armored cars patrolled the streets. In Madras, police fired on the protesters, two were dead, and 20 others were injured.…

Other articles written by Ho Chi Minh include *"Workers' Movement in India," "Indian Peasants," and "Peasant and Workers Movements in India,"* all published in *Inprekorr* in 1928. Certainly, these lucid, concise, and sharp articles on India's national struggle for independence written by Ho Chi Minh had a positive mobilizing effect on the Vietnamese people's struggle during the colonial period.

The Indian and Vietnamese nationalists had opportunities to meet each other when the Congress of Oppressed Nationalities was held in Brussels in February 1927. At this Congress, Jawaharlal Nehru met Ho Chi Minh for the first time. One year later, Jawaharlal Nehru's father, Motilal Nehru met the Vietnamese leader in Brussels while participating in the meeting of the Executive Committee of the League against imperialism. Both nurtured a good impression about each other, and Ho Chi Minh would often fondly recall his meetings with Motilal Nehru (Reddy, 2009, p. 5). Through these meetings, Ho Chi Minh had special respect for the Nehru family. Since then, Vietnamese nationalists occasionally attended the meetings of the Indian National Congress.

During the Second World War, the Vietnamese were among the Southeast Asian peoples who contributed to the independence movement of Subhash Chandra Bose. At that time, Vietnam was under French colonialism, and the French Government did not allow the setting up of a branch of the Indian Independence League in Sai Gon and Hanoi. Yet, the old Indian Association of Vietnam could carry out some of its activities and helped to collect about 1.5 million USD for Subhash Chandra Bose's movement (Minh, 2011, pp. 401–402). In 1945, the Provisional Government of Subhash Chandra Bose was allowed to set up a radio station as well as a purchasing mission in the city of Sai Gon.

On January 21, 1947, "Vietnam Day" was observed by students in India. The day was marked by a spirit of solidarity. Crowds of students demonstrated in front of the Consulate General of France in Bombay and Calcutta. They shouted slogans urging the French troops to withdraw from Vietnam. British soldiers opened fire and shot dead two Calcutta students, namely Sri Dhiranjan Sen and Sri Amalendu Ghosh, at the University of Calcutta (Sakhuja, 2011, p. 163). Sarat Chandra Bose, Subhash Chandra Bose's elder brother, proposed to recruit volunteers for Vietnam in fighting against the French. However, the proposal was not approved by J. Nehru as he was afraid that it would make the international issue more complicated (Reddy, 2009, p. 7).

On September 2, 1947, the interim government was established in India, and J. Nehru became the leader of the newly founded government. On this occasion, President Ho Chi Minh sent a congratulatory message to Jawaharlal Nehru. Ho Chi Minh wrote (Toan et al., 2019, p. 61 and p. 535):

> I am very happy to hear that the first free Indian Government was established. On behalf of the Democratic Republic of Vietnam, I would like to extend congratulations and best wishes. I strongly believe that the cordial ties between the two countries would help to bring happiness to the two nations...

Nehru responded the message with enthusiasm and conveyed to the President of Vietnam that he looked forward to promoting "close fraternal relations between free India and Democratic Vietnam" (Reddy, 2009, p. 7). In December 1946, Nehru stated that India would stand side by side with Vietnam in the country's national movement and that he was against the French's attempts to suppress the Vietnamese nationalists (Prasad, 1979, p. 198).

Hence, both India and Vietnam were under the domination of colonialism in the latter half of the nineteenth century and the first half of the twentieth century. Their friendship is also rooted in similar plights of colonial rule, struggle for independence and freedom, and shared values and benefits in rebuilding and protecting the countries. The mutual sympathy between the people who suffered from colonialism and imperialism is an important factor that binds India–Vietnam together.

1.2 India–Vietnam Political and Diplomatic Relations During the Cold War

Looking at the major events in Vietnam's Cold War history, it can be inferred that India–Vietnam relations went through two major phases: Phase 1 from 1947 to 1975, which is marked by Vietnam's great wars against the French and the U.S. and the division of the country into two Vietnams. Phase 2 is from 1975 to 1991, during which the country was liberated from foreign domination and got unified and began its reconstruction period. Grounded in terms of the Indian leadership, relations between India and Vietnam during the Cold War may also be divided into periods under Prime Minister Jawaharlal Nehru, L. B. Shastri, Indira Gandhi, Morarji Desai, and Rajiv Gandhi.

1.2.1 India–Vietnam Relations Under Jawaharlal Nehru (1947–1964)

Between 1947 and 1954, India under Nehru followed a policy of neutrality and noninvolvement in Vietnam as during this time, Vietnam had two governments (the Democratic Republic of Vietnam or DRVN and Republic of Vietnam or RVN). In 1947, India organized the Asian Relations Conference in New Delhi, and both the North and South regimes of Vietnam were invited to join the conference.

In 1954, India was concerned about the increasing conflict between France and Vietnam and the involvement of major powers, including the US and China, in Vietnam's internal affairs. The news of the serious battles at Dien Bien Phu came to India as a shock. The US planned to retaliate by the "United Action" in collaboration with France and Great Britain. In this situation, Nehru had to give up his policy of restraint. In his address to the Indian Parliament on February 22, 1954, he appealed for a ceasefire in Vietnam (Thien, 1960, p. 130). A six-point proposal was given in his address, and this proposal was later approved by the Colombo powers. It provided the basis of later negotiations on issues in Indochina. The proposal with six major points was: (1) to ensure a climate of peace and conciliation, (2) a ceasefire is desired, (3) to support independence of the three Indochina states, (4) to support direct negotiations between the parties immediately and principally concerned, (5) to ensure nonintervention, and (6) to inform the U.N. and to use its good offices (Reddy, 2009, p. 9).

1.2.1.1 India's Role in the International Control Commission (ICC)

The Geneva Conference on the Indochina issue was organized between May 9 and July 21, 1954. V. K. Krishna Menon was assigned by J. Nehru to take the responsibility of putting across opinions to help in resolving the Indochina conundrum. Krishna Menon reached Geneva on April 23, 1954. Initially, he planned to stay in Geneva for a few days, but he ended up staying there for three weeks (Reddy, 2009, p. 10). India had an important role in supervising the Geneva settlement of the Indochina issue (Sardesai, 1968, p. 47). Later, New Delhi were among the few places in the world where negotiations of the Indochina issue were held. In accordance with the Geneva Agreements, a ceasefire was declared. Thereby, Vietnam was divided into two parts, i.e., North and South Vietnams at the 17th parallel. India, as a credible nonaligned power, was appointed as the Chairman of the International Control Commission (ICC) along with two other countries, i.e., Poland and Canada. The ICC's task was to provide supervision of the ceasefire. In addition, it had to arrange for organizing elections by July 1956 in order to reunify the two Vietnams. The conference finally declared that Vietnam was divided provisionally, and it would hold elections by July 1956 (after two years) in order to unify the country.

It was India's desire that the Geneva provisions were implemented fully so that peace was ensured in Vietnam. However, despite India's support of election for the reunification of Vietnam, it finally agreed with the decision of the co-chairman that the election is postponed indefinitely. Thus, the political settlement of Vietnam was not carried out as scheduled. India's attitude might be explained by the fact that, at that time, India's foreign policy concerns were governed by global considerations rather than by the region's immediate interests (Sardesai, 1968, p. 254). It is to be noted that the majority of ICC's staff was Indians. Canada and Poland had about 160 people, while the number of Indians was 1086 as of March 25, 1955 (Reddy, 2009, p. 11). As the Chairman of ICC, India was to keep the even balance among the parties. Thus, it could easily become the target of criticism whenever ICC put forward unpopular decisions. India performed its duties well until mid-1955. From mid-1956 to the end of 1958, ICC was losing effectiveness as it could not settle the increasing opposition of South Vietnam. In the years 1959 and 1960, the increasing involvement of the US in Vietnam and the incurring hostilities between the North and South regimes of Vietnam led to the intense division among the parties which was reflected on ICC's discussion table. South Vietnam was against the Geneva Agreements, especially the election-related agreements. In addition, it was against the introducing of war equipment and troops and military bases from outside. As time went by, India had lesser chance to function effectively as Chairman of ICC when the scope of conflict in Vietnam was expanding. From 1965 onwards, India's stand toward the two Vietnams underwent some changes. India turned more critical toward South Vietnam and the US as they did not comply with the terms of the Geneva Agreements. India and ICC often criticized the US's bombings on Vietnam. In 1972, when India decided to upgrade its diplomatic mission in Hanoi to full ambassadorial level, there were fierce demonstration in front of the ICC headquarters in South Vietnam. The U.S. also protested against India's upgrading of diplomatic representation with North Vietnam.

However, it is noted that, as Chairman of the ICC, India could play the sterling role of a contributor to peace in Indochina, albeit with several challenges. In the beginning, it could do much to contribute to conflict resolution in Indochina. Later on, it could not be very effective in getting the provisions of Geneva Agreement implemented because South Vietnam became more and more hostile, and the US was involved more intensely in Vietnam (Reddy, 2009, p. 11).

1.2.1.2   India's Relations with South Vietnam

In 1956, India's relations with South Vietnam improved steadily. In May 1956, the Government of South Vietnam accorded India the benefit of the most-favored-nation. In August 1956, a South Vietnam trade delegation went to India to explore economic cooperation opportunities and to promote South Vietnam–India relations. The efforts of South Vietnam trade delegation were appreciated by India and thus soon after India and South Vietnam decided to open the Consulate General of South Vietnam in Delhi in February 1957. The year 1957 was remarkable in India–South Vietnam relations when the Vice President of India, Radhakrishnan made a visit to South Vietnam in September. During the visit, he invited President Ngo Dinh Diem to visit India at a suitable time.

President of South Vietnam Ngo Dinh Diem paid a reciprocal visit to India two months later, on November 4, 1957. Following Ngo Dinh Diem's visit, a number of Vietnamese engineers went to India to learn Indian hydroelectric projects. As a result of the cordial political relations, trade between India and South Vietnam also increased in 1957 and 1958. In the following year, a high-ranking delegation of South Vietnam went to India to participate in the India-1958 Exhibition which was held in Delhi. From the Indian side, there were two delegations visiting South Vietnam in 1958 to explore the possibilities of cooperation with the latter. During the 1962 India–China border war, South Vietnam, in contrast to North Vietnam, supported India and sided with her in condemning the Chinese attack. Evidently, India's relations with South Vietnam were on a positive trajectory.

1.2.1.3   India's Relations with North Vietnam

North Vietnam was fully cooperative with the ICC in supporting the implementation of the Geneva Agreements between 1954 and 1955; hence during this time, India had cordial relations with North Vietnam. Relations between India and North Vietnam were enhanced in October 1954, when J. Nehru became the first foreign leader to visit Hanoi on his way to Beijing.[1] During the visit, President Ho Chi Minh informed the Indian Prime Minister that he would provide maximum cooperation for the implementation of the Geneva Agreements. He also added that he would endeavor to settle the issues by peaceful, nonviolent means without any outside interference

---

[1] On September 3, 2016, Prime Minister Modi also visited Hanoi before his visit to Beijing.

(Sardesai, 1968, pp. 76–77). In April 1955, Foreign Minister of North Vietnam Pham Van Dong made a visit to India and reassured India of its cooperation in implementing Geneva Agreements (Sardesai, 1968, p. 88). In September 1957, S. Radhakrishnan, the then Vice President of India, visited North Vietnam, and he was given a very warm reception in Hanoi. Although India was also suffering from food shortages, it extended its help to North Vietnam by sending 7000 tons of rice to Hanoi (Reddy, 2009, p. 16). Between February 5–13, 1958, President Ho Chi Minh visited India and was given a rousing reception and was received at the airport by Nehru. Another landmark in India–Vietnam relations in 1959 was the official visit by the President of India, Rajendra Prasad, to both the North and South of Vietnam.

Towards the end of 1959, India changed its attitude toward both North and South Vietnams. This happened due to the subversive activities in South Vietnam and North Vietnam's pro-Chinese attitude in the India–China border war of 1962. The 1962 border war between India and China created some misunderstanding between India and North Vietnam because of the latter's decision to support China. The reason for Vietnam's support of China was that it received great support from China and the former Soviet Union during its war efforts against the United States. Possibly, Vietnam had limited option at that time (Chopra, 2000, p. 218). India was evidently disappointed. However, North Vietnam was also disappointed with India when she joined Canada in voting against North Vietnam in the ICC's special report of 1962 which criticized the role of North Vietnam in the subversive incidents in South Vietnam. This led to North Vietnam's suspicion of India. North Vietnam was not happy with India's close relations with South Vietnam. Vietnam's position during the India–China border dispute could be explained by taking into account the effect of the intensifying Cold War, and Vietnam was made a battle ground among the super powers.

Among the newspapers that published news on India–China border war, *Nhân Dân* (*The People*—a popular newspaper in Vietnam) issued on October 17, 1962, requoted the Pakistan's *Reviewer* issued on October 8, 1962, which expressed its support to China. The reaction towards India was negative, that India was "aggressively causing conflicts with China" (Cong & Thanh, 2021). Given the global context of the Cold War, China's material and spiritual support to North Vietnam, and India's cordial ties with South Vietnam as well as North Vietnam's war of resistance against the U.S.; this attitude of North Vietnam toward the India–China border war was understandable. During the 1962 India–China border war, North Vietnam was hostile, while South Vietnam extended support to India. Different reactions between North and South Vietnam toward the India–China border war in 1962 showed ideological polarization in Vietnam which was a manifestation of the Cold War in Vietnam.

Though this position was not published widely in Vietnamese media of the time, it was shared among the politicians and academicians (Huê, 2010).[2] Hence, when the China–India dispute manifested as a full-scale war and India had to appeal for

---

[2] In an interview between the authors and Prof. Do Thu Ha, Head of Department of Indian Studies, Faculty of Oriental Studies, Hanoi University of Social Sciences and Humanities, Vietnam National University on 13 August 2021, Prof. Ha expressed similar view.

military assistance from the US and Western countries, North Vietnam openly sided with China in condemning "Indian expansionism" and of "colluding" with the imperialists (Sardesai, 1968, p. 194). Despite Vietnam soon softening its criticism of India, relations between India and North Vietnam had been adversely impacted. The Indian Consulate General in Hanoi had to reduce its staff to a large extent, and the movement of the Indian staff was to be watched closely.

In the early years of J. Nehru's government, India had cordial relations with both North and South Vietnams. But toward the end of 1950s and early 1960s, India's relations with South Vietnam was friendly but its relations with North Vietnam was rather hostile due to the China factor.

1.2.2   India–Vietnam Relations Under L. B. Shastri (1964–1966)

When Lal Bahadur Shastri came to power in India in 1964, he continued Nehru's policy of nonalignment. Shastri retained many members of Nehru's Council of Ministers. With a socialist background, Shastri built closer ties with the Soviet Union. Shastri's tenure as Prime Minister of India lasted only nineteen months due to his sudden death in Tashkent (then the Soviet Union).

Prime Minister Shastri supported North Vietnam's cause in the war against the U.S. In 1964, before he visited the U.S., Shastri appealed to the U.S. to restore peace. Shastri tried hard to persuade other countries to convene a Geneva-type conference. Being annoyed with India's position in Vietnam, the U.S. requested for a postponement of the scheduled visit of Prime Minister Shastri to the U.S. which was considered by India as an embarrassment (Nga, 2018). Thus, India under Shastri supported North Vietnam at the cost of embittering its bilateral relations with the U.S. During this time, the Indian people were totally in favor of Vietnam which was proved by the fact that the people in Kolkata city echoed the slogan of "My name is Vietnam, Your name is Vietnam, All of our names is Vietnam" (Amar Nam, Tomar Nam, Vietnam, Vietnam) (Sakhuja, 2011, p. 160 and p. 163).

India's support of North Vietnam at the cost of its relations with the U.S. was a remarkable proof that India was a reliable partner of Vietnam in times of need. This support may have stemmed from India's independent and nonaligned foreign policy in the context of the ongoing Cold War. But at the same time, it may have been the result of the consideration that India's support of Vietnam would prevent the latter from inching even closer to China, as had happened during the India–China border war in 1962.

1.2.3   India–Vietnam Relations Under Indira Gandhi (1966–1977)

When Indira Gandhi became Prime Minister of India in 1966, the Indian position regarding Vietnam and the U.S. bombing of Vietnam gradually changed. Indira Gandhi's growing proximity with the Soviet Union helped improve India's relations with North Vietnam. When the U.S. bombed Hanoi and Haiphong in June 1966, India fiercely condemned the U.S.'s bombing activities. Since then, India's policy on Vietnam was to call for an unconditional bombing halt in the country. During Indira Gandhi's visit to the Soviet Union in July 1966, she had a joint communiqué with Kosygin, USSR's Prime Minister, in which she urged for an "immediate cessation of bombings and the resolution of the Vietnam conflict within the framework of Geneva accords" (Thayer & Thakur, 1992, p. 237). Indira Gandhi also gave several proposals in order to end the Vietnam War. She brought about a seven-point proposal which called "for (1) convening of a Geneva Conference by the Co-Chairmen, (2) immediate ending of bombing in North Vietnam to be followed by cessation of hostilities, (3) the ICC to safeguard the standstill arrangement, (4) willingness of India, as Chairman of the ICC, to accept additional responsibility, (5) withdrawal of all foreign forces in Vietnam, (6) the Geneva Conference to guarantee the integrity and independence of Indochina states, and (7) rehabilitation and development plan to repair the ravages of war" (Das, 1972, p. 69; also see Nga, 2018). Indira Gandhi was of the opinion that the Indochina war was "the most pointless conflict" of modern times and appreciated the heroic resistance of the Vietnamese people against foreign domination (Reddy, 2009, p. 22).

Changes in India's position on the Vietnam War led to transformed India–Vietnam relations. On September 2, 1969, Dinesh Singh, then Foreign Minister of India, was a representative of India at the funeral ceremony of President Ho Chi Minh and the Government of India, as a mark of respect, also hung a funeral flag all day. After Singh's return to India, India recognized the Provisional Revolutionary Government (PRG) of South Vietnam. In July 1970, Madam Nguyen Thi Binh, Foreign Minister of PRG, made a visit to India. From 1970 onwards, as India titled toward the Soviet Union, it became much closer to North rather than South Vietnam. India gave full support for the causes of the national freedom struggle in Vietnam and opposed U.S. interference inside the country. During Mrs. Indira Gandhi's visit to Moscow in 1971, she discussed the Vietnam issue with the Soviet Union and pledged India's support and commitment to fight for "the inalienable rights of all peoples, especially those of Vietnamese people, to national independence and freedom."[3]

On January 7, 1972, India and North Vietnam upgraded their diplomatic missions to the ambassadorial level. This signaled a new direction in India's policy of "equidistance" from the North and South Vietnam. According to the then Indian Foreign Minister Swaran Singh, the upgrade of the India–North Vietnam relations to full

---

[3] *Foreign Affairs Records*, Vol. XVII, September 1971. And Tridib Chakraborti, n. 4, p. 30.

diplomatic level was "recognition of the realities of the situation".[4] Vietnamese newspaper, *Nhan Dan*, described this action as "an inalienable step in conformity with the friendship between India and Vietnamese people and the reality in Vietnam."[5] There was strong reaction of the U.S. on the Indian position on Vietnam, and this attitude adversely affected the U.S.–India dialogue on future relations between the two countries. The U.S. bombing in Hanoi on October 11, 1972, also hit the Indian mission. According to Novosti Press Agency, the American reaction was "a new page in the chronicle of the United States blackmail of India" (Reddy, 2009, p. 22).

Between 1975–1991, with the victory of the Communist regime of North Vietnam, followed by the reunification of the two Vietnams, India–Vietnam relations got a further boost. Vietnam considered India one of the most crucial partners in its foreign relations. For India, Vietnam was an important country in Southeast Asia. Both countries have had convergent viewpoints on almost all regional and global political issues.

On April 30, 1975, India gave recognition of the Provisional Revolutionary Government (PRG) of South Vietnam as soon as it won the battle in Vietnam. The Indian Prime Minister Indira Gandhi immediately sent her congratulations message to Mr. Nguyen Huu Tho, President of the PRG on May 2, 1975: *"We welcome the good news of the successful culmination of the long and bitter struggle arrived by your valiant people at such great sacrifices. I send you and your Government my congratulations and good wishes in which my Government and the Indian nation join me"* (Reddy, 2009, p. 25). In June 1975, G. S. Dhillon, Speaker of the Lok Sabha led a delegation to visit to Vietnam, and he was welcomed with a very warm hospitality.

Along with the unification of North and South, Vietnam was to reconstruct its war-ravaged economy. In this context, India provided immense support, both spiritually and materially, through enhanced cooperation in various areas including science and technology, industry, and agriculture. India shared with Vietnam its rich experience and skills and thereby helped in building Vietnam's capacity. In May 1976, India received Madam Nguyen Thi Binh, the Foreign Minister of Vietnam, with great affability. During the visit to India by Madam Nguyen Thi Binh, discussions among the two countries' leaders revolved around the work of reconstruction of Vietnam, as well as the political developments in the region. Both sides shared views on the preparation of the then forthcoming Non-aligned Summit in Colombo. India was generous in offering its full support in the economic reconstruction of Vietnam. On July 2, 1976, when Vietnam adopted the new name "Socialist Republic of Vietnam" and a new government headed by Pham Van Dong, both the Indian President and Prime Minister sent congratulations messages to Vietnam which said, *"The Government and people of India rejoice with you at the successful reunification of your country…"* (Reddy, 2009, p. 27).

Thus, the most important turning point in India–Vietnam relations took place during the first tenure of Prime Minister Indira Gandhi when the two countries established full diplomatic relations at ambassadorial level on 7th January 1972. The

---

[4] Foreign Affairs Record, Vol. XVII, September 1971.

[5] See Footnote 4.

two countries began to cooperate in wider areas and supported each other in regional and international issues.

1.2.4 India–Vietnam Relations Under Morarji Desai (1977–1980)

In March 1977, when the new government headed by Morarji Desai was formed in India, Prime Minister Pham Van Dong sent greetings which stated that he hoped for the consolidation and development of Vietnam–India friendship and collaboration.[6] Under the Janata Government, India attached importance to the position of Vietnam. India provided its full support for Vietnam to become a member of the UNO and welcomed Vietnam's joining on September 20, 1977.

1978 was a remarkable year in India–Vietnam relations in terms of the depth of high-level visits between the two sides. In January 1978, Samarendra Kundu, Minister of External Affairs, led a high-level delegation to Vietnam. As a gesture of friendship, Prime Minister Pham Van Dong broke protocol by personally welcoming Samarendra Kundu. Photos of Kundu's visit were widely published in the newspapers of Vietnam. Mr. Vu Than, Minister in the Prime Minister's office, said "You came to Vietnam not as a close friend but as a member of the family..." (Reddy, 2009, p. 27).

In February 1978, the Prime Minister of Vietnam, Pham Van Dong, visited India. The visit was said to open a new chapter in Vietnam–India relations. Pham Van Dong's visit was the first one by a top Vietnamese leader to India after 20 years since the visit of President Ho Chi Minh to India in 1958. During the visit, Pham Van Dong had exchanges with the Indian Prime Minister Morarji Desai, Minister of External Affairs Atal Bihari Vajpayee, and gave an important speech at the Indian Parliament which was a rare gesture by a visiting foreign dignitary. Speaking at the Indian Parliament, Pham Van Dong described India–Vietnam relations as "as pure as a cloudless sky."[7] At the end of the visit, the two sides issued a joint communiqué. India reaffirmed its desire to share its experience, expertise, and skills with the people of Vietnam to contribute to its national reconstruction.

Several other important visits in 1978 included the visit to Vietnam by Madhu Limaye, Janata Party leader, when he took with him a delegation of nine members from all parties in India. On the Vietnam side, Foreign Minister Nguyen Duy Trinh visited India in December 1978. These visits helped strengthen mutual understanding and cooperation in various fields including economy and trade, agriculture and industry, education and culture, and science and technology. The two countries affirmed their shared perception of the regional and global situation. Both supported

---

[6] *The Hindustan Times*, September 8 1975.

[7] *Tạp chí Cộng sản* (*Communist Review*), 12 August 2015. https://www.tapchicongsan.org.vn/tru yen-thong-hien-tai/-/2018/34649/moi-quan-he-huu-nghi-truyen-thong-viet-nam---an-do-%E2% 80%9Ctrong-sang-nhu-bau-troi-khong-gon-bong-may%E2%80%9D.aspx.

the principles of "nonalignment" and "peaceful coexistence" among the countries of the world and of Southeast Asia (Reddy, 2009).

The special place of Vietnam in India's foreign policy was well depicted in India's strong support to the Heng Samrin regime of Cambodia in 1979. This regime was disapproved by China and most of the regional countries. India was the only non-Communist nation that extended recognition to Vietnam—supported Heng Samrin regime in Phnom Penh. India did that at the cost of its relations with the regional organization ASEAN which was prepared to extend the dialogue partnership to India and start a new phase in India–ASEAN association in mid-1980s. (Chopra, 2000, p. 218). In a sense, this also shows Vietnam's importance in India's China policy. India considered Vietnam an important partner in India's mission to contain the Chinese influence in the Southeast Asian region long before the rise of China as a major power (Bhattacharya, 2018, p. 30).

1.2.5   India–Vietnam Relations Under Indira Gandhi (1980–1984)

When Indira Gandhi entered the Prime Minister's Office again in 1980 and formed the new Government of India, Vietnam Prime Minister Pham Van Dong made a second official visit to India. India–Vietnam relations continued the momentum under Indira Gandhi's leadership. On February 13, 1982, P. V. Narasimha Rao, External Affairs Minister of India, visited Vietnam. During the visit, he held talks with Prime Minister Pham Van Dong. A joint statement was issued which affirmed that the two sides would "continue to reduce the tensions in the region through dialogue." The two visits to India by Nguyen Co Thach, Foreign Minister of Vietnam in April and December, in the same year suggest that both India and Vietnam attached great importance to holding high-level talks on matters of mutual concern. During the December visit of Foreign Minister Nguyen Co Thach in 1982, India and Vietnam decided to set up an "Indo-Vietnam Joint Economic Commission."[8] Vietnam and India began an exchange of visits of their army chiefs when in April 1984, Vietnam's Army Chief Le Trong Tan made a visit to India. In reciprocity, the Chief of Army Staff of India Gen. K. V. Krishna Rao visited Vietnam. In September 1984, Le Duan, Secretary-General of the Communist Party of Vietnam, made an official visit to India. This was Le Duan's first foreign trip to a non-Communist country. Vice Prime Minister Tran Quynh continue to stay in India for one more week to continue discussing issues of bilateral cooperation after Le Duan returned to Vietnam. The visit of Le Duan was a landmark in India–Vietnam relations under Indira Gandhi's Prime Ministership and opened new vistas for bilateral cooperation in all areas, particularly in science and technology. When Prime Minister Indira Gandhi was murdered on October 31, 1984, Vietnam "declared state mourning throughout the country for three days, from 3 to November 5 and flew the national flag half-mast at all government offices and

---

[8] Bhattacharya (1983), p. 626.

suspended all entertainments." (Reddy, 2009, p. 34) Vietnam only gave such long duration and mode of mourning to the highest senior most member of the family.

1.2.6 India–Vietnam Relations Under Rajiv Gandhi (1985–1991)

Under the prime ministership of Rajiv Gandhi, India and Vietnam promoted party to party relations between the Communist Party of Vietnam and the Communist Party of India (CPI). Between June 21–25, 1985, a delegation of the Communist Party of India (CPI) led by Ch. Rajeswara Rao, General Secretary, visited Vietnam. After the visit, a press communiqué was issued expressing the two countries' shared viewpoints on "the aims and activities of the two parties in the domestic and external policies." (Reddy, 2009, p. 34).

In November 1985, Prime Minister Rajiv Gandhi made a two-day visit to Vietnam which was the first visit by an Indian Prime Minister to the country after 30 years. During his visit, the Vietnam Government conferred the highest and most prestigious award—the order of the Golden Star—posthumously on the late Prime Minister Indira Gandhi for her great support to Vietnam during its struggle for national unification and her firm position on opposing imperialism and colonialism. Receiving the award on his mother's behalf, Mr. Rajiv Gandhi described the honor accorded on his mother as an expression of the traditional friendship between the two nations. In a joint statement issued after Mr. Rajiv Gandhi's visit, the two sides emphasized its call for "complete disarmament and an end to all vestiges of colonialism and racism." In Rajiv Gandhi's words, "Vietnam is a true and sincere friend of India with whom we enjoy… many shared geopolitical perceptions. We have established a strong political understanding that will strengthen and safeguard the forces of peace and stability in Asia." (Reddy, 2009, p. 34).

In 1986, Vietnam began its Innovation period or Doi Moi, and there was a change in the country's leadership. The new leadership did not have much contact with their Indian counterparts, yet Vietnam continued maintaining its time-tested friendship with India. To warm ties, in January 1987, Prime Minister Rajiv Gandhi sent a high-level ministerial delegation to Hanoi led by External Affairs Minister, N. D. Tiwari. During the visit, N. D. Tiwari stated: *"Indo-Vietnamese relations are neither based on temporary and narrow considerations of self-interest nor are directed against any other nation and fully derive their inspiration and sustenance from the deep-rooted and abiding friendship of peoples of the two countries"* (Reddy, 2009, p. 34).

Minister of State for External Affairs, Natwar Singh made a visit to Vietnam twice—the first one in July 1987 and the second one in November–December 1988. During his visit to Vietnam, he helped Hanoi in solving the Cambodian problem. On April 16, 1988, Rajiv Gandhi visited Vietnam the second time on his way back from Japan. He had to cancel his scheduled visit to Hiroshima so that he could stay briefly in Ho Chi Minh City which affirmed the importance of the visit. Rajiv Gandhi held talks with Nguyen Van Linh, Secretary-General of the Vietnam Communist Party. In the words of Rajiv Gandhi, "*On my way back from Japan, I stopped at Vietnam to meet the new leadership that has taken over. Vietnam is a true and sincere friend of India with whom we enjoyed shared geopolitical perceptions. My visit reaffirmed strong historical ties between the two countries. We have established a strong political understanding with the Vietnamese leadership, an understanding to promote all-round cooperation in economic, social and cultural development, an understanding that will strengthen and safeguard the forces of peace and stability in Asia*" (Reddy, 2009, p. 34).

The last Cold War years were replete with diplomatic activities between India and Vietnam. In an interview to the authors, Mr. Saxena shared that Rajiv Gandhi, who visited Beijing 26 years after the Sino-India war of 1962, stopped in Ho Chi Minh City for four hours on his return to New Delhi. Mr. Gandhi, it is believed had been requested by the Vietnamese to convey a conciliatory message on their behalf to Beijing. This reiterates the level of confidence in the bilateral relations.

In January 1989, Nguyen Van Linh, Secretary-General of Vietnam Communist Party, became the guest of honor at India's 39th Republic Day celebrations. In an interview with the Vietnamese News Agency, Nguyen Van Linh underlined that India–Vietnam relations were "an example for South-South cooperation among the nonaligned countries" (Chakraborti, 1990, pp. 55–56). On April 10, 1989, General Vo Nguyen Giap, Deputy Prime Minister of Vietnam, visited India. Nguyen Co Thach, Foreign Minister of Vietnam, visited India later in the same month. From April 13–15, 1990, the Minister for External Affairs, I. K. Gujral made a visit to Vietnam to inaugurate the fourth meeting of the India–Vietnam Joint Commission in Hanoi. On April 24, 1991, President of India, R. Venkataraman, made a visit to Vietnam. All these visits boosted Vietnam–India political and diplomatic relations.

Thus, during the Cold War period, India tried to maintain cordial relations with North and South Vietnam between 1947 and 1975 and promoted relations with the Socialist Republic of Vietnam after the unification in 1975. During this period, bilateral relations were strongly affected by the imperatives of the superpower politics and India's policy of nonalignment.

1.3   India–Vietnam Political and Diplomatic Relations Post-cold War

From the 1990s, with the end of the Cold War and in the vigorous trends of international integration and globalization, Vietnam–India relations have undergone significant changes. Before the 1990s, Vietnam–India relations were primarily focused on political relations. After the 1990s, bilateral relations became more comprehensive as cooperation in security and defense, economy, culture, education, and technology was also promoted. Crucial factors for the strengthening of bilateral relations during this period are Innovation Policy (*Đổi Mới*) of Vietnam from 1986, India's economic reforms in 1991 and especially India's Look East Policy in 1991 which, since 2014 is the Act East policy.

1.3.1 Towards a Comprehensive Partnership (1991–2003)

In the post-Cold War era, the two governments continue to make great efforts at maintaining healthy political relations and uplifting them to even higher levels. It was only in 1991 that India also initiated its Look East Policy, with the view to engage neighbors in India's extended neighborhood. This is reflected in the exchange of various state visits of leaders of the two countries: Indian Prime Minister R. Venkataraman visited Vietnam in April 1991, Vietnam Secretary-General Do Muoi visited India in September 1992, Deputy Prime Minister cum Minister of Foreign Affairs Nguyen Manh Cam visited India in 1992, and Indian Prime Minister Narasimha Rao visited Vietnam in September 1994. In December 1999, President Tran Duc Luong led a delegation including ministers and vice-ministers to India. In 2000, with *Vientiane Declaration*, India and Vietnam joined the Mekong–Ganga cooperation, combining bilateral cooperation with regional cooperation in order to ensure greater mutual benefits. This helped to create a framework for the relations between the two countries in the twenty-first century.

Entering the twenty-first century, Vietnam–India political relations continue to be promoted. 2001 was marked by the official visit of the Indian Prime Minister Atal Bihari Vajpayee to Vietnam in January. In May 2003, the Secretary-General of Vietnam Communist Party, Nong Duc Manh made a visit to India. This visit was an important landmark in the history of bilateral relations. During this visit, the "Joint Declaration regarding the Framework for Comprehensive Cooperation between the two countries entering the twenty-first century" was signed. This was the first joint declaration of comprehensive partnership that Vietnam signed with another country.

1.3.2 Toward Strategic Partnership (2003–2007)

Between 2003–2007, the Comprehensive Cooperation was fortified, culminating in the elevation of bilateral relations to a Strategic Partnership during the visit to India by Vietnam Prime Minister Nguyen Tan Dung in July 2007. The significance of the India–Vietnam Strategic Partnership is in the fact that Vietnam is the only country in ASEAN with which India had signed one such so far (Sakhuja, 2011, p. 153).

The Strategic Partnership was not merely confined to the military arena, and it was a commitment to deepen bilateral relations in the political, economic, security, defense, cultural, science, and technological dimensions. The Strategic Partnership agreement also called for mutual cooperation in regional and multilateral institutions.

1.3.3 Toward Comprehensive Strategic Partnership (2007–2016)

New developments in bilateral relations continued to be fostered through exchanges of high-level visits. Important visits to India from the Vietnamese side during this period include the visit of Vice President Nguyen Thi Doan in 2009; Chairman of the National Assembly Nguyen Phu Trong in 2010; President Truong Tan Sang on October 12, 2011; Vice Prime Minister Nguyen Thien Nhan in March–April 2012; Vice Prime Minister in January 2013; Minister of Foreign Affairs Pham Binh Minh in July 2013; Minister of Public Security Tran Dai Quang in October 2013; Secretary-General Nguyen Phu Trong in November 2013. From the Indian side, Speaker of Lower House Somnath Chatterjee visited Vietnam in March 2007; Minister of Defence A. K. Antony in December 2007; President Pratibha Patil in November 2008, Prime Minister Manmohan Singh came to Hanoi in October 2010 and Speaker of the Lower House, Madam Meira Kumar visited Vietnam in May 2011; Vice President of India Mohammad Hamid Ansari in January 2013.

When Narendra Modi came to power since May 2014, there were new adjustments in foreign policy. He focused on engaging with neighboring countries in South and Southeast Asia through the Neighborhood First and Act East policies. He made his initial visits to Bhutan, Nepal, Bangladesh, Myanmar, Singapore, Japan, and Vietnam. In fact, the term "Act East" was first mentioned by the Minister of External Affairs Sushma Swaraj during her visit to Hanoi in 2014 when she underlined that India was not only "Looking East" but also "Acting East."[9]

During the first tenure of Prime Minister Modi, several important high-level visits of both sides include the visit to Vietnam by President Pranab Mukherjee from September 14–17, 2014; Prime Minister of Vietnam Nguyen Tan Dung visited India for the third time on October 27–28, 2014.

In this context, the visit to Vietnam by President Pranab Mukherjee in September 2014 can be highlighted. It was then that a joint statement was issued, and many cooperation agreements were signed. An important symbolic event was that President Pranab Mukherjee presented to Vietnam a small Bodhi tree originating from Bodhgaya (where the Buddha was enlightened) and a symbol of the cohesion between both nations from historical times to the present. President Pranab Mukherjee affirmed that India–Vietnam relations were in an excellent state and that "India has always stood by and supported the Vietnamese people. In the past, India was besides Vietnam, today and in the future, India will continue to strongly support Vietnam. Vietnam is a reliable and worthy partner of India's trust."[10]

Assessing Vietnam's role in ASEAN and India's policy, President Mukherjee stated that Vietnam is an important pillar in India's Look East Policy, a strategic partner of India within ASEAN as well as in the wider region (Tien, 2021). Both

---

[9] Anand and Mishra (2014), tr. 27.

[10] Minh Lý, Tổng thống Mukherjee: Việt Nam là đối tác đáng tin cậy của Ấn Độ (http://www.vietnamplus.vn/tong-thong-mukherjee-viet-nam-la-doi-tac-dang-tin-cay-cua-an-do/281975.vnp, accessed on January 12, 2015).

countries cooperate closely in many regional forums such as ASEAN, East Asia Summit (EAS), Mekong-Ganga cooperation, ASEM, and many multi-organizations such as U.N. and WTO.[11]

After the visit of President Pranab Mukherjee, in the same month, Vietnam Prime Minister Nguyen Tan Dung made the third trip to India on September 27–28, 2014 (He visited India in 2007 and 2012 also). During this visit, Prime Minister Nguyen Tan Dung held private talks with Indian Prime Minister Narendra Modi, held meetings with President Pranab Mukherjee, Vice President Mohammad Hamid Ansari, Lower House Speaker Sumitra Mahajan, and Minister for External Affairs Sushma Swaraj. In addition, Prime Minister Dung visited Bodhgaya and met with the Chief Minister of Bihar Jitan Ram Manjhi. During the visit, the two sides' leaders reaffirmed their commitment to the strengthening of the bilateral Strategic Partnership.[12]

Nine years of an evolved Strategic Partnership led to another milestone in India–Vietnam relations when Prime Minister Narendra Modi made an official visit to Vietnam on September 3, 2016. During this visit, the two sides upgraded bilateral relations from "Strategic Partnership" to "Comprehensive Strategic Partnership".[13] In the words of the Spokesman of the Ministry of External Affairs of India, Vikas Swarup, P.M. Modi's visit has brought about a "new benchmark for India–Vietnam ties which will take the relationship to a whole new level."[14] This was the first visit to Vietnam by an Indian Prime Minister after 15 years. Speaking at a press conference at the Government Office of Vietnam on September 3, Prime Minister Modi said that "the decision to upgrade our Strategic Partnership to Comprehensive Strategic Partnership captures the intent and path of our future cooperation. It will provide a new direction, momentum, and substance to our bilateral cooperation. Our common efforts will also contribute to stability, security, and prosperity in this region."[15] The Vietnam side also affirmed its consistent support to India in its implementation of this policy.

In a one day working agenda, Prime Minister N. Modi attended various meetings and had many activities in Hanoi: meeting with Vietnamese counterpart Nguyen Xuan Phuc, witnessing the signing of 12 cooperation documents between the two countries; calling on Secretary-General Nguyen Phu Trong; meeting the President Tran Dai Quang and the Chairman of the National Assembly Nguyen Thi Kim Ngan; laying a wreath at the memorial of national heroes and martyrs, paying homage to the President Ho Chi Minh, visiting Uncle Ho's stilt house, and visiting Quán Sứ Pagoda in Hanoi (Nga, 2017, pp. 400–409).

The visit to Vietnam of Prime Minister Modi was very successful (Nga, 2017, pp. 400–409): both sides signed a Joint Statement, 12 cooperation documents in

---

[11] See Footnote 10.

[12] Tuyên bố chung Việt Nam - Ấn Độ (http://baodientu.chinhphu.vn/Hoat-dong-cua-lanh-dao-Dang-Nha-nuoc/Tuyen-bo-chung-Viet-Nam-An-Do/212180.vgp, accessed on January 12, 2015).

[13] Vietnam has signed a "Comprehensive Strategic Partnership" with three countries, i.e., China (2008), Russia (2012), and India (2016).

[14] Sarma (2016).

[15] *Pmindia* (2016).

which there was an MOU on the cooperation between the Vietnam Academy of Social Sciences (VASS) and Indian Council of World Affairs (ICWA). The signing of these cooperative documents has helped consolidate the strong traditional ties on the one hand and enhanced and expanded bilateral cooperation in new fields such as cooperation in the exploitation and use of Outer Space for Peaceful Purposes, cooperation on cybersecurity, exchange of non-military marine information, cooperation in the construction of infrastructure for the training of high-quality information and technology... During the visit, the two sides also agreed that the year 2017 would be made the "Vietnam–India Friendship Year" to celebrate the 45th anniversary of the establishment of full diplomatic relation (1/1972–1/2017) and the 10th anniversary of the establishment of Strategic Partnership (7/2007/–7/2017) between the two countries. The official visit to India shortly afterward by Vietnam Defense Minister Ngo Xuan Lich and National Assembly Chairperson Nguyen Thi Kim Ngan in December 2016 has helped realize the Comprehensive Strategic Partnership's objectives during Prime Minister Modi's visit to Vietnam (Binh & Anh, 2018).

1.3.4 Strengthening Comprehensive Strategic Partnership (2016–2020)

From 2016 to 2020, India and Vietnam took various steps to strengthen their Comprehensive Strategic Partnership. There were many more high-level visits from both sides between August 26–28, 2018. These include the visit of Minister of External Affairs Sushma Swaraj when she co-chaired the 16th Joint Commission meeting and attended the 3rd International Conference on the Indian Ocean in Hanoi; between November 18–20, 2018, President Ram Nath Kovind visited Vietnam, the first visit to Asian countries after assuming office; between May 9–12, 2019, Vice President Venkaiah Naidu visited Vietnam; attended the 16th U.N.'s VESAK. From the Vietnam side, between January 24–26, 2018, Prime Minister Nguyen Xuan Phuc was among the chief guests of the Indian Republic Day celebration; attended India–ASEAN Summit; between March 2–4, 2018, President Tran Dai Quang visited India officially; between February 11–13, 2020, Vice President Dang Thi Ngoc Thinh visited India.

These high-level visits have not only helped heighten the political trust between the two sides and the importance that the two sides attach to each other, but also demonstrated their efforts in implementing the Comprehensive Strategic Partnership in areas of trade and investment, defense and security. As a result of these visits, direct flights between India and Vietnam were established in 2018 and the first direct flights were operated in 2019. Also in 2018, the Centre for Vietnam Studies was established in New Delhi.

1.3.5 *Promoting India–Vietnam Relations in the Context of COVID-19 Pandemic*

The outbreak of the COVID-19 pandemic has not stalled the development of political and diplomatic relations. On April 13, 2020, the two Prime Ministers Nguyen Xuan Phuc and Narendra Modi made a phone call to discuss cooperation in epidemic prevention and in deepening the bilateral Comprehensive Strategic Partnership. On August 25, 2020, Foreign Ministers Pham Binh Minh and Subrahmanyam Jaishankar were the co-chairs of the 17th Meeting of the Joint Commission on economic, trade, scientific, and technical cooperation. The success of the 17th Session of the Vietnam–India Joint Commission despite COVID-19 proves that bilateral engagements have not lost pace. On the contrary, after the initial disruption, the relationship has further strengthened. In the past, and despite the absence of the pandemic, continuous sessions of the Joint Commission could not be held. Sometimes the interval between the sessions was 4 or 5 years. Prior to 2018, Joint Commission meetings were held in 2013, 2011, and 2007.

On December 21, 2020, Prime Ministers Narendra Modi and Nguyen Xuan Phuc held a virtual summit successfully. During the meeting, the two sides exchanged views on wide-ranging bilateral, regional, and global issues. Most importantly, they set forth the Joint Vision for Peace, Prosperity and People to guide the future development of India–Vietnam Comprehensive Strategic Partnership. Three days later, the Indian Navy Ship, INS KILTAN docked at Ho Chi Minh City on December 24, 2020, carrying 15 tons of humanitarian assistance and relief supplies for the victims of the fatal flooding and landslides that were inflicting several provinces in Central Vietnam. The ship's visit is part of India–Vietnam ever-growing bilateral relations which were also highlighted during the Virtual Summit between the leaders.

1.4 Visionary Leaders

The above description shows that despite various changes in governments and leadership, India–Vietnam relations have been on an upward trajectory. Bilateral relations have been sustained thanks to the frequent exchanges of visits among high-level leaders of the two sides. Generation of leaders from Mahatma Gandhi, Jawaharlal Nehru, Indira Gandhi, Rajiv Gandhi, A. B. Vajpayee, to Ho Chi Minh, Pham Van Dong, Nguyen Thi Binh, Nguyen Van Linh, Nguyen Co Thach, Nong Duc Manh, Tran Duc Luong, Nguyen Tan Dung, Nguyen Phu Trong, Tran Dai Quang, Pham Binh Minh… and many others has consistently tried to cultivate, strengthen, and build the Comprehensive Strategic Partnership in all fields.

In this context, it is pertinent to delve a little deeper into the relationship between the two leaders who are considered Fathers of the two nations, i.e., Mahatma Gandhi and Vietnam and Ho Chi Minh with India.

1.4.1 Mahatma Gandhi

Mohandas Karamchand Gandhi (October 2, 1869–January 30, 1948) belonged to a family of vaishya caste in Porbandar, Gujarat, India. His father was Karamchand Gandhi, a Porbandar "diwan" whose mother was Putlibai, a devout Hindu. M. K. Gandhi is respectfully referred to by millions of Indian people as Mahatma, meaning "A Great Soul". Not only a great national leader and hero, Mahatma Gandhi is revered by many Indians as "Bapu" which means Father. Gandhi left India for South Africa in 1893 when he was 24 years old for a temporary law case for a local Indian businessman. However, he ended up staying in South Africa for about 20 years to champion the cause of the struggle against racial discrimination and social injustice. In South Africa, Mahatma Gandhi evolved the Satyagraha strategy (using soul force or truth force as a weapon of fighting). Upon returning to India in 1914, Mahatma Gandhi led the freedom movement against British colonialism and won independence for India with the complete support of the Indian people, especially those of the lowest order of the society. Throughout his life, he opposed all forms of violence; contrarily, he insisted on using the method of nonviolent struggle (Ahimsa). Gandhi's Satyagraha is well-known and has impacted many nonviolence movements in India as well as in other countries, including the Civil Rights Movement in the United States led by Martin Luther King, Jr.

Though Mahatma Gandhi never visited Vietnam, the Vietnamese people, including Ho Chi Minh, greatly admired and respected him. Gandhi did influence Ho Chi Minh, though less directly than Lenin.[16] On one occasion of Mahatma Gandhi's birthdays, Ho Chi Minh sent a message to the Mahatma through the Indian Government in New Delhi. The message reads: "I would like to send to you my warmest congratulations on the occasion of your 77th birthday and wish you a double 77 years old" (Toan et al., 2019, p. 64 and p. 538). On another occasion, Ho Chi Minh said, "I and others may be revolutionaries, but we are disciples of Mahatma Gandhi, directly or indirectly, nothing more nothing less."[17]

In Vietnam, in recent years, awareness about Mahatma Gandhi has increased, and some books about Gandhiji have been translated, including Gandhi's Autobiography or "The Stories of my experiments with Truth", "The Essence of Hinduism", books on Gandhiji's political activities and thought. Awareness about Gandhiji has increased since 2007, and Vietnam has celebrated *International Nonviolence Day* on Gandhiji's birthday (October 2). In 1918–1919, in celebration of the 150th Birth Anniversary of Mahatma Gandhi, various activities were held in Vietnam, including seminars, exhibitions, screening of award-winning film "Gandhi" at various universities in Vietnam, a Quiz, and drama shows by school children on Gandhi's life, an online narration of stories of Mahatma Gandhi, presenting of books compiled by Gandhi to the National Library of Vietnam and the inauguration of Gandhi's bust in Hanoi. Mahatma Gandhi has inspired a large number of Vietnamese people from all sections

---

[16] "Ho Chi Minh: Remembering the King and the Saint". https://thewire.in/history/ho-chi-minh-vietnam.

[17] See Footnote 16.

of the society. Especially, Vietnamese school children have also developed much love and respect for the great Father of India. Indians settled in Vietnam affirm that Indian festivals and special historic occasions are celebrated with great enthusiasm.

1.4.2 President Ho Chi Minh

President Ho Chi Minh (May 19, 1890–September 3, 1969) is considered Father of the nation of Vietnam. He was born in a Confucian family, in Hoang Tru village of Kim Lien commune, Nam Dan district, Nghe An province, a central region of Vietnam. In June 1911, Ho Chi Minh went abroad and began his 30 years of traveling worldwide to find a way to liberate his home country from foreign domination; he went to many countries in Europe, Asia, Africa, and America. Like Mahatma Gandhi, President Ho Chi Minh discovered how to serve his homeland and his life mission during the time traveling abroad. After 30 years of activities abroad, in 1941, he returned to the homeland and directly led the revolutionary movement of Vietnam. With the success of the August Revolution, Vietnam officially became an independent nation. On September 2, 1945, President Ho Chi Minh read the Declaration of Independence, giving birth to the Democratic Republic of Vietnam.

President Ho Chi Minh had a special connection with India and contributed significantly to the promotion and consolidation of Vietnam–India relations. During his lifetime, Ho Chi Minh visited India three times. His first visit to India was in 1911 when he traveled to secure his mission of saving his country; the second time was in 1946 when he was the President of the newly founded nation of Vietnam and on his way to France to attend the peace negotiations; the third time was in 1958 when he made an official visit to India for 10 days as the President of the Democratic Republic of Vietnam. President Ho Chi Minh's visits to India left a deep impression in the hearts of the Indian people. In this official visit to India thousands of Indian people took to the streets to greet him warmly and solemnly. Indian people often tell each other about the visit of President Ho Chi Minh to India in 1958 (Van, 2019). In the words of Ambassador Pham Sanh Chau (Toan et al., 2019, p. 18):

> "When Uncle Ho came to India, the whole country of the Ganga River welcomed the Viet-
> namese leader with the warmest, sincerest and most respectful affection. Indian people still
> tell the story of the red carpet and the throne in the meeting to welcome Uncle Ho with tens
> of thousands of people gathering at Red Fort in New Delhi, India. India, the host country,
> rolled out the red carpet to welcome President Ho Chi Minh, but he refused to walk on the
> carpet; the Indian host prepared a golden chair (looked like a golden throne) for Uncle Ho
> on the honor podium, while Prime Minister J. Nehru sat on an ordinary chair. When Prime
> Minister Nehru invited Uncle Ho to sit on that chair, he politely refused to do so, and he just
> sat on the ordinary chair like everyone else, even though Prime Minister Nehru said, "You
> are our honored guest. It is our honor if you sit on that chair!"

During his lifetime, Ho Chi Minh wrote over 60 articles, including research papers, poems, letters, telegraph messages, speeches, etc., about India and his experience with Indian leaders and people. In the words of Geetesh Sharma, Ho Chi Minh "left an everlasting impression over the people of India. He won the hearts of one and all by his affability, cordiality, humility and austerity…" (Toan et al., 2019, p. 9). Ho Chi Minh has been compared to Gandhi and Lenin. "There were always many admirers of Ho Chi Minh (1890–1969), the paramount leader of Vietnam during his lifetime. Indeed, he had become the symbol of all that was good in Vietnam—because of his charisma, will power and perseverance" (Chopra, 2000, p. 202).

1.5 Conclusion

Thus, the story of India–Vietnam relations in more than 2000 years of history is a profound and continuous one. Like a river that flows incessantly, it may have twists and turns; sometimes it is wide, sometimes it is narrow, but it never stops. Despite the fluctuations of history, the change of regimes and governments, the relationship continues to be maintained and enhanced to new heights. It is also like a colorful picture. There was a time when it was like a beautiful sky full of stars (in ancient times when the Indianized kingdoms were established in Vietnam); sometimes it is like a clear, cloudless sky (in the late 1970s and 80s), but sometimes it can also be cloudy and gray (like in the early 1960s). In fact, India had to bear the costs of her unflinching support for the Vietnamese people during their struggle against French colonialism as well as against intervention by USA. India also supported Vietnam when it had sent its army to Cambodia to clamp down on the genocide by the Pol Pot regime in 1978. New Delhi stood by Hanoi, despite this causing tremendous diplomatic loss, in terms of its relations with ASEAN and the West. ASEAN condemned India's stand of supporting the Heng Samrin regime and the Vietnamese aggression that went against the tenets of peace, and tranquility of ASEAN and its principle of non-interference in internal affairs of neighbors (Ghoshal, 2021: 351). Despite various difficulties and challenges due to internal and external circumstances, the two countries have become real comprehensive partners who have "strategic trust" in each other, a rarity in today's global scenario of uncertainty and mistrust.

The bilateral relationship has been cultivated constantly and nurtured by generations of leaders and the people of the two countries, and that is why the friendship has become more intense and durable. While Vietnamese leaders such as Ho Chi Minh are greatly respected by the Indian people, Indian leaders like Mahatma Gandhi and Jawaharlal Nehru were also greatly revered by the Vietnamese people. However, the cordial bonds are not only promoted from above, and it is also bolstered from below through the people-to-people contacts at local levels. Bilateral interaction is now taking place not only in the top-down direction but also in the bottom-up direction. The momentum for this direction has also been given by the "Joint Vision for Peace, Prosperity and People" between India and Vietnam issued during the virtual meeting between Prime Ministers Narendra Modi and Nguyen Xuan Phuc on December 21, 2020. "People" has become an important pillar in our bilateral Comprehensive Strategic Partnership. The significance of "people" as also the historical context and connect will provide the milieu for the subsequent chapters. The next chapter takes the reader to the realm of culture from the fourth century AD to the present.

References

Anand, V., & Mishra, R. (2014, September–October). India's' act east policy: A perspective. *VIVEK: Issues and Options, III*(V).

Bhattacharya, S. S. (1983, January). Co Thach visit to India. *Strategic Analysis, VII*(10).

Binh, N. X., & Anh, N. T. (2018). Promotion of Vietnam–India comprehensive strategic partnership. *International Studies.*

Chakraborti, T. (1990, April–June). India and Vietnam: A new dimension in South-South economic cooperation. *Asian Studies (Calcutta), 8.*

Chopra, V. D. (2000). *Vietnam today and Indo-Vietnam relations.* Gyan Publishing House.

Cong, P. X. C., & Thanh, V. N. (2021). Pakistan's reactions to the India–China border war in 1962 [Phản ứng của Pakistan với cuộc chiến tranh biên giới Ấn Độ - Trung Quốc năm 1962]. *Journal for Indian and Asian Studies, 8.*

Das, P. K. (1972). *India and Vietnam war* (p. 69).

Foreign Affairs Records, Vol. XVII, September 1971. And Tridib Chakraborti, n. 4.

Ghoshal, B. (2021). Vietnam in India's foreign policy. In E. Sridharan (Ed.), *Eastward Ho? India in the Indo-Pacific* (p. 351). Orient Blackswan Publishers.

Ho Chi Minh: Remembering the king and the saint. https://thewire.in/history/ho-chi-minh-vietnam

Huệ, N. C. (2010). Quan hệ Việt Nam-Ấn Độ từ năm 1956 đến những năm đầu thế kỷ XXI [Vietnam–India relations from 1956 to the first years of the 21st century], MãSố: CS.2009.19.56; DTKH Cấp Trường; Đại học Sư phạm Tp. HCM, 2010.

Lý, M. (2015). *Tổng thống Mukherjee: Việt Nam là đối tác đáng tin cậy của Ấn Độ.* http://www.vietnamplus.vn/tong-thong-mukherjee-viet-nam-la-doi-tac-dang-tin-cay-cua-an-do/281975.vnp

Minh, H. C. (2011). Toàn tập, Nxb. Chính trị quốc gia, H. 2011, t. 2, tr. 350–352.

Nga, L. T. H. (2017). India–Vietnam relations since September 2016: From the symbolic to practical results. *China report* (Vol. 53, No. 3, pp. 400–409). Sage Publication.

Nga, L. T. H. (2018). *Quan hệ Ấn Độ - Hoa Kỳ (1947-1991) [India–U.S. relations (1947-1991)].* National Political Publishing House.

Pmindia. (2016). *Press statement by Prime Minister during his visit to Vietnam.* http://www.pmindia.gov.in/en/news_updates/press-statement-by-prime-minister-during-his-visit-to-vietnam/

Prasad, B. (1979). *Indian Nationalism in Asia, 1900-1947.*

Reddy, R. (2009). *India and Vietnam: Era of friendship and cooperation (1947-1991).* Emerald Publishers.

Sakhuja, V. (Ed.). (2011). *India–Vietnam strategic partnership: Exploring vistas for expanded cooperation.* Pentagon Press.

Sardesai, D. R. (1968). *Indian foreign policy in Cambodia, Laos and Vietnam 1947-1964, Berkeley.*

Sarma, S. (2016, September 5). India–Vietnam relations after Modi's Visit. *The diplomat.* http://thediplomat.com/2016/09/india-vietnam-relations-after-modis-visit/

Sinha, S., & Trivedi, S. (2018). *Emerging horizons in India–Vietnam relations.* Pentagon Press (Paper: Subhadeep Bhattacharya, "Growing significance of Vietnam in India's Act East Policy", pp. 28–43).

Thayer, C., & Thakur, R. (1992). *Soviet relations with India and Vietnam, 1945-1992, Delhi.*

Thien, T. T. (1960). *India and Southeast Asia, 1947-1960, Geneva.*

Tien, T. N. (2021). The Rise of India in the new balance of power in Asia since the beginning of 21st century: Impacts on India–Vietnam relations. *Humanities and Social Sciences Reviews.*

Toan, L. V., Jayachandra Reddy, G., & Thảo, N. T. P. (2019). *Hồ Chí Minh với Ấn Độ (Ho Chi Minh with India)*, Nxb. Lý luận chính trị, Hà Nội.

Tuyên bố chung Việt Nam - Ấn Độ. http://baodientu.chinhphu.vn/Hoat-dong-cua-lanh-dao-Dang-Nha-nuoc/Tuyen-bo-chung-Viet-Nam-An-Do/212180.vgp

Van, V. H. (2019). The foundation of Vietnam and India relations, historical values. *Asian Social Science*.

Chapter 2
India–Vietnam Cultural Linkages

The previous chapter highlighted the bilateral relations through history. This chapter focuses on the abundance and richness of the transmission of Indian culture to Vietnam, even as cultural connectivity with India has permeated Southeast Asian nations.

The year 2020 saw some significant developments in the promotion of cultural links between India and Vietnam. On December 21, 2020, the two Prime Ministers held a virtual meeting and issued the Joint Vision for Peace, Prosperity and People. For the first time, "People" has become one of the pillars of bilateral relations in official documents. There are three cooperation programs announced as a result of the virtual summit out of which two are about culture. There is one program on the development assistance projects related to the preservation of the historical heritage of Vietnam (group F tower in Mỹ Sơn, Đồng Dương Buddhist Monastery in Quảng Nam, and Nhạn Stupa in Phú Yên) and one program on writing an encyclopaedia of cultural and civilizational relations between Vietnam and India.

On December 31, 2020, the Prime Minister of Vietnam signed decision number 2283/QĐ-TTg which recognizes the National Treasures, and two artifacts at the Champa Sculpture Museum in Đà Nẵng are in this list, i.e., Ganesha and Gajasima sandstone statues. These are unique artifacts with particular forms and value which are typical of the religious art of Champa through the ages.[1] In May 2020, there was a discovery of a sandstone Linga dated ninth century in Central Vietnam by the Archeological Survey of India (Walter de Gruyter GmbH, 2021). Thus, the story of India–Vietnam cultural interaction which began in about the third century before Christ, during the time of the Great Emperor Ashoka, continues to tell new stories with new illuminating discoveries. Indian Foreign Minister Mr. Jaishankar referred to the new discovery as a "great cultural example of India's development partnership"

---

[1] Bảo tàng điêu khắc Chăm Đà Nẵng có thêm hai hiện vật được công nhận bảo vật quốc gia. http://www.chammuseum.vn/view.aspx?ID=499&title=bao_tang_dieu_khac_cham_da_nang_co_them_hai_hien_vat_duoc_cong_nhan_bao_vat_quoc_gia.

© The Author(s), under exclusive license to Springer Nature Singapore Pte Ltd. 2021   25
R. Marwah and L. T. Hằng Nga, *India–Vietnam Relations*, Dynamics of Asian Development, https://doi.org/10.1007/978-981-16-7822-6_2

and reaffirmed "the civilizational connect" between India and Vietnam.[2] It is evident that there are still many more Indian cultural imprints embedded in the country's landscape that are yet to be explored.

2.1 India, Vietnam, and Southeast Asia—Cultural and Civilizational Links

India is well-known as one of the most flourishing cultures of human civilization. Therefore, the influence of Indian culture on the outside world is also powerful. Throughout its history, Indian culture has absorbed external influences and spread outward in every direction. Southeast Asia is one of the areas most strongly affected by Indian culture. In the words of Pandit Nehru, "Indian civilization took root especially in the countries of Southeast Asia, and the evidence for this can be found all over the place today" (Nehru, 2010 edition, pp. 211–219). The spread of Indian culture to Vietnam is part of India's cultural influence in the Southeast Asian region. This exchange has left indelible marks in almost every aspect of the lives of many countries in Southeast Asia including Malaysia, Indonesia, Myanmar, Thailand, and Vietnam. The strong imprints of Indian culture in the region continue to be found in the literature, culture, language, religion and philosophy, art and architecture, customs, and practices of these countries. A Malaysian scholar, namely Farish A Noor, wrote, "the development of Southeast Asian civilization goes hand in hand with the development of the Indian civilization" (Suryanarayan, 2013, p. 6).

The term "Southeast" bears an essential connotation in the context of the identity of this region—a region which is "South" of China and "East" of India. European anthropologists and historians considered Southeast Asia a faraway region in Asia sandwiched between the two rich civilizations of India and China. The nationalist historians of India called Southeast Asia the "Greater India" in the early twentieth century (Roy & Bhattacharya, 2015, p. 1; Marwah, 2020, p. 7). Indian elements like the Sanskrit language, the Hindu–Buddhist cults, Dharmashastras, and the Indian concept of kingship became essential features of the early states of Southeast Asia. Indian cultural elements influenced the ordinary people in Southeast Asia as Indian deities became popular and the stories of the epics like Ramayana and Mahabharata were indigenized (Guy, 2018, pp. 253–273; Dhar, 2018, pp. 325–345). Nobel Laureate Rabindranath Tagore traveled to several countries in Southeast Asia including Thailand and Vietnam and wrote about the deep connections between India and these two nations. Such deep cultural connections acted as the foundation of India's Southeast Asia relations in the post-colonial and post-Cold War periods.

Several important favorable conditions facilitated the dynamic interaction between India and Southeast Asia. First, it is essential to understand the importance

---

[2] Archeological Survey of India discovers ninth-century sandstone Shiva Linga in Vietnam. https://theprint.in/india/archaeological-survey-of-india-discovers-9th-century-sandstone-shiva-linga-in-vietnam/430366/, accessed on July 15, 2020.

of India's geographical proximity to this region. It is evident that this proximity facilitated the movement of people from India to the lands lying eastward (Liên, 2018, p. 109; Marwah, 2020, p. 5). Looking at the world map, it can be seen that Southeast Asia is India's extended neighbor. The island of Pu Breush, located in the Northwest of Sumatra, is only 92 nautical miles from the Indira Point (which is less than the distance between Chennai and Tirupati). Similarly, in Thailand, Phuket is only 273 nautical miles away from Indira Point (which is less than the distance between Chennai and Madurai) (Marwah, 2020, pp. 5–6). Secondly, in the spread of Indian culture in all directions in Southeast Asia, the sea plays a key role. As is well documented, sea trade developed quite strongly in the early centuries before Christ. Tamralipti port at the mouth of the Ganges was one of the first departure points of traders from India. From there, various ships sailed toward the Malay Peninsula. The classical Chinese bibliographies did mention this fact (Mishra, 2001, tr. 107). One of the reasons that may explain the "sea crossing" which was a taboo in Indian culture was the development of Indian maritime trade. By this time, the Indians had learnt the ship building techniques from the countries in the Persian Gulf and built large ships that could carry between 600 and 700 passengers (Coedes, 2008, p. 55). Thirdly, there was the spiritual factor that encouraged the Indians to cross the "black water", i.e., the evolution of Buddhism. Buddhism helped its believers to remove caste barriers and at the same time to remove the converts' fear of being polluted by touching with the "barbarians" during sea trips (Coedes, 2008, p. 58). Fourthly, the legendary wealth of Southeast Asia was of great attraction to the Indian traders. It was referred to as Suvarnabhumi (the Land of Gold) or Suvarnadvipa (the Golden Island or Peninsula), Narikeladvipa (Coconut Island), Karpuradvipa (Camphor Island), and Yavodvipa (Barley Island) in Ramayana, and Pali Nidesa are only some references in Sanskrit. Sylvain Lévi emphasized the role of gold seeking in the "expansion" of the Indian diaspora in Southeast Asia. It was gold that attracted India to the Far East's rich "golden island" (Coedes, 2008, p. 56).

Archeological evidence found in the Korat Plateau (Thailand), Bali and Java (Indonesia), and Đông Sơn, Óc Eo (Vietnam) indicates intense contact between India and Southeast Asia from the first millennium before Christ (Mishra, 2001, p. 106). Therefore, the contact between the Indians and the inhabitants of Southeast Asia around the beginning of the Christian era was not the first one. However, it was only that this time the Indians had come here in larger numbers, and this was the first time that they brought along the intellectual elements to propagate their religion, art, and language in these lands (Coedes, 2008, tr. 49).

Most archeological evidences show that there have been two main phases of contacts and exchanges between Southeast Asia and the Indian world in ancient time. Phase I was from the fifth century BCE to early CE. During this phase, there were regular exchanges, but these were on a small scale; in Phase II from the first half of the first millennium CE, there was the rapid development of trading networks and the emergence of early Southeast Asian states. Changes in social life, burial customs, and religious practice allowed them to be called "Indianized states" by R. C. Majumdar (1952) (Liên, 2018, p. 108). Studies by Liên (2018) indicate that in the centuries before the Christian era, the sea trade route was conducive to making

Image 2.1 My Son Temple, Village of Dui Phu, Vietnam. *Source* https://commons.wikimedia.org/wiki/File:My_Son,_Vietnam.jpg; Accessed on May 31, 2021

several Indian products known. According to Liên, these products "became favorite goods for the ancient communities in Vietnam. However, Indian civilization did not yet play a role in the social structure; Indian beliefs and religions were not yet commonly practiced among the local communities, until the appearance of the first states" (Liên, 2018, p. 114).

Scholars in India and elsewhere know about the Ayutthaya Kingdom of Siam (Thailand), the great Borobudur temple in Indonesia, vast Indian influence in Java, Sumatra and Bali (Indonesia), and Angkor Wat of Cambodia. However, it is less well known that the first Hindu kingdoms outside India were established in the region that is now the territory of Vietnam. Few people know that the first imprints of Hinduism or Indian culture were also found in Mỹ Sơn (Đà Nẵng) and Võ Cạnh (Nha Trang) in Vietnam. When Indian President Ram Nath Kovind visited Vietnam in 2018, he began his journey from Da Nang, where the World Heritage Site of My Son is located; this has a significant symbolic meaning. In the words of President Ram Nath Kovind, "this temple complex is a reminder of the unique culture that developed on the coast of present-day Vietnam thousands of years ago, a culture that drew from the spiritual depth of Hinduism in India. It was truly remarkable to see the Shiva Linga and the many sculptures of Shiva adorning this ancient temple complex built by the Champa kings."[3] Refer Image 2.1.

Apart from Mỹ Sơn (Đà Nẵng), archeological evidences related to the evolution of coastal cultures in the late Neolithic Age reveal trace of cultural exchanges between India and Vietnam in all three regions of North, Central, and Southern Vietnam, most probably via the sea routes (Liên, 2018, pp. 107–127). In the North, evidences of cultural exchanges were found in Hạ Long–Quảng Ninh, Hải Phòng provinces.

---

[3] Address by the President of India, Shri Ram Nath Kovind on the occasion of Mahashivratri celebrations at Isha Yoga Center.

According to Lê Thị Liên, in the region of the Northern central coast (including Nghệ An, Hà Tĩnh, and Quảng Bình provinces), "artifacts of Bau Tro culture reflect the interchange with the Hoa Loc and Ha Long cultures to the North, the Xom Con culture to the South and the mountainous areas of Nghệ An, Quảng Bình, Upper Laos and Bien Ho in Tây Nguyên highland" (Liên, 2018, p. 111). In the Southern parts, various sites have been excavated along the coast of central provinces including Th`ưa Thiên Huế, Quảng Nam, Quảng Ngãi, Bình Định, Khánh Hòa, Ninh Thuận, Đồng Nai, Sài Gòn-Gia Định (Hồ Chí Minh City), Bình Dương, Lâm Đồng, Đồng Tháp (Liên, 2018, pp. 107–127).

2.2 Indian Cultural Imprints in Vietnam

Any writing on India–Southeast Asia cultural relations will remain incomplete without referring to the eternal linkages between India and Vietnam. Hinduism and Buddhism are the two pillars that provide the conduits for cultural and civilizational exchanges. This is proved by hundreds of Hindu and Buddhist temples and stupas scattered in Central and Southern Vietnam (Sharma, 2012).

2.2.1 Buddhist Imprints

For a long time, most of the people in Vietnam believed that Buddhism reached them indirectly through China. However, recent research has shown that Indian Buddhism was introduced to Vietnam directly in the third and second centuries BC during the reign of Emperor Ashoka (Nga, 2020; Toan, 2017). It is now well known that Indian Buddhism had been first introduced to the Do Son area, Hai Phong province of Northern Vietnam before it went to China (Toan, 2017). Archeological sites in Kien An, Thuy Nguyen, Tien Lang, An Lao districts, Hai Phong depict that the land covers nine mountains jutting out to the East Sea, creating rich archeological value in Hai Phong in prehistoric period. During this time, Do Son, Hai Phong was a busy trading center under the Hung King dynasty of Vietnam. It was from here that several routes originated to reach other trading centers in Northern Vietnam, such as Luy Lau, Ke Cho, and Pho Hien. Among these trading centers, Luy Lau in Bac Ninh province became a famous Buddhist center in Vietnam in the early times.

Later, in the latter half of the second century BC, two Indian Buddhist monks, namely Mahajavaka and Kalyanacuri, came to Luy Lau. These traces can still be seen at Đậu pagoda in Bac Ninh province (Nga, 2020). Thus, historical evidence has proved that, instead of receiving Buddhism from China, Vietnam has transmitted Buddhism to China. Scholars are now of the opinion that Buddhism was transmitted to Banh Thanh, Lac Duong of China through Luy Lau of Vietnam (Toan, 2017). This was even acknowledged by Chinese scholars of the twentieth century such as Hu Shih (Ho Thich), Feng Youqing (Phung Huu Thanh) in their works. Thus, it is affirmed that Indian Buddhism was directly introduced to Vietnam before it spread to China.

Other sources also point to the fact that Indian Buddhism was transmitted to China from the Funan kingdom in the second century AD. According to Thái Nguyễn Đức Minh, in the book "Cao Tăng truyện" [Tales of Senior Monks], Volume 1 recorded: During the reign of Tấn Huệ Đế (290–306), the Indian monk, Mahajivaka, came to Funan to propagate dharma. The book titled "Nam Tề Thư" recorded an event: in 484, a Funan monk, Nagasena, went to (China) to invite the Southern emperor (hoàng đế Nam Tề) to come to help Buddhism flourish because the number of monks increased in large number and Hindu Dharma was expanding. During the reign of King Jayavarman (484–514), there were two Funan monks, i.e., Sanghapala and Mandra who went to China to translate Buddhist sutras, bringing Funan sutras to China. The book "Tales of Senior Monks" recorded that, in 548, (Chinese) Emperor sent an envoy to Funan to ask for Buddhist scriptures. The Funan King agreed to give monk Gumrata several sutra books to carry to China (Quân, 2017). The book titled "Lương Thư" also informs that the Lương dynasty sent a delegation to Funan to ask for Buddhist sutras and request senior monks to come to China to teach Buddhist Dharma in the period 535 to 545. The Funan King sent the Most Venerable Paramantha (or Gunatatna)—an Indian monk practicing Dharma in Funan—who brought 240 sets of Buddhist scriptures to China in 546 (Nhuệ, 2008). These facts are significant for the Indology in Vietnam, as it reaffirms that the Buddhism that traveled to Vietnam is "original" Buddhism and not diffused by Chinese Buddhism (Toan, 2017).

In the sixth century, Virutaruci, a Zen Buddhist monk, came to Giao Châu (Bac Ninh, Vietnam) and formed the first Zen Buddhist school in Vietnam, known as Virutaruci Zen School (Tỳ Ni Đa Lưu Chi). This Zen School was mainly influenced by Indian Buddhism and marginally by Chinese Buddhism. This school was transmitted through 19 generations and was lost in the thirteenth century.[4]

At the beginning of the eleventh century, a Zen monk, namely Sùng Phạm (passed away in 1087), belonging to the eleventh generation of Virutaruci Zen School, went to India to study Buddhism for nine years. When he returned, he started a school in Pháp Vân pagoda. Many disciples followed him, including Đạo Hạnh, a Zen monk known for his esoteric Buddhism. Sùng Phạm helped in promoting and strengthening Buddhism in Vietnam. The King Lê Đại Hành (Lê Dynasty) sought his advice many times. Apart from Sùng Phạm, some other Indian Tantric monks also came to Vietnam later on, such as Yogibrahman (thirteenth century), other Buddhist monks (fourteenth century), and were warmly welcomed by the Trần Dynasty.

Archeological findings and other sources revealed that Indian Buddhism penetrated and diffused into local societies of Vietnam since early history. As pointed out by Liên, in Northern Vietnam, "the most interesting story is the origin of the Four Dharma Buddhas" (Liên, 2018, p. 114). The local people also refer to the "Four

---

[4] Thiền phái Tỳ-ni-da-lưu-chi. http://langmai.org/tang-kinh-cac/vien-sach/giang-kinh/viet-nam-phat-giao-su-luan/chuong-05-thien-phai-ty-ni-da-luu-chi?set_language=vi, accessed on October 1, 2019.

Dharma Buddhas as the Four Lady Buddhas: Pháp Vân (Cloud Lady), Pháp Vũ (Rain Lady), Pháp Lôi (Thunder Lady), and Pháp Điển (Lighting Lady)." The tradition of worshipping the Four Dharma Buddhas is witnessed in various areas of the Red River delta. According to Liên, this is an old tradition that the Indian Vedic cult could have influenced, even as it was overlaid with Chinese elements during the Hán domination in the early Christian era. Other areas in Northern Vietnam, such as Lạch Trường in the old Mã river mouth (Thanh Hóa province) and Vinh in Lam river mouth (Nghệ An province), were dynamic centers from the early first millennium CE. The Tháp Nhạn Buddhist stupa (Nam Đàn, Nghệ An) is "the outcome of a mixture between Việt, Chinese, and Indian elements during the seventh–ninth centuries" (Dũng & Cường, 1987). Another interesting discovery is the tenth-century stone pillars inscribed with Indian Buddhist sutra using an old Chinese alphabet at Hoa Lư ancient capital, Ninh Bình province. This indicates that, although veiled by "an imposed layer of Chinese culture, the earlier Việt culture which was strongly dominated by Indian elements still survived" (Liên, 2018, p. 116).

In the present times, a large number of Buddhist monks and nuns from Vietnam travel to India to study Buddhism, thereby strengthening the Buddhist links. In 2016, Prime Minister Modi took time to visit Quan Su pagoda, reminiscing and affirming the more than 2000 years of Buddhist linkages between India and Vietnam. When the late President Tran Dai Quang visited India in March 2018, he began his trip by visiting Bodhgaya Temple, the sacred place of Buddhism. This shows the importance of Buddhist imprints for the peoples of both countries.

2.2.2 Hindu Imprints

In addition to Buddhism, Hinduism came to Vietnam in a later period, at the beginning of the CE due to the commercial contacts between India and Vietnam. When the first wave of Indian merchants came to Vietnam, they were accompanied by priests and religious artifacts. They played a remarkable role in molding the history, culture, and civilization of the people of Vietnam (Mazumdar, 1979). Scholars in Vietnam are of the view that, "the Đồng Nai and Mekong river systems played essential roles in the diffusion of Indian civilization to the inland areas of what is now Southern Vietnam and Southern Cambodia. Phallic type Sivalingas, representing the earliest Hindu beliefs, have been unearthed at the late prehistoric sites at Giồng Nổi (Bến Tre province) and Gò Cao Su (Long An province)" (Dũng & Tới, 2007, pp. 13–15). Archeological evidence shows the influence of Hinduism in Funan (*Phù Nam*), Oc Eo, and Champa cultures. Funan and Champa were the first Hindu kingdoms in Vietnam that were established in the first centuries AD. Several monuments dating from the second half of the first millennium CE stand testimony to this influence. To name a few, these are the Vĩnh Hưng tower (Minh Hải province), Bình Thạnh and Chót Mạt (Tây Ninh province) and several ruins of the Cát Tiên temple complex in Lâm Đồng province (Liên, 2018, p. 120). According to Lê Thị Liên, all these monuments are "dated to the flourishing period of the Óc Eo culture. The artifacts found inside the temples' foundation demonstrate a rich and diverse Hindu pantheon.

The art, iconographic features, and Hindu architecture reflect a long history of cultural interaction with various Indian areas and art centers" (Liên, 2018, p. 120).

According to an inscription in the My Son Sanctuary, King Bhadravarman I in the fourth century AD offered this land to the god and built Bhadresvara temple. Therefore, this land is considered the holy land of the Champa kingdom. According to *Associate Professor Dr. Dang Van Thang, Deparment of Archeology, Faculty of History, University of Social Sciences and Humanities—Vietnam National University, HCMC-cum-Standing Vice Chairman of Ho Chi Minh City Historical Science Association,*[5] "My Son Sanctuary was forgotten after the reign of King Jaya Paramesvaravarman II, XIII century. The Champa kings, after taking the throne, often went to My Son Sanctuary to build temples to dedicate to the gods, to restore, and embellish the old temples."

At present, My Son Heritage Site is the living proof of the Hindu connection between the two nations. Over time, Indian emigrants became permanent settlers in what was known as Champa and in parts of Funan (Cochin China) by inter-marrying local women, but at the same time, they maintained regular and close links with their homeland. Thus, a process of "Indianization" was begun by which the Indian literature, language, philosophy, beliefs, art and architecture, customs, and manners were spread to Vietnam through peaceful means (Coedes, 1996). Funan and Champa, located in the central coastal and Southern parts of Vietnam, became the first Indianized kingdoms in Vietnam. Various Hindu dynasties ruled over the kingdom of Champa from different capitals such as Amaravathi (Dong Duong), Panduranga (Phan Rang), Sri Vyaya (Binh Dinh), and Kauthara (Nha Trang) until the middle of the fifteenth century. Even the name Champa is derived from the province of Bhagalpur in Bihar, India. Perhaps, the original inhabitants of Champa originated from the Indian city of that time. It was mainly in the nineteenth century, when from French colonies in India, including Pondicherry, Karaikal, and Mahe that Indian migration to Indochina took place. These Indian migrants had a salient role in spreading Indian culture.

The statistics of the 2009 census in Vietnam showed that there were 161,729 Cham people, mostly living in the Southwest and Southeast provinces of Vietnam, including Thuan Hai, Nghia Binh, Phu Khanh, An Giang, Dong Nai, Tay Ninh, and Ho Chi Minh City.[6] Champa chose to adopt Indian manners, language, and religion and thus was entirely influenced by Indian culture. The influence of Shaivism, Vaishnavism, and Buddhism on the Chams was so significant that "their social organization, marriage, and inheritance rules have not changed despite their conversion to Islam later on. They changed their religion so as to protect themselves from the Muslim invasion" (Dutt, 1985, p. 181). Refer Image 2.2.

---

[5] Associate Professor Dr. Dang Van Thang, Deparment of Archeology, Faculty of History, University of Social Sciences and Humanities—Vietnam National University, HCMC-cum-Standing Vice Chairman of Ho Chi Minh City Historical Science Association, shared details about the My Son sanctuary in a seminar held on August 23, 2021.

[6] Committee for Ethnic Minority Affairs (Ủy ban Dân tộc), http://www.cema.gov.vn/gioi-thieu/cong-dong-54-dan-toc/nguoi-cham.htm.

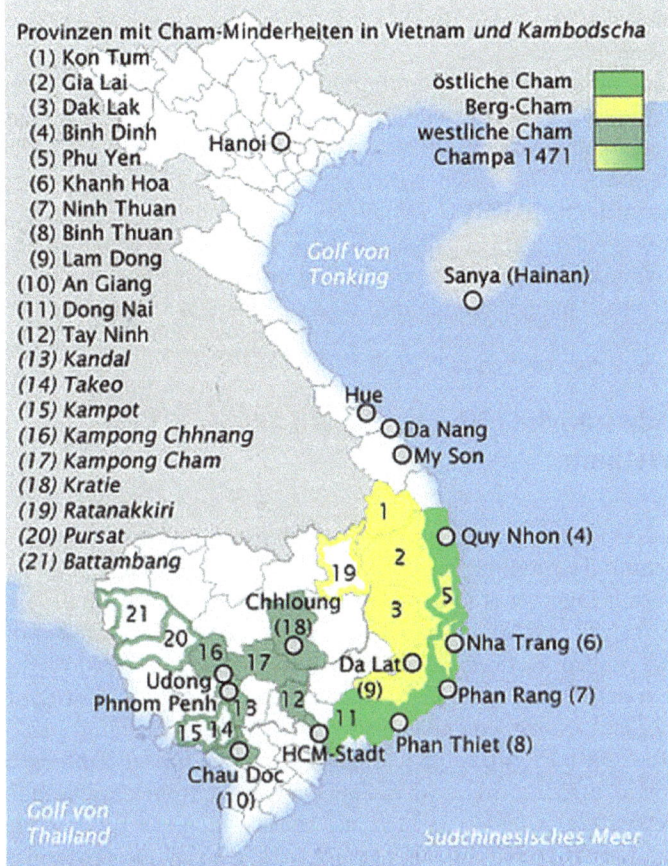

Provinzen mit Cham-Minderheiten in Vietnam *und Kambodscha*
- (1) Kon Tum
- (2) Gia Lai
- (3) Dak Lak
- (4) Binh Dinh
- (5) Phu Yen
- (6) Khanh Hoa
- (7) Ninh Thuan
- (8) Binh Thuan
- (9) Lam Dong
- (10) An Giang
- (11) Dong Nai
- (12) Tay Ninh
- *(13) Kandal*
- *(14) Takeo*
- *(15) Kampot*
- *(16) Kampong Chhnang*
- *(17) Kampong Cham*
- *(18) Kratie*
- *(19) Ratanakkiri*
- *(20) Pursat*
- *(21) Battambang*

östliche Cham
Berg-Cham
westliche Cham
Champa 1471

Image 2.2 Cham People in Vietnam and Cambodia. *Source* https://commons.wikimedia.org/wiki/File:Cham_People_in_Vietnam_and_Cambodia.jpg; November 25, 2010; accessed on May 31, 2021

Thus, it is not possible to deny the profound imprints of Indian culture and civilization on the everyday life of the ancient people in Vietnam from various sources. Since early time, Indian Buddhism and Hinduism had come and coexisted with local beliefs and later with other religions such as Christianity and Islam. More recently, during the French colonial period in the late nineteenth and early twentieth centuries, several Hindu temples were built in Saigon (Ho Chi Minh City) to serve as places of worship and community activities for the Indian diaspora when they came to the city. Mrs. Sadhana Saxena, in an interview to the authors, confirmed that the people of Vietnam are very warm and affectionate toward Indians and enjoy participating in all Indian festivals. She also explained that her Hindi language students learn various forms of Indian dances and art.[7]

The unique proofs of the modern imprints are the existence and functioning of the Hindu temples in Ho Chi Minh City. The three remaining active temples include Subramanyam Swamy Temple (98 Nam Kỳ Khởi Nghĩa street), Sri Thenday Yuthapani Temple (66 Tôn Thất Thiệp street), and Mariamman Temple (45 Trương Định street), all are in district 1 of Ho Chi Minh City. Thus, from ancient to modern periods, imprints of Buddhism and Hinduism have been found in Vietnam. Traces of Indian religions have integrated into Vietnamese culture and have become an inseparable part of Vietnamese indigenous culture.

2.3   People Imprints: Rabindranath Tagore's Visit to Vietnam

People are a representation of culture. Rabindranath Tagore is perhaps the most exemplary cultural representative of India who visited Vietnam in 1929.

Rabindranath Tagore was supposed to visit Vietnam in 1924, but the visit did not materialize. Instead of Rabindranath, his close associate and a Professor of History, Kalidas Nag, visited Vietnam in 1924.[8] It was Vietnamese social reformers, Bùi Quang Chiếu and Dương Văn Giao, who requested Tagore to visit Sai Gon. Bùi Quang Chiếu and Dương Văn Giao also visited Tagore's Shantiniketan School in India (Smith, 2008). In Japan, the representative of the French Embassy extended the invitation to Tagore to stop over at Sài Gòn enroute from Canada and America. Tagore accepted the invitation in 1929 and became the State Guest of the French Government. On his arrival, he was heartily welcomed by the people of Sài Gòn. A reception committee including French, Indian, and Vietnamese community was formed to receive Rabindranath at Sài Gòn.[9] Vietnamese members of the reception committee included Bùi Quang Chiếu, Dương Văn Giao, Diệp Văn Kỳ, Luu Văn Lang, Nguyễn Văn San, and Lê Trung Nghĩa. During his brief stopover at Saigon, the print media was replete with illustrated reports on the poet's visit along with translations of his speeches, treatise, and poems in Vietnamese.

Rabindranath Tagore stayed at Saigon between the twenty-first and twenty-third June 1929. Twenty-first June was declared a public holiday in Saigon to show special honor to the visiting Poet. His brief and only visit to Saigon was eventful. He wore a Vietnamese outfit—a black tunic and white trousers—specially designed for him during his visit. Though he was physically exhausted during his visit to Saigon after

---

[7] Mrs. Sadhana Saxena teaches Hindi at the HCMC University of Social sciences and Humanities. She shared her views with the authors on August 13, 2021.

[8] Speech by Professor Bidyut Chakrabarty, Vice Chancellor of Visva-Bharti University, Shantiniketan at a seminar to celebrate the 90th year of Gurudev Rabindranath Tagore's visit to Saigon, Vietnam Academy of Social Sciences, Hanoi, 29 March 2019.

[9] See Footnote 8.

trips to distant Canada and America, he delivered moving and inspiring speeches in Saigon. In his speeches, he emphasized the ancient cultural linkages between the peoples of India and Vietnam:

> Before human joys and human miseries, my heart always beats with the same rhythm as that of those of my predecessors who in the most distant past lived among you, I bring you the greetings of that radiant India, who lavished her sight on this land as well as the message of sympathy and brotherhood of present India who lives separated from you by geographic distance and by the dead solitude of her own darkness. (Reddy, 2009, p. 6)

And more:

> In the past, people from my country used to come to your land dreaming their dreams under your beautiful skies, singing their songs, creating beautiful things and building their temples. Nevertheless, in the centuries that followed, the facts of history and the barriers of geography had succeeded in interrupting that wonderful relationship. I have come to your shores today with nothing to offer you but my songs. Can I not beg of you to give me a small corner of your heart?[10]

At the Municipal Theatre of Sai Gon, Bui Quang Chieu said, "...*the Poet Tagore does not cultivate a narrow nationalism... Far from being hostile to Western Civilisations, the illustrious inhabitant of Shantiniketan wishes with all his soul of a poet to combine the civilizations of the East and of the West in order to give to the world their full value-generating beauty and goodness.*"[11] In the words of Duong Van Giao, "*And you have come here today, Teacher, to give us proof of [India's] extraordinary vitality. Thanks to you, our traditions and our relationships are going from now on to be renewed usefully.*"[12]

At Rabindra-Bhavana Museum in India, there is a handwritten citation in French, addressed to Tagore by Duong Van Giao. It reads.

> As you are, Master, not only the Poet of Asia but according to the word of the most significant contemporary politician Gandhi, the Poet of the world. You not only bring honor to your motherland but also to the humanity to whom you devote even now all your thought and activity in spite of your advanced age.
>
> … Master, your arrival heralds peace and freedom in the Indochinese Union. We welcome you with all humility.[13]

Vietnamese famous poet, Xuan Dieu, remembering Rabindranath Tagore's visit to Sai Gon, later said: "I thought that our city of Sai Gon then was holding the precious thing of human intelligence."[14]

In March 2019, the Institute for Indian and Southwest Asian Studies (VIISAS), Vietnam Academy of Social Sciences (VASS), organized an international seminar and photo exhibition to celebrate Gurudev Rabindranath Tagore's 90 years visit to

---

[10] Requote from the speech by Professor Bidyut Chakrabarty.

[11] See Footnote 8.

[12] Speech by Professor Bidyut Chakrabarty.

[13] See Footnote 10.

[14] See Footnote 8.

Saigon (today Ho Chi Minh City). The Vice-Chancellor of Visva-Bharti University, Professor Bidyut Chakrabarty, came to Vietnam to deliver the keynote address. Gurudev Tagore's visit to Vietnam and the excitement and inspiration that he brought to the Vietnamese people in the 1920s is also a landmark in India–Vietnam cultural interaction. As pointed out by the Indian President Ram Nath Kovind in his speech at the Vietnam National Assembly in Hanoi in November 2018: "In the ultimate analysis, the people-to-people network between Vietnam and India… is the foundation and the edifice of our partnership."

Frequent exchange of visits by later generations of great personalities of the two countries which were mentioned in the previous chapter also helps strengthen the cultural connection between the two sides. Culture has always been quintessential in all high-level visits. In 1959, Indian President, Rajendra Prasad, gifted Vietnam a Boddhi tree planted at Trấn Quốc pagoda (National Defence pagoda) in Hanoi capital. In 2014, President Pranab Mukherjee also presented Vietnam with another Boddhi tree originating from Bodhgaya where Lord Buddha got enlightenment. These are pieces of evidence of India–Vietnam friendship sustained by cultural linkages.

2.4 India–Vietnam Cultural Cooperation in the New Millennium

In the new millennium, India is trying to reconnect with the Southeast Asian region including Vietnam with its "Look East" policy and to strengthen its engagement by "Acting East". Also, the prerequisites for the cultural cooperation between Vietnam and India are the historical foundation of cultural–religious interactions between the two countries and the strategy of cultural diplomacy promoting the soft power of each country in the twenty-first century. Though culture is not the focus at the meeting table of the two sides' leaders, it has always been important aspect of their bilateral relations. On September 3, 2016, while visiting Quán Sứ Pagoda, Prime Minister Modi affirmed: "The advent of Buddhism from India to Vietnam and the monuments of Vietnam's Hindu Cham temples stand testimony to these bonds…".[15]

2.4.1 Cultural Cooperation Activities

Along with the development of political, economic, security, and defense cooperation, cultural cooperation has also been strengthened by implementing several cultural exchange programs between the two sides.

---

[15] Press Statement by Prime Minister during his visit to Vietnam, http://www.pmindia.gov.in/en/news_updates/press-statement-by-prime-minister-during-his-visit-to-vietnam/ accessed 29th December 2017.

Annually, on India's Independence Day (August 15), the National Day of Vietnam (September 2), and the anniversary of the establishment of diplomatic ties between the two countries (January 7), many exhibitions and art performances are organized to showcase the beauty of both India and Vietnam to the common people of the two countries. The dynamic cultural cooperation between the two countries in the past decades can be shown through a long list of cultural activities in Table 2.1.

Table 2.1   Major activities of cultural cooperation between Vietnam and India (2000–2020)

Time	Contents
March 2010	A ceremony was held in New Delhi to launch the book *Traces of Indian culture in Vietnam* by Geetesh Sharma. The book was translated into Vietnamese and the Vietnamese version was launched in Hanoi on May 23, 2012
July 5, 2011	The Government of Vietnam decided to establish the Institute for Indian and Southwest Asian Studies, under the Vietnam Academy of Social Sciences. So far, the institute has conducted various research projects on Indian studies and maintained a monthly journal about India and promoted international cooperation with several research institutions in India
September 15, 2014	Indian President Pranab Mukherjee Vietnamese President Trương Tấn Sang attended the opening ceremony of the Center for Indian Studies at the National Academy of Politics and Public Administration
From March 5–15, 2014	Indian Festivals were organized in Hanoi, Danang and Ho Chi Minh City. Various cultural activities were held, including classical dance performances and poetry citations by Sangeet Natak Academy; Buddhist Festival of the Himalayan Central Research Institute; Food Festival, folk dance by Kalbelia Group, Mehendi and Yoga... All the activities received an enthusiastic response from Vietnamese side
From June 25–29, 2014	A Bollywood dance troupe of 12 members came to Vietnam under the auspices of the Indian Council for Cultural Relations (ICCR). The dance troupe performed in Hanoi, Phú Thọ, Yên Bái and got the love of Vietnamese audience
From September 14–17, 2014	Indian President Pranab Mukherjee visited Vietnam. In addition to the signing of Joint Statement and many other cooperation agreements, an important symbolic event was that President Pranab presented Vietnam a Bodhi tree originating from Bodhgaya, where Lord Buddha got enlightenment, and is a symbol for the consolidation between Vietnam and India in terms of culture, religion, and history. During his stay in Vietnam, President Mukherjee also visited Trấn Quốc pagoda. A Bodhi tree was planted by the first President of India, Rajendra Prasad, in 1959 and is growing as a beautiful proof of the sustainability of Vietnam–India friendship

(continued)

Table 2.1 (continued)

Time	Contents
September 27–28, 2014	Vietnamese President Nguyễn Tấn Dũng visited India. This was the third visit of Nguyễn Tấn Dũng to India (the previous visits were made in 2007, 2012). Of the seven MoUs signed between Vietnam and India during the visit of Prime Minister Nguyễn Tấn Dũng on October 27–28, 2014, there are up to five MoUs related to culture, education, and media connections. This shows that cultural cooperation has become a significant part of bilateral relations. These cooperation agreements include MoU on the establishment of Nalanda University; MoU on Conservation and Restoration of the World Heritage Site of Mỹ Sơn, Quảng Nam province, Vietnam; MoU on establishing the Centre for English Language and Information Technology Training at the Telecommunications University; Cultural Exchange Programme 2015–2017; MoU on Exchange of Audio-Visual Programmes. These cooperation agreements have pushed cultural cooperation between the two countries. According to Indian Ambassador Preeti Saran, cultural cooperation has been the highlight in India–Vietnam ties[a]
August 20, 2015	At the Vietnam Academy of Social Sciences, the Hanoi Union of Friendship Organizations (HAUFO), in collaboration with the Institute for Indian and Southwest Asian Studies, organized a ceremony to celebrate the 68th years of India's Independence and the opening of three new branches of the HAUFO. HAUFO was set up in Hanoi and many other cities of Vietnam in 2002, promoting people-to-people and cultural contact between the two countries (Binh & Anh, 2018)
June 21, 2015	The First International Yoga Day was held at Quần Ngựa Sports Complex in Hanoi with nearly 5000 people and about 900 Yoga performers. This was a Yoga festival, attracting many Vietnamese people. Currently, the Government of India has sent one professional Yoga teacher to Hanoi to teach Yoga for the Vietnamese people. The first Yoga class has been opened at Hanoi University of Social Sciences and Humanities in January 2016 (Nga & Quang, 2021)
From December 12–13, 2015	Indian Film Festivals were held in Hanoi, Danang, and Ho Chi Minh City, attracting many Vietnamese audiences
March 2018	Among the many cultural events organized to celebrate 45 years of diplomatic relations and ten years of Strategic Partnership between Vietnam and India, Indian Buddhist Days Festivals at the Mandala Great Stupa, Tay Thien Pagoda, Vinh Phuc province in Vietnam is an important one. The event has helped revive the cultural and spiritual connections between Vietnam and India through Buddhism (Nga, 2017)

(continued)

Table 2.1 (continued)

Time	Contents
October 2020	Indian Cultural Days were jointly organized by the Institute for Indian and Southwest Asian Studies, Swami Vivekananda Cultural Centre, and School of Social Science Education at Vinh University, Nghệ An province, which attracted many researchers, teachers, and students

Source Compilation by the authors
[a]Speech by Ambassador Preeti Saran at the end-year meeting at Hanoi Union of Friendship Organizations, on January 19, 2016

In addition, many academic conferences on Indian cultural values, India–Vietnam cultural interaction have been held in Vietnam. To name a few: international conference on "Buddhist linkages between India–ASEAN and Vietnam", jointly organized by Indian Embassy in Hanoi and Vietnam Academy of Social Sciences in April 2011; international conference on "Cham civilization, Vietnam and India Linkages", jointly organized by Indian Embassy in Hanoi and the Institute of Culture and Art, Ministry of Culture, Sports and Tourism in Da Nang in June 2012; international conference on "Indian traces in the acculturation of Vietnam and Southeast Asia", at Ho Chi Minh City University of Social Sciences and Humanities in May 2013. A national conference on "Indian Values in Asia" was organized at the Ho Chi Minh City University of Social Sciences and Humanities on January 8, 2016.

Vietnam and India have been engaging in new development partnership projects in heritage conservation. Cooperation in the conservation of the Mỹ Sơn Heritage Site has been actively promoted in the last decade. Mỹ Sơn Heritage Site was recognized as a World Heritage Site in 1999 and is one of the 23 Special National Heritage Sites of Vietnam. In November 2010, India sent a delegation from the Archeological Survey of India to survey the Champa tower relics in Vietnam. After the survey, ASI experts made a report about the possibility of joint cooperation in the conservation of the Champa towers at Mỹ Sơn. The report also mentioned setting up a conservation project at Mỹ Sơn Heritage Site in 5 years. The Indian Government announced the funding of nearly 3 million USD for this project. In 2018, after the visit to India by Vietnamese President Trần Đại Quang, India provided a credit package to restore and renovate the Hoa Lai and Champa Po Klong Garai Stupas and nonrefundable aid to the Cham communities in Ninh Thuan province (Nga & Quang, 2020).

Currently, Vietnam and India are working together to preserve the temple at Mỹ Sơn, Đồng Dương Buddhist Monastery in Quảng Nam, and the Nhạn Chăm Tower in Phú Yên. According to Ambassador of India to Vietnam, Pranay Verma, "heritage conservation is an excellent way of reminding us how profoundly and deeply we are connected historically as culture, as civilization. This is an area where India has lots of expertise because we have some of the oldest institutions in the world engaging in archeological conservation."[16]

---

[16] Vietnam, India cooperation in heritage conservation, m.vovworld.vn.

The Mỹ Sơn complex is a huge temple complex. Vietnam and India are currently engaged in three projects: block H, block K, and block A inside the Mỹ Sơn complex. Blocks H and K are complete; the work on block A has begun. The idea of the preservation work is not to construct a new building but to preserve heritage values and enable it to retain its originality as a ruined building for posterity. It is not about transforming the complex into modern structures but preserving their antiquity, as they hold precious memories and stories about the historical connect.[17]

To commemorate the 50th anniversary of bilateral diplomatic relations in 2022, the governments of the two countries are engaged in a compilation of an encyclopedia of India–Vietnam cultural and civilizational relations.[18] This project is to be conducted jointly by the Institute for Indian and Southwest Asian Studies (VIISAS), Vietnam Academy of Social Sciences (VASS), the Indian Council for Cultural Relations (ICCR), and Swami Vivekananda Cultural Centre, Hanoi (SVCC).

The dense list of cultural exchange activities between Vietnam and India suggests that India–Vietnam cultural cooperation has been growing strongly since the beginning of the twenty-first century.

The most significant new development in Vietnam–India cultural cooperation in the new millennium is the formal inauguration and effective functioning of the Indian Cultural Centre (later renamed as Swami Vivekananda Cultural Centre) in Hanoi and the Centre for Vietnam Studies in New Delhi (Nga & Quang, 2021).

2.4.2   Swami Vivekananda Cultural Centre, Hanoi

The Indian Cultural Centre (ICC) was established in September 2017 on Prime Minister Modi's visit to Vietnam and was formally inaugurated on April 21, 2017. Its headquarters are at No. 63, Trần Hưng Đạo street, Hoàn Kiếm Lake, Hanoi. It was renamed Swami Vivekananda Cultural Centre in 2019 due to the celebration of the 125th anniversary of Swami Vivekananda's speech at the Chicago Parliament of World Religions. Since its establishment, SVCC has been very active in organizing cultural events and promoting India–Vietnam cultural interaction. It regularly organizes events to popularize India's vast and colorful culture in Vietnam and receive positive responses from the Vietnamese people. The inaugural ceremony of the SVCC was marked by the charming performances of Indian classical dances at Hanoi Opera House on April 21, 2017, including Kuchipudi, Bharatanatyam, Odissi, and Kathak, together with a concert between the Indian Army and the People's Army of Vietnam which have left a deep impression on the Vietnamese audience, increased the admiration among the Vietnamese about the rich culture of India. Similar cultural activities are organized monthly, even weekly at the center, for example: famous Bollywood movies screenings (*3 idiots*, *Paheli*, *Mary Kom*, *Tanu Weds Manu*, *Bhaag Milkha*

---

[17] See Footnote 16.

[18] India–Vietnam Joint Vision for Peace, Prosperity and People. https://www.mea.gov.in/bilateral-documents.htm?dtl/33324/India_Vietnam_Joint_Vision_for_Peace_Prosperity_and_People.

Bhaag); inviting specialists from India to come to Hanoi to conduct workshops on Indian music, dances and Yoga (Kuchipudi and Odissi workshop; Bharatanatyam and Kathak workshop); Buddhist exhibitions, food festivals, textile and fashion shows, among others. Apart from regular events, SVCC Hanoi also collaborates with other organizations in organizing large-scale events such as the International Yoga Day in Hanoi, attracting thousands of Vietnamese Yoga-lovers from all parts of the country. The celebration of Diwali festival with lights and special shows also attracted thousands of Vietnamese people. On March 26–27, 2019, it organized a two-day workshop introducing Kuchipudi–Indian classical dance to the Vietnamese people. A quiz contest about Mahatma Gandhi was organized to celebrate the 150th birth anniversary of the Mahatma. All these activities have helped SVCC Hanoi to build up a base of regular visitors and a reputation for being a cultural hub sharing the Indian way of life with the Vietnamese people.

In present times, SVCC is the key agency in promoting cultural interactions in Hanoi. It is equipped with a library of more than 2000 books about India, both in English and Vietnamese. ICC also offers regular Yoga and traditional Indian dance classes for months at an affordable cost. The Yoga classes are always full, and people who want to register may have to wait for sometime before they are enrolled into a class.

2.4.3 Centre for Vietnam Studies, New Delhi

The Centre for Vietnam Studies was also formally established during the official visit to India by Vietnamese President Tran Dai Quang on March 4–6, 2018 (Nga & Quang, 2021). The center organized its inaugural ceremony on May 15, 2018. Since then, the center has organized many events including the Anniversary of President's Birthday, India–Vietnam Youth Dialogue, Screening of movies, International Conference "India–Vietnam: Strengthening Economic Ties" on July 26–27, 2018. In 2020, in the context of the COVID-19 pandemic, the Centre for Vietnam Studies, in collaboration with the Society for Policy Research and Empowerment and Embassy of the Socialist Republic of Vietnam New Delhi, organized an international video symposium on "Public Diplomacy and India–Vietnam Engagements" on June 12, 2020 (Nga & Quang, 2021).

In addition, research institutes like Vietnam Institute for Indian and Southwest Asian Studies (VIISAS), Vietnam Academy of Social Sciences, and Vietnam–India Friendship Organizations in Vietnam are active agencies in promoting cultural exchanges and people-to-people contact between the two countries. The Union of Friendship Organizations of Vietnam and the Association of Friendship and Cultural Cooperation of India signed an MOU on cooperation between the two sides for 2017–2022. The overall objective of the MOU is to enhance mutual understanding between the peoples of Vietnam and India, to foster cooperative partnership between the two countries in the fields of politics, economics, tourism, science and technology, and people exchange. Significantly, the two sides will vigorously promote its role as a bridge linking the two countries' media in exchanging programs and introducing attractive tourist destinations of the two countries.

2.5 Conclusion

India and Vietnam established contacts very early in history which led to the depth of their cultural–religious interactions. Through these contacts, local Vietnamese culture has been attracted by India's rich and diverse culture. As pointed out by the leaders and scholars of both sides, Indian culture reached Vietnam mainly through overtures of peace and hence could easily be implanted in the hearts of the Vietnamese people. The intermingling of Indian and Vietnamese communities inevitably led to the transformation and adaptation of both cultures. It has not led to the disappearance of one culture but has created unique features for both sides. Both the cultures have been enriched and renewed.

India–Vietnam cultural relations are integral to India–Southeast Asian cultural relations, in the past, present, and will continue in the future. Like many other countries in Southeast Asia, the early and prolonged cultural interaction has blended the two cultures and made it inseparable. Indian culture has become an integral part of Vietnamese national culture. The ancient and early medieval periods may be considered the golden periods of India–Vietnam cultural and civilizational links. The modern period saw revivalism of these cultural and civilizational linkages: Hindu temples were built in Southern Vietnam; visit to Vietnam by Rabindranath Tagore brought a new impetus to the bilateral cultural and civilizational relations.

It is important to emphasize that India–Vietnam relations are not only historical, but cultural and civilizational too. This implies that the people of our two nations established relations not due to narrow economic and commercial motivations, but at much more intense and experiential levels. It is the cohesion in terms of culture and civilization that makes the bilateral relationship inseparable. If interests and benefits control only commercial ties, these would be transient and short-lived. However, it is the enduring cultural and civilizational relationship, through which connections, though invisible, are time-tested and eternal. Like the core layer of an onion, cultural links at a deeper level exude the energy that keeps moving the wheels of our relations. The cultural strands of our two nations are woven together through the architectonics of temples, their varied materials and milieus, patronage and transregional connections, ritual observances and performance traditions, among several others. The current revivalism of India–Vietnam cultural and civilizational ties is an embodiment of recognizing the importance of the cultural aspect in bilateral engagement. These strong bonds of friendship help surmount challenges in the bilateral relationship.

To comprehend the bilateral aspects of the relationship, it is important to situate these within the multilateral framework of ASEAN. The next chapter comprises a discussion of the foreign policies of India and Vietnam, especially within India's

LEP and the Act East Policy (AEP) of 2014. India's convergence of interests with Southeast Asian nations provided a fillip to its economic, scientific, and strategic pursuits.

References

Address by the President of India, Shri Ram Nath Kovind on Mahashivratri celebrations at Isha Yoga Center.

Archaeological Survey of India discovers 9th century sandstone Shiva Linga in Vietnam. https://theprint.in/india/archaeological-survey-of-india-discovers-9th-century-sandstone-shiva-linga-in-vietnam/430366/

Bảo tàng điêu khắc Chăm Đà Nẵng có thêm hai hiện vật được công nhận bảo vật quốc gia. http://www.chammuseum.vn/view.aspx?ID=499&title=bao_tang_dieu_khac_cham_da_nang_co_them_hai_hien_vat_duoc_cong_nhan_bao_vat_quoc_gia

Binh, N. X., & Anh, N. T. (2018). Promotion of Vietnam–India comprehensive strategic partnership. *International Studies*.

Coedes, G. (1996). *The Indianized states of Southeast Asia*. University of Hawaii Press.

Coedes, G. (2008). *Cổ sử các quốc gia Ấn Độ hóa ở Viễn Đông*. NXB Thế giới.

Committee for Ethnic Minority Affairs (Ủy ban Dân tộc). http://www.cema.gov.vn/gioi-thieu/cong-dong-54-dan-toc/nguoi-cham.htm

Dhar, P. P. (2018). Monuments, motifs, myths: Architecture and its transformations in early India and Southeast Asia. In S. Saran (Ed.), *Cultural and civilizational links between India and Southeast Asia*. https://doi.org/10.1007/978-981-10-7317-5_19

Dũng, T. A., & Cường, N. M. (1987). *Tháp Nhạn ở Nghệ Tĩnh qua hai lần khai quật [Tháp Nhạn site in Nghệ Tĩnh province after the two excavations]*. Document of Vietnam Institute of Archaeology.

Dũng, T. A., & T´ời, L. V. (2007). Di chỉ Giồng Nổi (Bến Tre) qua ba lần khai quật [Giồng Nổi site (Bến Tre province) after the three excavations]. *Khảo Cổ học [Archeological Review], 2*(146).

Dutt, A. K. (1985). *Southeast Asia: Realm of contrast, Boulder*.

Guy, J. (2018). Shiva's land: Understanding the religious landscape of early Southeast Asia. In S. Saran (Ed.), *Cultural and civilizational links between India and Southeast Asia*. https://doi.org/10.1007/978-981-10-7317-5_15

India–Vietnam joint vision for peace, prosperity and people. https://www.mea.gov.in/bilateral-documents.htm?dtl/33324/India__Vietnam_Joint_Vision_for_Peace_Prosperity_and_People

Liên, L. T. (2018). Indian–Southeast Asian contacts and cultural exchanges: Evidence. In S. Saran (Ed.), *Cultural and civilizational links between India and Southeast Asia*. https://doi.org/10.1007/978-981-10-7317-5_7

Marwah, R. (2020). *Re-imagining India-Thailand relations: A multilateral and bilateral perspective*. World Scientific.

Mazumdar, A. C. (1979). *India and Southeast Asia, Delhi*.

Mishra, P. P. (2001). India–Southeast Asian relations: An overview, Teaching South Asia. *An Internet Journal of Pedagogy, 1*(1).

Nehru, J. (2010). *The discovery of India*. Penguin.

Nga, L. T. H. (2017). *Vietnam-India relations since September 2016: From the symbolic to practical results*. Sage.

Nga, L. T. H. (2020). Hindu temples in Ho Chi Minh City: Living proof of Vietnam–India religious interaction. *Vietnam Social Sciences Review, 3*(197), 3–18. ISSN: 1013–4328.

Nga, L. T. H., & Quang, T. H. (2020). Tightening India–Vietnam cultural and educational ties. In G. Jayachandra Reddy & N. X. Trung (Eds.), *India and Vietnam: New horizons*. Narendra Publishing House.

Nga, L. T. H., & Quang, T. H. (2021). Public diplomacy in strengthening India–Vietnam relations. *India Quarterly: A Journal of International Affairs.*

Nhuệ, N. Đ. (2008). *Phù Nam: Huyền thoại và những vấn đề lịch sử (Funan: Mythology and historical issues).* http://nghiencuuquocte.org/2017/11/03/phu-nam-huyen-thoai-va-nhung-van-de-lich-su

Press Statement by Prime Minister during his visit to Vietnam. http://www.pmindia.gov.in/en/news_updates/press-statement-by-prime-minister-during-his-visit-to-vietnam/. Accessed December 29, 2017.

Quân, T. N. Đ. M. (2017). *Vương Quốc Phù Nam (Funan Kingdom).* http://sites.google.com/site/quankhoasu/vuong-quoc-phu-nam-1

Reddy, C. R. (2009). *India and Vietnam: Era of friendship and cooperation (1947-1991)* (p. 6). Emerald Publishers.

Roy, A. B., & Bhattacharya, S. (2015). *India and Southeast Asia: States, borders and culture.* Shipra, Maulana Abul Kalam Azad Institute of Asian Studies.

Sharma, G. (2012). *Những dấu vết Văn hóa Ấn Độ tại Việt Nam (Traces of Indian culture in Vietnam)* (Translated by Thich Tri Minh), Nxb. Văn hóa Văn nghệ Tp. Hồ Chí Minh, Tp. Hồ Chí Minh.

Smith, R. B. (2008). Bui Quang Chieu and the Constitutionalist Party in French Cochinchina, 1917-30. *Modern Asian Studies.*

Speech by Ambassador Preeti Saran at the end-year meeting of Hanoi Union of Frienship Organizations, on 19th January 2016.

Speech by Professor Bidyut Chakrabarty, Vice Chancellor of Visva-Bharti University, Shantiniketan at a seminar to celebrate the 90th year of Gurudev Rabindranath Tagore's visit to Saigon, Vietnam Academy of Social Sciences, Hanoi, 29 March 2019.

Suryanarayan, V. (2013, March). India and Southeast Asia, a personal narrative from Chennai. *IPCS special report.*

Thiền phái Tỳ-ni-đa-lưu-chi. http://langmai.org/tang-kinh-cac/vien-sach/giang-kinh/viet-nam-phat-giao-su-luan/chuong-05-thien-phai-ty-ni-da-luu-chi?set_language=vi

Toan, L. V. (2017). *Ngọn nguồn giao lưu văn hóa việt Nam - Ấn Độ (Trường hợp Chùa Đót Sơn, xã Cấp Tiến, Huyện Tiên Lãng, Hải Phòng) (Phần 1) (Origin of Vietnam–India Cultural Interaction, The case of Dot Son Pagoda, Cap Tien commune, Tien Lang district, Hai Phong province).* http://cis.org.vn/article/2235/ngon-nguon-giao-luu-van-hoa-viet-nam-an-do-truong-hop-chua-dot-son-xa-cap-tien-huyen-tien-lang-hai-phong-phan-1.html

Walter de Gruyter GmbH. (2021). *Primary sources and Asian pasts.*

Chapter 3
Foreign Policies of Vietnam and India: Articulating Convergences

The previous chapter underlined the cultural and soft power connections. India's relationship with Vietnam, as has been articulated often by diplomats, "has no clouds and is clear as blue skies." Prof. Reddy echoed the same view, "There are no punctuation marks in this relationship as it stands the test of time over several decades." The strategic partnership of 2007 prospered into a Comprehensive Strategic Partnership in 2016, soon after 2014, when India's LEP advanced to the Act East Policy (AEP). Vietnam has always attached importance to the Indian factor in its foreign policy, since it promoted a multilateral and diversified foreign policy. This chapter analyses the importance of India in Vietnam's foreign policy since its reform by examining its relations with India in strategic politics, security, and defense which were specified in the important political documents of the Communist Party of Vietnam (CPV).

3.1 Vietnam's Position in India's Foreign Policy

3.1.1 Overview of India's Foreign Policy

There are various ways of periodization of India's foreign policy from independence to the present. According to J. N. Dixit, India's foreign policy in the post-independence period can be divided into four major phases: the first phase from 1946 to 1954; the second phase from 1954 to 1962; the third phase from 1962 to 1984; the fourth phase from 1984 to 2014. From 2014 up to now may be termed as the current phase.

During the first phase (1946–1954), the main concerns in India's foreign policy included: national consolidation and territorial integration; the evolution of a political and strategic worldview amid the confrontation between the US-led Western allies and the Soviet-led group of socialist countries; establishment of relations with two of India's most important neighbors, Pakistan and China, with one displaying its hostile attitude (Pakistan) and the other ambiguity (China) (Springer Science and Business

© The Author(s), under exclusive license to Springer Nature Singapore Pte Ltd. 2021   45
R. Marwah and L. T. Hằng Nga, *India–Vietnam Relations*, Dynamics of Asian
Development, https://doi.org/10.1007/978-981-16-7822-6_3

Media LLC, 1984). India was also concerned about the existence of colonialism in Asian and African countries. India's foreign policy during this period had several key features: (1) a non-aligned stance in the context of the Cold War (Mukherjee, 2020); (2) an assertive political and military attitude in consolidating India's territorial integrity in its dealings with Pakistan and the princely states; (3) striving to maintain a reasonable, friendly balance with China (India gave concessions to China on the issue of Tibet and supported China's entry in the United Nations and the Security Council); (4) banding together newly independent states on matters of common concern. The objective here was to ensure that these countries retain the right to strategic autonomy in decision-making on internal affairs, foreign and defense policy without any pressure by external powers.

During the second phase (1954–1962), India went through a turbulent period that culminated in a military defeat against China in 1962. India's concerns over Pakistan increased significantly after Pakistan entered a defense and military pact with the U.S. in 1954 and participated in the Treaty of Southeast Asia (SEATO) and the Central Treaty Organization (CENTO). Meanwhile, the West's economic, political and defense aid to India was somewhat modest.

During the third phase (1964–1984), there was a change in the focus and direction of India's foreign policy (Springer Science and Business Media LLC, 2020). Under the leadership of Prime Minister Indira Gandhi, India's foreign policy shifted in the direction of political realism, much different from the romantic illusions and moral idealism that was once imbued in India's foreign policy Nehru period. As stated by Indira Gandhi: "My father (Nehru) is a saint who has strayed into politics, but I am a tough politician" (Nga, 2017a, b). During this period, Indira Gandhi implemented a foreign policy with two main objectives: to restore India's economic development and thereby maintain India's security and strengthen her position in the international arena. Indira Gandhi expanded India's defense cooperation with the Soviet Union and its allies, signed the Indo-Soviet Treaty of Peace, Friendship and Cooperation in August 1971 (Kumar, 2008).

However, India's close association with the Soviet Union, consolidated through the Treaty of friendship and cooperation led to skepticism toward India's ambitions in the wider region. In the 1980s, India's naval expansion was also viewed with suspicion by ASEAN countries as Indonesia, which shared the maritime space. During the height of the cold war, there was also a debate over India's recognition of the Heng Samrin regime in Cambodia in 1980, an initiative that the entire ASEAN region did not view as a positive one. Hence, India's engagement with most ASEAN countries, excluding Vietnam, was limited to cultural and diasporic exchanges (Sundararaman, 2021, pp. 386–387).

The fourth phase (1984–2014) began when Prime Minister Rajiv Gandhi came to power in 1984. Rajiv Gandhi's policies were lucid even as India reacted cautiously to new challenges and trends (the Cold War was on the verge of collapse, the Soviet Perestroika, China's Reform, Pakistan's possession of nuclear weapons causing a change in the military balance in South Asia. Rajiv Gandhi opened the possibility of drawing closer to the U.S. and the West while maintaining moderate relations with the Soviet Union; diversifying supplies and technology for defense; improving and normalizing relations with China, and liberalization of the economy). Since 1991, under the leadership of Prime Minister Narasimha Rao, India made significant adjustments to adapt to the new international environment of post-Cold War time. India implemented various economic and foreign policy reforms. With the end of the Cold War, India had to reconsider the appropriateness of the principle of non-alignment. India's security linkages with the Soviet Union had altered too. The collapse of the bipolar world system did not give way to a harmonious new world order, but it created new competition modes. Along with that, the acceleration of globalization and an information revolution created complexities that made it imperative for India to evolve a new agenda to find a foothold in the new world context.

Interestingly, on May 11 and 13, 1998, India conducted five nuclear tests, justified by both domestic and external transformations. Evidently, these stunned the world. According to Indrani Bagchi, "the tests set India on a road that led to a global acknowledgment of India not merely as a nuclear power. Very simply, it helped to get the global high table to make space for India."[1] India was also keen to be viewed as a responsible state. This change in India's stature was not lost on neighboring Southeast Asia. America too changed its attitude toward India (Talbott, 2006).

- *Adjustments of India's Foreign Policy Under Prime Minister Narendra Modi*

When Prime Minister Modi came to power in 2014, India's foreign policy turned a new page, marked by a dynamic, proactive, and assertive character. A key feature was India's unprecedented diplomatic access to all continents and hemispheres, covering big, medium, and small countries. Besides, Prime Minister Modi encouraged the greater engagement of states in the federal government's foreign affairs. The number of foreign visits by the Indian President, Prime Minister, Vice-President, Minister of External Affairs and other Ministers reached record levels. Prime Minister Modi is sometimes referred to as a "Diplomatic Prime Minister/Foreign Affairs Prime Minister". As of October 2019, he had visited 60 countries.

In some cases, like in neighboring countries, the Prime Minister's visits took place after a period of interruption that spanned many years, between 10 and 60 years. For Vietnam, the visit by Prime Minister Modi in 2016 was the first visit by an Indian prime minister in 15 years. Overall, the top leaders' visits and outreach with countries in all regions underline the commitment of the Indian government to building a relationship with all large and small nations in the spirit of "Vasudhaiva Kutumbakam," which means "the whole world is one family."

Based on the diplomatic legacy of the predecessor governments, the Modi administration has made crucial foreign policy adjustments (Binh, 2019).

Firstly, in terms of foreign policy objectives, the Modi government has prioritized economic development concomitant with geoeconomic factors. During previous governments, promoting economic development was not the key priority; those preceding it included territorial integrity, policy independence, and international

---

[1] Bagchi, I. https://economictimes.indiatimes.com/news/politics-and-nation/how-1998-pokhran-tests-changed-indias-image/a-sudden-decision/slideshow/64135032.cms, May 13, 1998; accessed on August 26, 2021.

peace and security. Physical location of a country can no longer constrain its economic choices as long as it is functionally connected with the larger web of cooperation (Yasmin, 2019: 325). Research on India in Vietnam emphasizes the criticality of the geoeconomic factor in shaping the country's foreign policy and at the same time points to the decline of the geopolitical factor in international relations. India has demonstrated alacrity in grasping reality when it defines economy and knowledge as critical attributes of the "new strategy of a New India" (Binh, 2019).

Secondly, in terms of foreign policy content, the Modi government has made significant changes; viz., from one of "neighborhood priority" to a policy of "neighborhood first," from an ambiguous maritime policy to a lucid policy toward the Indian Ocean and for the Indo-Pacific (Springer Science and Business Media LLC, 2019); from "Look East" to "Act East"; from being "non-aligned" to being "multi-aligned," and from an unclear strategy for promoting soft power to a robust soft power strategy. A significant factor has been India's bonding with Japan and the United States. According to Tellis, India–US relations had been tempered by Donald Trump's new transactionalism, and an awkward hesitation in standing up to China despite its continuing hostility—all of which have taken the oomph out of his audacious embrace of the United States (Tellis, 2019). With Biden in office, India–US relations are once again, on an upward trajectory.

The emphasis on development issues in India's foreign policy in recent years has resulted in a "Diplomacy for Development." During Prime Minister Modi's first tenure, the enhanced engagement and integration with external partners has catalyzed foreign investment and technology cooperation. Diplomacy has helped India promote its key programs that aim at achieving the goal of creating a new India by 2022. Other growth pathways include "Make in India," Skill India, Smart Cities, infrastructure development, Digital India, Clean India among others. Diplomacy has boosted inward FDI to India, viz UAE: 75 billion USD; Japan: 33 billion USD; China: 22 billion USD; South Korea: 11 billion USD, to mention a few (Bình, 2019).

Indian diplomacy in recent years is focused on promoting connectivity, even as it attaches importance to infrastructure, institutional and digital connectivity to enhance regional integration in South Asia, Southeast Asia, and Central Asia. Within South Asia, the Bangladesh, Bhutan, India, Nepal (BBIN). Motor Vehicles Agreement provides seamless connectivity for the vehicles and passengers of these four countries. Besides, the 1360 km trilateral highway between India, Myanmar, and Thailand is near completion (Springer Science and Business Media LLC, 2018). Once this project is completed, it will help connect India's Northeast region with ASEAN. India has also proposed to connect this highway with Cambodia, Laos, and Vietnam. Both Vietnam and India seek Japan as a partner in this initiative.

3.1.2 Vietnam in India's Act East Policy

Vietnam's position in India's foreign policy is to be identified based on the two countries' historical relations; the convergence of national interests; mutual support in regional, multiregional and international organizations; as well as acceleration of reforms in India and Vietnam. In the post-Cold War period, in general, Vietnam enjoyed a salient position in India's foreign policy. However, Vietnam's position in India's foreign policy has not been static, as this has transformed in the context of regional and global dynamics, as well as the influence of major powers.

Vietnam's position in India's policy can be identified in India's AEP and in the Indo-Pacific Oceans Initiative (IPOI). These are comprised within the framework of several regional and multiregional groupings including among others, India–ASEAN cooperation, Mekong–Ganga Cooperation, East Asia Summit, ASEAN Defense Ministers Meeting Plus among others.

India's LEP, undergirded through its Northeast provinces, promotes connectivity with East Asia and Southeast Asia–India's extended neighborhood. One of the reasons why India promoted its LEP was the lackluster progress in India's cooperation with South Asian countries, especially through the South Asian Association for Regional Cooperation (SAARC) (Marwah & Ramanayake, 2021). Since its inception, India's LEP has gone through three significant phases. The first phase from 1992 to 2002 focused on trade and investment linkages with ASEAN. During this period, India entered into the Sectoral Dialogue Partnership with ASEAN in 1992 and was upgraded to a Full Dialogue Partner in 1996 when it joined the ASEAN Regional Forum (ARF). Since 2002, India has started to hold annual India–ASEAN Summit level meetings.

The second phase of the LEP began in 2003 when Foreign Minister Yashwant Sinha (at Harvard University, September 29, 2003) shared an expanded view of the government on the "Eastern region," including Australia, New Zealand, China, Japan, and Korea, with ASEAN being at the center. This phase marked a shift from trade to broader security and economic issues. In 2012, the 20th anniversary of the India–ASEAN Dialogue Partnership was marked by an upgrade of India–ASEAN relations to a strategic partnership level. The new phase of the LEP was termed as "enhanced LEP."

In 2014, the Modi government gave an impressive new name to this policy, i.e., "Act East" policy (AEP). Interestingly, this term was first mentioned during India's Foreign Minister Sushma Swaraj's visit to Vietnam in August 2014. The change in nomenclature was to be matched by new initiatives, and game-changing drivers to alter the dynamics of India–ASEAN relations in general, India's relations with each member state, and specifically, India–Vietnam relations. Since then, the Government of India has adopted an "action oriented" and holistic policy approach toward its relations with ASEAN. A significant manifestation of the AEP was the presence of ASEAN Heads of Government at the Republic Day of India on January 26, 2018. India has devoted considerable attention to promoting economic connections between India and the CMLV countries (Cambodia, Myanmar, Laos, and Vietnam), a subregion within ASEAN that has the advantage of its relative proximity to India's Northeastern (NE) region. One of the most important initiatives for the NE region was to set up a Project Development Fund, of approximately $71.5 million in 2016 with India's Export–Import Bank to boost Indian investment in this region (Nga, 2019, pp. 28–36).

India's AEP has evolved to become more comprehensive, practical, and flexible. Cooperation between India and ASEAN member countries has been vigorously promoted, creating a revived genre with new regional cooperation mechanisms in Asia. A clear policy direction has been India's building up strategic partnerships with many countries in the region (Springer Science and Business Media LLC, 2018). India views the Look East as a "highway" that directly brings India into the Asia–Pacific integration and participates in the "Asian century."

The policy adjustment from "Look East" to "Act East" under Prime Minister Modi has many implications. According to Dhruva Jaishankar, *first*, it shifts from economic emphasis to more inclusive cohesion, with particular emphasis on the security aspect. *Secondly*, the scope of the policy extends from the initial Southeast and East Asia to a much broader region, i.e., the Indo-Pacific. *Thirdly*, this policy adjustment urges action on feasible issues on the agenda. This is what differentiated the AEP from the LEP in the past: greater security, greater scope, and greater impulse. Though not always publicly stated, the goal of the AEP is to maintain a balance of power in India's favor in the Indo-Pacific region.[2]

Assessing Vietnam's role in ASEAN and India's LEP, President Mukherjee (September 2014) said that Vietnam is a very important, strategic pillar in India's LEP, within ASEAN as well as in the wider region. This was reaffirmed during mutual visits by senior leaders of the two countries. In March 2018, during a meeting with Vietnamese President Trần Đại Quang in New Delhi, Prime Minister Modi affirmed that India would continue to promote the AEP to strengthen cooperation with the Indo-Asia–Pacific region in which Vietnam plays a key role and commands a priority position.[3] According to the Indian Ambassador to Vietnam, H. E. Pranay Verma,[4] "India's view of Vietnam as an essential pillar of its AEP is beyond doubt. Through this policy, India looks forward to integrating and engaging with the maritime and mainland space in the Eastern region by better connectivity, more interaction and greater institutional cohesion. India supported Vietnam during the tenure of the latter's chairmanship of ASEAN in 2020".

3.1.3 Vietnam in India's Indo-Pacific Oceans Initiative (IPOI)

It is remarkable that, before U.S. President Donald Trump announced the "Indo-Pacific strategy" in Đà Nẵng, Vietnam in October 2017, India already had a vision for this region. In 1941, Kalidas Nag, an Indian scholar, historian, senator, and politician, used the term "Indo-Pacific Domain" to confirm the ancient imprints of Indian

---

[2] Dhruva Jaishankar, Look East to Act East, xem: Dhruv Katoch (Editor), *India's Foreign Policy towards resurgence*, Pentagon Press LLP, tr. 117.

[3] Toàn văn tuyên bố chung Việt Nam - Ấn Độ. https://vnexpress.net, accessed on March 6, 2018.

[4] Interaction with the Indian Ambassador Pranay Verma at the Institute for Indian and Southwest Asian Studies, Hanoi, September 17, 2019.

civilization in the Indo-Pacific region.[5] Khurana (2007), Director of the National Maritime Foundation, New Delhi, is the first scholar to use the term with geopolitical implications. In the article "Maritime Security: Prospects of India–Japan Cooperation," Khurana argues that India and Japan's common and core interests in the maritime domain will be difficult to secure if the Indo-Pacific oceans are divided in strategic perception (Nga & Thuong, 2021).[6] Since 2010, the term Indo-Pacific has become popular in scholarly discourse on New Delhi's broad strategic and economic interests in its expanding neighborhood.

Since 2015, the Modi government uses the term "Indo-Pacific" frequently; the country's vision is articulated through several official documents, viz. Strategy for maritime security of India (October 2015), Joint Statement on the India and Japan Vision 2025 (December 12, 2015), The India–Australia Joint Statement (April 10, 2017); the U.S.–India Joint Statement on prosperity though a partnership (June 27, 2017), Joint Vision Statement on India–Indonesia Maritime Cooperation in the Indo-Pacific (May 30, 2018). A comprehensive vision of the Indo-Pacific region was expressed in the Indian prime minister's keynote address at the Shangri-La Dialogue, Singapore on June 1, 2018. At the Shangri-La Dialogue, Modi affirmed that India's vision in the Indo-Pacific is an integral part of India's shared vision for the future of India and the world and is described in one word—SAGAR (which is 'Ocean in Hindi), i.e., "Security and Growth for All." He underlined ASEAN's inclusiveness, openness, and centrality in the new Indo-Pacific region. He also asserted that, among other things, the Indo-Pacific represents a free, open, inclusive region that includes everyone, all states within and beyond region having interest in it. ASEAN has been and will continue to be the hub of the Indo-Pacific region.[7] Thus, the vision of India in the Indo-Pacific region is open, inclusive, and has a dialectical unity with the philosophical foundation throughout the history of India, that is "*Vasudhaiva Kutumbakam*" (The Whole World is One Family).

In April 2019, India set up an Indo-Pacific wing in the Ministry of External Affairs. The division is meant to integrate under one Indo-Pacific umbrella, the Indian Ocean Rim Association (IORA), ASEAN and the Quad (the U.S., Japan, Australia, and India). An Oceania division was created in the MEA in September 2020 to bring India's administrative and diplomatic focus on the region stretching from the Western Pacific to the Andaman Sea.

On the question of Vietnam joining the Quad, in an interview to Business Standard, Excellency Chau, Vietnam's ambassador in India, said, "We are following the evolution of Quad very closely. We are of the view that any idea or movement that contributes to the peace and stability in the region, that contributes to upholding international law and that contributes to the peaceful settlement of dispute through

---

[5] Ganguly (2018), tháng 8/2018, tr. 18.

[6] Khurana (2007).

[7] See more Nga (2019).

dialogue—should be welcomed." In his view, if Vietnam was invited to join the supply chain or the fight against climate change, the response would be in the affirmative.[8]

As in India's AEP, in India's vision of the Indo-Pacific region, Vietnam also has an important role. Indian Ambassador to Vietnam Pranay Verma opined that India's Act East Policy and Indo-Pacific Vision are based on the *terra firma* of deeper integration between India and ASEAN and the centrality of ASEAN in India's action plans, with Vietnam being a vital conduit connecting India with ASEAN.[9]

On December 13–14, 2019, the Indian Ministry of External Affairs held two important conferences on foreign affairs in New Delhi: the 6th Indian Ocean Dialogue and the 11th Delhi Dialogue (December 10, 2019). At the events, Indian Minister of External Affairs, S. Jaishankar analyzed India's Indo-Pacific strategy, which has different characteristics in comparison with Washington's Indo-Pacific strategy. While India's Indo-Pacific (I-P) strategy covers a larger geographical area, the U.S.'s I-P strategy "stretches from the West coast of India to the West coast of the United States, excluding the Gulf States in the Arabian and African Sea (on the Western coast of the Indian Ocean)" (Loan & Tung, 2021). India's I-P strategy, on the other hand, "would cover the Western Indian Ocean region, Gulf countries, island countries in the Arabian Sea and Africa" (Loan & Tung, 2021). This permits India to strengthen its cooperation with East Asia, the Gulf, and Africa, thereby placing India at the center. Along with the other Indo-Pacific countries, India will balance a rising China and play a leading role in the region (Loan & Tung, 2021).[10]

India's Indo-Pacific Vision has become more concrete with the launching of India's Indo-Pacific Oceans Initiative (IPOI) at the East Asia Summit in Thailand in November 2019. While revealing the future roadmap of IPOI, Prime Minister Modi emphasized the multilateral cooperation between India and ASEAN and stated: "We should recognize the imperative for all states in the regions with interests in it, to work collaboratively to safeguard the oceans; enhance maritime security; preserve marine resources; build capacity and fairly share resources; reduce disaster risk; enhance science, technology and academic cooperation; and promote free, fair and mutually beneficial trade and maritime transport."[11]

IPOI is considered "a landmark intervention" by India and "a potential game-changer" in pushing and directing a robust engagement between India and ASEAN partners based on convergence of strategic interests in politico-economic and socio-cultural frontiers while "ensuring safety, maritime security and stability in the crucial Indo-Pacific region" (Loan & Tung, 2021). IPOI is being built on India's AEP (focusing on the Eastern Indian Ocean and the Western Pacific) and Act West policy

---

[8] Manish Kumar Jha, Business World, http://www.businessworld.in/article/We-Are-Determined-To-Protect-Our-Sovereignty-On-The-Sea-As-China-Transgressed-Into-Our-Area-Vietnam-Ambassador-Pham-Sanh-Chau/16-10-2020-332394/; October 16, 2020, accessed on May 19, 2021.

[9] See Footnote 4.

[10] Prof. T. V. Paul in a lecture, chaired by Dr. Reena Marwah, on July 15, 2020, on Sino-India rivalry: Explaining Anomalies, organised by the Association of Asia Scholars.

[11] India–ASEAN strategic cooperation: Impacting security and stability in the Indo-Pacific region, https://www.orfonline.org/expert-speak/india-asean-strategic-cooperation-impacting-security-stability-indo-pacific-region/, accessed on May 19, 2021.

(focusing on the Western Indian Ocean).[12] "The newly adopted plan of action (2021–2025) during India–ASEAN Ministerial Meeting held in September 2020 is all set to add further momentum to the roadmap articulated by IPOI in bringing India and ASEAN members closer, working together as natural partners in tactical and strategic manner".[13]

Vietnam is an important partner in India's IPOI, based on shared values and interests in promoting peace, stability, and prosperity in the region. At the 17th Meeting of the India–Vietnam Joint Commission on Trade, Economic, Scientific and Technological Cooperation that took place on August 25, 2020, the two countries were determined to promote their bilateral cooperation in line with India's IPOI and the ASEAN's Outlook on Indo-Pacific. The objective was to "achieve shared security, prosperity and growth for all in the region" (Loan & Tung, 2021). India invited Vietnam to partner on one of the seven pillars of the IPOI.[14] In the area of capacity building and information sharing, India and Vietnam pursue naval cooperation, which includes composite training programs in submarines, aviation, and dockyard training. In the past, both countries' coast guards signed an MOU for the establishment of collaborative relationships to combat transnational crime and develop cooperation in 2015. In 2016, after India and Vietnam upgraded their ties to the level of a Comprehensive Strategic Partnership, both sides have signed an agreement to exchange white shipping information. India is also exploring the possibility of selling warships to the Vietnamese Coast Guard.[15]

- *Assessment of Vietnam's Position in India's Foreign Policy*

Through the analysis of India's AEP and IPOI, it is evident that Vietnam has an important position in India's foreign policy direction including the political, economic, strategic, and cultural dimensions.

Politically, India views Vietnam as a trusted traditional friend of India. Indian Ambassador to Vietnam, Pranay Verma, said that, in the context of an increasingly complex world and lack of trust, having someone who understands you, is sensitive to your worries, and always stands by your side is truly precious.[16] India's respect for Vietnam is reflected in the frequency of high-level visits and the degree of commitment of India's leaders for Vietnam. Since Prime Minister Modi took power, there has been a dense list of high-level visits between the two sides. From the Indian side, a few notable are the visits of President Pranab Mukherjee (2014), Prime Minister Narendra Modi (2016), President Ram Nath Kovind (2018), and Vice-President V. Naidu (2019). Besides, there are various other ministerial-level visits. After the

---

[12] The Indo-Pacific Oceans Initiative: Towards a coherent Indo-Pacific policy for India, https://www.orfonline.org/research/indo-pacific-oceans-initiative-towards-coherent-indo-pacific-policy-india/.

[13] Ibid., accessed on October 17, 2019.

[14] India–Vietnam Relations: Strong and Getting Stronger, https://thediplomat.com/2020/08/india-vietnam-relations-strong-and-getting-stronger/, accessed on October 17, 2019.

[15] Ibid.

[16] Views expressed by scholars at the monthly seminar at Vietnam Institute for Indian and Southwest Asian Studies, on October 17, 2019.

outbreak of the COVID-19 pandemic, the two sides have maintained regular inter-action through virtual meetings. The 17th Joint Commission between the two sides was successfully held virtually in August 2020. In December 2020, Prime Ministers Narendra Modi and Nguyễn Xuân Phúc held a video meeting to discuss issues of bilateral cooperation. All these high-level meetings have had spillover effects toward the lower strata of the political system, thereby promoting effective implementation of government policies. In the regional and international arena, India and Vietnam have shared concerns and interests. India has been appreciative of the close coordi-nation and support from Vietnam at multilateral forums, especially within the United Nations framework. Vietnam supported India for the position of a non-permanent member of the Security Council of the United Nations for the term 2021–2022.

Economically, India highly appreciates Vietnam's economic development achievements after more than 30 years of "Đổi Mới" (Innovation and Reforms). The rapid growth of Vietnam's economy with a market of more than 90 million people and Vietnam's priorities for foreign investment and its rich resources holds promise for several opportunities. Vietnam has "officially replaced Thailand to become India's fourth largest trading partner in ASEAN, after Indonesia, Singapore and Malaysia" (Jha & Vinh, 2020). India's fast and sustainable growing economy makes greater demands on alternative energy sources and hence has turned its attention to oil and gas exploitation in the East Vietnam Sea (South China Sea). India has started to partic-ipate in oil and gas exploitation in the East Sea since the 1980s. As of 2018, India invested in 182 projects worth $816 million, ranking 28/126 countries/territories investing in Vietnam; while Vietnamese businesses have seven investment projects in India, reaching nearly $6,15 million (VNMedia, 2018). India encourages cooper-ation between the Vietnam Oil and Gas Group (PVN) and the National Petroleum Company of India (ONGC) to explore and exploit oil and gas on the mainland, continental shelf, and exclusive economic zones of Vietnam.

Strategically, India's policy toward Vietnam should be placed in the context of the constantly changing geopolitics in the Indo-Asia–Pacific region. In recent times, China's growing sway and weight among India's neighboring countries (Sri Lanka, Pakistan, Maldives, Nepal, and Bhutan) has made India wary and cautious. There-fore, the rapid development of relations between India and Vietnam—a neighboring country of China—is seen as a move to balance and compete for influence in strategic areas. China's maritime and territorial advances in the region have fueled anxieties and a build-up of alliances among extra-regional powers, e.g., the Quadrilateral Security Dialogue. The China factor has also led India to expand defense and naval cooperation with Vietnam and support efforts to modernize its military force. India believes that Vietnam–India relations enhance each other's country's influence and contribute to peace and stability in the wider region.[17]

In terms of culture and civilization, Vietnam is considered an important partner in India's soft power diplomacy. The Swami Vivekananda Cultural Center was set up

---

[17] View expressed by scholars at the monthly seminar at the Insitute for Indian and Southwest Asian Studies, on October 17, 2019.

in Hanoi (2016) and contributes to the promotion of India–Vietnam cultural interactions and understanding (Nga & Quang, 2021). India has always treasured, through history, its cultural and civilizational connections with Vietnam. During the official visit to Vietnam in November 2018, Indian President Ram Nath Kovind visited Mỹ Sơn Sanctuary before arriving in Hanoi. India also supports the conservation and embellishment of the Mỹ Sơn Sanctuary, a vivid demonstration of the cultural and civilizational linkages between the two countries. Every year, the Government of India allocates grants (Grant-in-Aid) to support cultural activities in Vietnam.[18] As a result of the virtual summit on December 21, 2020, between Prime Ministers Narendra Modi and Nguyen Xuan Phuc, the two sides issued the Vietnam–India Joint Vision Statement for Peace, Prosperity, and People. A bilateral project for Encyclopedia on Vietnam–India Civilizational and Cultural Interaction was also launched during the virtual summit.

3.2 India's Position in Vietnam's Policy

3.2.1 Overview of Vietnam's Foreign Policy

Vietnam's foreign policy can be understood through three major periods: 1945–1975; 1975–1986; 1986–present. Between 1945 and 1975, Vietnam had to undergo two major wars of independence, to liberate the country from French colonialism (1945–1954) and American imperialism (1954–1975). Immediately after the establishment of the Democratic Republic of Vietnam (1945), under the astute leadership of President Ho Chi Minh and other senior leaders of the Communist Party of Vietnam (CPV), diplomacy played a pioneering role in maintaining Vietnam's national independence and protecting the new-born revolutionary government (*Nhân Dân*, August 27, 2020).[19] According to former Foreign Minister, Nguyễn Dy Niên, diplomatic activities were indeed one of the war fronts, contributing to garner the support of the world's people, especially the socialist countries in helping and supporting Vietnam (*Nhân Dân*, August 20, 2005).[20] Both Nehru and Ho Chi Minh were keen on the support and cooperation of Asian countries under colonial rule. Hence, the two leaders were good friends and worked to bring peace to the region. Refer Image 5.1.

In the words of Foreign Minister Phạm Bình Minh, during this period, "Diplomacy raised the banner of peace, national independence, perseverance in combining the political struggle with legal struggles, enlisting the support of the Soviet Union,

---

[18] VTV News (2018).

[19] Ngoại giao Việt Nam: 75 năm đồng hành cùng dân tộc, *Nhân Dân*, August 27, 2020, https://nhandan.com.vn/tin-tuc-su-kien/ngoai-giao-viet-nam-75-nam-dong-hanh-cung-dan-toc--614495/, accessed on October 19, 2019.

[20] *Nhân Dân*, Ngoại giao Việt Nam nắm bắt đúng thời cơ, hóa giải nhanh thách thức, August 20, 2005, https://nhandan.com.vn/tin-tuc-su-kien/ngoai-giao-viet-nam-nam-bat-dung-thoi-co-hoa-giai-nhanh-thach-thuc-411173, accessed on October 19, 2019.

China, and other socialist countries, broadening relations with nationalist countries and forming the world people's front to support the nationalist cause of the Vietnamese people. As an outcome of the above and with decisive victory on the battlefields, the French colonialists and the American imperialists were compelled to sit at the negotiating table to end the war." The French Indochina War lasted from 1946–1954, i.e. until the French rule came to an end with their defeat by the Viet Minh at the Battle of Dien Bien Phu. The final Geneva Accords were produced in July 1954; these accords helped establish the 17th parallel (latitude 17°N) as a temporary, demarcation line separating the military forces of the French and the Viet Minh. The signing of the Paris Peace Accords in 1973 officially called the "Agreement Ending the War and Restoring the Peace in Vietnam," marked a formal end to the devastating war, which had claimed a million Vietnamese lives and thousands of American lives (Image 3.1).

After the unification of Vietnam in 1975, Vietnam's foreign policy underwent essential changes. At the fourth Congress of the Communist Party of Vietnam (CPV), Vietnam stated its "aspiration to establish and enlarge its normal relations with all countries based on respecting independence, sovereignty, equality, and mutual interests" (Vinh, 2019, p. 1). Between 1975 and 1986, diplomatic activities contributed significantly to breaking the embargoed position of Vietnam, creating a conducive international environment for the Innovation Period that followed.

Vietnam officially entered the Innovation and Reform period (Đổi Mới) in 1986. At the Sixth National Congress of the CPV in 1986, Vietnam emphasized "solidarity

Image 3.1 Indian Prime Minister Jawaharlal Nehru with Vietnamese President, Ho Chi Minh, in Hanoi on October 18, 1954. *Source* https://commons.wikimedia.org/wiki/File:Jawaharlal_Nehru_with_Ho_Chi_Minh.jpg

and comprehensive cooperation with the Soviet Union as a cornerstone of the foreign policy of the Party and the State…" and at the same time was "ready to improve relations with the United States for the sake of peace and stability in Southeast Asia." (Vinh, 2019, p. 1). Resolution 13 of the Politburo in 1988 stated that Vietnam was to adopt a foreign policy of diversification in order to "make more friends and fewer enemies" (Vinh, 2019). Since the Seventh Congress of CPV in 1991, Vietnam has pursued "a multidirectional foreign policy" which is considered optimal policy by smaller countries while coping with "asymmetrical relations". The Seventh Congress of CPV emphasized a foreign policy of "equal cooperation based on the principle of peaceful coexistence that was to the mutual benefit of all countries, regardless of their sociopolitical ideology" (Vinh, 2019).

At the eighth Congress of the Party in 1996, for the first time, the policy of international economic integration was mentioned: "To build an open economy with regional and international integration" (Loan, 2018, p. 10). The ninth Congress elaborated on the interconnection between independence, self-reliance, and international economic integration: "Proactively integrate into international and regional economy in the spirit of maximizing inner-strength, enhancing the effectiveness of international cooperation, ensuring independence, self-reliance and socialist orientation, protecting national interest and security, preserving national cultural identity and protecting environment." (Communist Party of Vietnam, 2016, p. 120)[21] Documents of the tenth, eleventh, twelfth, and thirteenth Party Congresses continued to affirm the foreign policy of independence, multilateralization and diversification; proactively integrate into the world in a comprehensive, extensive, and effective manner; firmly protect the homeland, maintain a peaceful and stable environment, and continuously improve Vietnam's international position and reputation (Loan, 2018).

Thus, Vietnam is diversifying and multilateralizing its foreign relations and signaling intent and willingness to be friends and reliable partners of all countries in the world community, striving for peace, independence and development, contributing to ensuring security, preserving a peaceful environment, taking advantage of international cooperation and support for the cause of its national development.[22] Vietnam speeded up its international cooperation after its Doi Moi (Innovation policy) in 1986. In 1985, it had diplomatic relations with only 23 countries. But in 1995, the number of its partners increased to 163 countries. By August 2020, "Vietnam had established diplomatic relations with 189 countries out of 193 UN member countries; set up a long-term and stable cooperation framework with 30 strategic and comprehensive partnerships".[23] Multilateral diplomacy has matured and gained significant achievements, affirming that Vietnam is a responsible member of the international community. Vietnam has successfully organized many important international events, such as being the Chairs of the Francophone Summit (1997), ASEAN summits (1998, 2010, 2020), ASEM (2005), and APEC (2006, 2017).

---

[21] Document of the 9th National Party Congress, Communist Party of Vietnam (Hanoi: The National Political Publishing House, 2016, p. 120).

[22] See Footnote 20.

[23] See Footnote 19.

Vietnam contributed significantly to the organization of the second US–North Korea Summit in Hanoi (2019) thereby promoting dialogue, reconciliation and peace in the Korean peninsula. As the Chair of ASEAN 2020, with virtual formats, Vietnam successfully led the ASEAN and carried out its scheduled activities. In the context of the unprecedented impact of the pandemic, Vietnam's slogan of "Responsive and Cohesive" ASEAN acquired a new meaning for the grouping (*Thế giới và Việt Nam*, February 14, 2021).

Vietnam's relations with India are placed in its overall foreign policy of openness, multilateralization and diversification. India's salience in Vietnam's external engagement can also be understood by the fact that India is currently one of the only three comprehensive strategic partners of Vietnam (Nga, 2018; Solanki, 2021). Hence, India is important in Vietnam's policy in terms of political, strategic, economic, and cultural dimensions.

3.2.2 Political and Strategic Dimensions

As a traditional partner, Vietnam considers India a priority partner in its policy of building a strategic partnership. Even before Vietnam signed its first strategic partnership with Russia in 2001, the term "strategic" was used to describe Vietnam–India relations in 1999 by Vietnamese President Trần Đức Lương (Vinh, 2019). He had told the Indian Minister of External Affairs, Jaswant Singh, in mid-November 2000 that "Vietnam treats India with strategic importance" (Vinh, 2019, p. 6). Thus, the Vietnam–India Strategic Partnership agreement of 2007 was a formalization of their continuing strategic relations. The enhancement from a strategic to a Comprehensive Strategic Partnership in September 2016 was an "inevitable development" (Nga, 2017a, b). To date, India is one of the three countries that have established a Comprehensive Strategic Partnership with Vietnam, besides China and Russia. The development of India–Vietnam relations from a comprehensive partnership in 2003 to a strategic partnership in 2007 and Comprehensive Strategic Partnership in 2016 is concrete evidence of the importance of India in Vietnam's policy.

Vietnam has also repeatedly affirmed its support for various policies of India. During his visit to India (2014), Prime Minister Nguyễn Tấn Dũng affirmed that the party, the state and people of Vietnam are conscious of the great support and assistance extended to Vietnam by India in the years of its struggle for national independence and reunification as well as national construction and defense in contemporary times. Additionally, Vietnam supports India's Look East/Act East Policy, pledges its support to India to strengthen its relations with ASEAN, to engage in East Asian cooperation, and to support India in becoming a permanent member of the U.N. Security Council (Loan, 2018, p. 20).

Vietnam has always supported India in its cooperation in the region (Jha & Vinh, 2020). This is proved by the fact that Vietnam supported India to be a member of crucial cooperation mechanisms in the region such as ARF, ASEAN–India summit meeting, EAS, ADMM+ and Expanded ASEAN Maritime Forum (EAMF). In the

ADMM+ forum, India and Vietnam had cochaired the Expert Working Group on Humanitarian Mine Actions. Four Indian Naval ships with around 1200 officers and sailors visited Da Nang on June 6–10, 2013. In the past few years, there have been visits by Indian vessels to Vietnam (Jha & Vinh, 2020, p. 70).

The frequent visits of top leaders of Vietnam to India in the past decade underline India's ascendant position in Vietnam's policy. Here, it is noteworthy to mention the visits of Nguyễn Phú Trọng, Chairman of National Congress (2010) and Secretary General of CPV (2013); State President Trương Tấn Sang (2011); Prime Minister Nguyễn Tấn Dũng (2012, 2014); Chairwoman of the National Congress Nguyễn Thị Kim Ngân (2016); President Trần Đại Quang (2018), Prime Minister Nguyễn Xuân Phúc (2018), Vice-President Đặng Thị Ngọc Thịnh (2020), etc.

Vietnam perceives India as a strategic partner to balance its relations with other major powers and to protect its national interests. In the emerging Indo-Pacific geopolitics, Vietnam's views converge on many aspects with India's vision with both countries emphasizing inclusivity, i.e., the participation of all countries in these two oceans. Both countries have shared interests in "maintaining peace, stability, cooperation and development in the Indo-Pacific region, on the basis of respect for international laws" (Loan & Tung, 2021). Vietnam also welcomes India's IPOI. In Vietnams' view, India's IPOI helps facilitate conducive conditions to reap advantages in implementation of its multidirectional, multilateral and diversified foreign policy. IPOI will also enable Vietnam balance its relations with major countries, increase its political and economic security and develop its multifaceted relations, particularly with regional and global powers (*Nhân Dân*, December 21, 2020).

3.2.3   Economic Dimension

Vietnam has set specific time-bound targets for development. In the next three decades, it will achieve the following milestones: first, by 2030, Vietnam will become an industrial country with a high average income, linking this objective with the 100th anniversary of the establishment of the Communist Party of Vietnam, and secondly, Vietnam will become a socialist-oriented-developed country by 2045 when Vietnam celebrates 100 years of its independence (1945–2045) (Central Office of the Vietnam Communist Party, 2021, p. 48). For the realization of these goals, Vietnam considers it imperative to tighten economic cooperation with India. Through IPOI, India is the gateway for facilitation of exchanges with Central Asia, a crucial area with a strategic location and rich source of oil. In addition, IPOI will help in connecting Vietnam's economy with coastal countries in Central Asian region. Moreover, strengthening economic cooperation and connectivity with India and other countries in the region will elevate Vietnam's capability to balance foreign investment from China. Vietnam is concerned about the fact that China is the largest foreign investor in Vietnam. Chinese investment accounted for 27.5% of total registered capital in 2019. This worries Vietnam. Therefore, Vietnam hopes to reduce long-term investment from China, particularly in the arena of infrastructure development.

On the other hand, in the context of rising tensions between Vietnam and China in the South China Sea, there are potential risks of being overly dependent on the latter. Vietnam–China trade turnover increase rapidly over the years. In 1997, trade with China accounted for only 4.23% of Vietnam's total trade (Vinh, 2019, p. 3). But this number increased to 14.69% in 2007 and 20.04% in 2017, respectively (Vinh, 2019, p. 3). As Vietnam is a highly open economy, and trade accounted for more than 200% of Vietnam's Gross Domestic Product (GDP) in 2017, its economic dependence has also resulted in its political dependence on China. Thus, Vietnam is keen to expand engagement with new markets to reduce its dependence on China. In this context, India has shown its willingness to replace China in supplying textile materials to Vietnam.

3.2.4 Cultural Dimension

India is also an important partner of Vietnam in terms of culture. Chapter 2 has explored the profound cultural linkages between India and Vietnam. Both governments have developed strategies to promote cultural diplomacy of the countries. Over the past decade, cultural cooperation has been the highlight of bilateral relations.

In Vietnam, Resolution No. 4 of the fourth Session of the Central Executive Committee of the Communist Party of Vietnam (January 14, 1993)[24] affirmed that culture is the spiritual foundation of the society, expressing the height and depth of the development level of a nation, and is the crystallization of the best values in the relationship among people, between the individuals and the society, between the people and nature. It is both a driving force for socioeconomic development and one of Vietnam's goals. Resolution No. 33 of the ninth session of the Central Executive Committee of the Communist Party of Vietnam (June 9, 2014)[25] provided the government's views on building and developing Vietnamese people and culture to meet the requirements of sustainable development. One of the tasks pointed out by the Resolution is: "To build culture in politics and economy (political culture and economic culture), in which regular attention is being put on economic culture. Human beings are really at the center of the socioeconomic development process; to create a legal cultural environment and a transparent, progressive and modern market for cultural products for enterprises to take part in the building and development of culture; to build corporate culture and business culture with a sense of respect for the law, respect for the credibility, healthy competition, for sustainable development

---

[24] Tư liệu văn kiện, Đảng Cộng sản [Documents of the Communist Party], https://tulieuvankien. dangcongsan.vn/van-kien-tu-lieu-ve-dang/hoi-nghi-bch-trung-uong/khoa-vii/nghi-quyet-so-04-nqhntw-hoi-nghi-lan-thu-tu-bchtw-dang-khoa-vii-ve-mot-so-nhiem-vu-van-hoa-van-nghe-nhung-nam-truoc-1129, accessed on July 15, 2021.

[25] Tư liệu văn kiện, Đảng Cộng sản [Documents of the Communist Party], https://tulieuvankien.dan gcongsan.vn/van-kien-tu-lieu-ve-dang/hoi-nghi-bch-trung-uong/khoa-xi/nghi-quyet-so-33-nqtw-ngay-962014-hoi-nghi-lan-thu-9-ban-chap-hanh-trung-uong-dang-khoa-xi-ve-xay-dung-va-phat-trien-590, accessed on July 15, 2021.

and national protection." Besides, the Resolution emphasizes the proactiveness in international integration in terms of culture: "To proactively integrate into the international culture, to absorb the quintessence of culture of mankind: to implement diverse forms of cultural diplomacy, to deepen culturally related international relations and to make it more effectively implemented…" In the present times, cultural diplomacy, along with political and economic diplomacy, is one of the three pillars of Vietnam's comprehensive diplomacy. As one of the three pillars of Vietnam's diplomacy, cultural diplomacy has been deployed at many levels throughout the country.

India is also a treasure house and repository of culture. Its cultural power is demonstrated in its unity in diversity, unbroken continuity, eternal religions, philosophy, art, literature, etc. India is home to many wonders of the world. The spread of Indian culture all over the world confirms its appeal and attractiveness which is a source of India's soft power. As soft power is becoming an engine to enhance countries' status, the Government of India has long been interested in taking advantage of its strong cultural traditions to enhance its national soft power.

Along with China, India is the cradle of Asian civilization. However, compared to China, the influence of Indian culture is much more significant. Chinese civilization and culture mainly spread in neighboring countries in East and Southeast Asia. The world knows little about Confucianism or Taoism, but many countries and people worldwide know about Indian Buddhism. The development of Buddhism is seen as a link connecting India with the world and helping India expand its influence.

The Modi government attaches importance to promoting cultural diplomacy, emphasizing traditional Indian culture (Yoga, Ayurveda, Hinduism, Buddhism) and contemporary Indian culture (through Bollywood). Yoga diplomacy has greatly promoted the image of India. Yoga has become "India's gift to the world" (Binh, 2019). Thanks to the active involvement of the Modi administration, June 21 has become the International Yoga Day, held in great popularity all over the world. The traditional Indian medicine, Ayurveda, is also increasingly known to the world.

The Government of Vietnam considers India an important partner in terms of culture. This is reflected in various joint statements being signed between the two countries over the years. The Joint Statement on the Vision for Peace, Prosperity, and People signed by the two governments on December 21, 2020, also emphasizes the deep cultural and historical bonds between the two countries. It states: "the two sides will commemorate and promote understanding and research of their shared cultural and civilizational heritage, including Buddhist and Cham cultures, traditions and ancient scriptures. Cooperation in the conservation of shared cultural heritage will be pursued as a key pillar of their development partnership. Traditional systems of medicine are of great significance for both countries in achieving Sustainable Development Goal 2 and 3. Owing to cultural exchange between the two countries for the past thousands of years, the traditional systems of medicine like Ayurveda and Vietnamese traditional medicine share many common threads of rich knowledge of health. Yoga has emerged as a symbol of peace and harmony and shared pursuit of spiritual well-being and happiness…".[26]

3.2.5 Other Dimensions

– *The East Sea (South China Sea)*

The resolution of territorial sovereignty disputes on land and at sea by peaceful means on the basis of international law is Vietnam's consistent policy. As for maritime sovereignty disputes, although Vietnam has sufficient historical evidence and legal basis to prove its indisputable sovereignty over islands in the East Sea, including the Spratly and Paracel islands, Vietnam is willing to negotiate peacefully to settle disputes on the basis of the provisions of the 1982 UNCLOS. While continuing to search for a long-term solution to this issue, Vietnam advocates that all parties exercise self-restraint and strictly implement the ASEAN–China Declaration on the Conduct of Parties (DOC), toward building a Code of Conduct (COC), to achieve a fair and long-term solution to this complicated issue so that the East Sea will be a sea of peace, friendship and prosperity.[27]

Vietnam appreciates India's strong stance on the East Sea issue. (For Vietnam, China's South China Sea, is its East Sea). Facing China's challenge over Vietnam's maritime boundary, besides implementing multilateral diplomacy, Vietnam aims at fostering closer ties with India, urging India to be more active in dealing with the East Sea issue. As a regional and global power, Vietnam hopes that India will actively support the parties concerned in resolving the disputes peacefully (Tiến, 2016, p. 133).

– *Defense*

As highlighted earlier, Vietnam follows a defense policy of "three nos"[28] and considers maintaining a peaceful and stable environment for socioeconomic development, industrialization and modernization of the country the highest national interests. Vietnam has been implementing a defense policy of peaceful and self-defensive nature which is reflected in the policy of not using force or threatening to use force in international relations, settling all disagreements and disputes with other countries by peaceful means. However, it is ready and resolute to respond to any external aggression. Implementing the independent and self-reliant defense policy, Vietnam has been building its defense strength with all-round resources of the country and its people. At the same time, Vietnam focuses on developing defense cooperation with

---

[26] Full Vietnam–India Joint Vision Statement for Peace, Prosperity, and People, http://news.chi nhphu.vn/Home/Full-Viet-NamIndia-Joint-Vision-Statement-for-Peace-Prosperity-and-People/ 202012/42482.vgp, accessed on July 15, 2021.

[27] Ministry of Defence of Vietnam, Basic issues of Vietnam's defence policy [Những vấn đề cơ bản của chính sách quốc phòng Việt Nam]. www.bqp.vn, accessed on July 15, 2021.

[28] See Footnote 27.

all countries on the basis of respecting each other's independence and sovereignty and for mutual benefits. Vietnam attaches importance to defense cooperation with neighboring countries, traditional friends as well as countries that share the same goal for peace, independence, and prosperity.[29]

Since Vietnam attaches importance to defense cooperation with traditional friends and desires to acquire military equipment from traditional trading partners, India has become one of Vietnam's most reliable partners in the realm of defense in recent years. Bilateral defense cooperation became institutionalized in 1994. India has emerged as an important partner of Vietnam in important areas of Vietnam's defense, including military training and education. India has helped train Vietnamese sailors to operate the Vietnamese people's Navy's Kilo-class submarines and Vietnamese Air Force pilots for years. India has also helped in giving English language training to Vietnamese military personnel. The two countries have negotiated for the sale of the BrahMos and Akash missiles to Vietnam, though some technical issues related to the possible exports of BrahMos missiles still need to be resolved.

During the official visit of Prime Minister Narendra Modi to Hanoi in 2016, 12 agreements were signed, including one with Larsen & Toubro (L&T) for utilizing $100 million of the $500 million defense line of credit given by India to Vietnam to build patrol boats (Nga, 2017a, b). India is one of the very few countries with whom Vietnam has held joint naval exercises. A Vietnam–India joint naval exercise took place in the South China Sea on June 8, 2013, and another joint exercise was carried out in May 2015. Indian naval ships have been visiting major ports in Vietnam annually, including ports at Dinh Vu (Hải Phòng), Tiên Sa (Đà Nẵng), Sài Gòn (Hồ Chí Minh City), and Nha Trang (Khánh Hòa). The Indian Navy is "perhaps the only foreign Navy in recent times to have been given the privilege to dock at ports other than the Halong Bay, near Hanoi" (Ghoshal, 2013, p. 134). As the Cam Ranh Bay (Nha Trang, Vietnam) is increasingly becoming important as one of the most strategic naval ports in Southeast Asia, it is significant that the Indian Navy has been granted permission to drop anchor at Cam Ranh Bay (Ghoshal, 2013, p. 134). These developments are a demonstration of India's prominence in Vietnam's policy (Vinh, 2019).

– *Science–Technology*

Vietnam sees India as an essential partner in scientific and technological cooperation and promotes cooperation in this area. Vietnam's Science and Technology Law 2000 affirms that the goal of scientific and technological activities is to build an advanced and modern science and technology hub to develop productive forces, improve management qualifications; rationally use natural resources, protect the environment; promote industrialization and modernization; build an advanced culture imbued with national identity; build a new people in Vietnam; contribute to rapid and sustainable socioeconomic development, improve the quality of life for the people, and ensure national defense and security. India has substantial advantages in sciences

---

[29] Ibid.

and technology, its IT industry is developing very fast, and Vietnam attaches importance to promoting scientific and technological cooperation with India. This aspect
is elaborated in Chap. 5.

3.3 Implications for Strengthening India–Vietnam Relations

The above description shows the mutuality of importance for both countries foreign
policies. This is a highly conducive factor for the two countries to promote bilateral
cooperation in all fields. Thus, it can be affirmed that the impediments to practical
cooperation between the two sides do not germinate from the official policies of the
two governments. The fact that the results of bilateral cooperation have not been as
good as expected shows that the two countries need to identify barriers in non-policy
related issues.

Perhaps, it is to be noted that, although India's official stance always emphasizes
Vietnam as an essential stanchion of India's AEP, the Vietnamese side should note
that India also considers several other Southeast Asian countries as crucial anchors of
this policy. India also values its relations with Myanmar, Indonesia, Singapore, and
Thailand, among SEA. Hence, Vietnam should understand that Vietnam's important
position in India's foreign policy is not unchanged, and that Vietnam should compete
with other Southeast Asian countries to attract India's attention, to continue to be the
authentic bolsterer of India in Southeast Asia.

Although Vietnam considers India as a comprehensive strategic partner, yet
Vietnam has not extended that prime position in actual practice. By highlighting
a minor incident, this can be amplified. When the Indian Embassy organized India's
Independence Day ceremony in Hanoi, the guest of honor from the Vietnamese side
would often be a Vice-Minister (not a Minister as in the case of the Independence
Day celebration of some other countries). Additionally, cooperation between the two
countries in some areas is still one way (e.g., in educational and technological cooperation, Vietnam has not given scholarships to Indian students who want to study
Vietnamese language and culture).

As regards Vietnamese perception about India, particularly within Vietnam's
diplomatic arena, India is ranked fifth, and hence is not among the coveted destinations for diplomats of the Ministry of Foreign Affairs. Vietnamese diplomats are
often hesitant to choose India for a diplomatic posting because diplomats face the
twin challenges of handling complex tasks, due to the frequency of high-level visits
as well as weather conditions of extreme summer and winter. Thus, there is a paradox
in Vietnam–India relations, that is, the paradox of excellent political relations at the
top level and ineffective or inadequate implementation at lower levels.

3.4 Conclusion

Indian foreign policy since independence demonstrates how lofty ideas have yielded space to parochial pragmatism. According to former diplomat, Rajiv Bhatia, "A strong streak of realism marks New Delhi's decisions today. The tone of moral superiority of yore has disappeared. But a striking commonality between Nehru and his successors persists—the idea of universality and exceptionalism. Nehru had said that India's dreams were 'also for the world.' In his address at the U.N. in September 2019, PM Modi echoed it in asserting that '…the very core of our approach is public welfare through public participation and this public welfare is not just for India but for the entire world'" (Bhatia, 2019).

Evidently, India's position and stature in international affairs has increased dramatically in recent years. Along with its military-economic growth and its assertiveness in foreign affairs under Prime Minister Modi, India has occupied an increasingly pivotal role in shaping the global agenda. India is gradually playing the role of "rule-maker" rather than a "rule-taker" and is emerging as a powerful player in the multipolar world. Strong ties with Vietnam significantly help pave the way for India to play a conspicuous role in shaping the regional security architecture. Increasing economic and strategic engagement with the United States, Japan, and the European Union by both countries underlines their mutual desire to break away from China's tight embrace. Yet, Vietnam maneuvers its relations with great powers with caution as it always faces the threat of being used as a pawn in great power politics between the US and China (Pant, 2018, p. 10).

Southeast Asia is central to India's vision of the Indo-Pacific as well as in its Act East Policy. As a relatively large market with a dynamically developing economy, Vietnam is an attractive destination for foreign investment, including investment from India. Vietnam's capacity to organize and coordinate international events, multilateral summits, and successes as the Chair of ASEAN in 2020, in its dealing with the COVID-19 pandemic, has raised Vietnam's prestige in the international arena. In the process of implementing its national economic, political and cultural renovation policies, Vietnam attaches a salient position to India. The bilateral felicitations and adulations must also be bolstered with a pragmatic, programmatic push.

For India, Vietnam enjoys an important position in the AEP, Vietnam is also a country that can actively participate in the Indo-Pacific Oceans Initiative. For Vietnam, India is an emerging power with ascendant influence in the region and the world; Vietnam considers India one of its three comprehensive strategic partners; India is important to Vietnam in terms of political, strategic, military, economic, cultural, and other dimensions. Both India and Vietnam need to take advantage of stated foreign policies at the two levels to promote effective cooperation programs in all fields. The futuristic template of bilateral relations will be tempered by the altered foreign policies impacted by the pandemic, the robustly entrenched China in South and Southeast Asia as well as the emergent theatrical subsets within the Indo-Pacific. Vietnam's affinities with the great powers and India's burgeoning alliances with like-minded democracies will find the greatest convergence in securing the maritime spaces of the seas and oceans. America's Vice-President Kamala Harris's visit to Hanoi in August 2021, succeeded by Secretary of State, Anthony Blinken's visit to New Delhi in the last week of July 2021 is an affirmation by the Biden administration that both countries are significant for USA's strategy for a rules-based order in the Indo-Pacific. Harris, who is the first US Vice-President to visit Vietnam, while imploring Hanoi to join the US in countering a bullying China, told the nation's president that "our relationship has come a long way in a quarter of a century."[30] While USA's trade war with China continues, both India and Vietnam are endeavoring to reduce their economic dependence on this large neighbor.

Prof. Do Thu Ha, underlining the salience of economic capabilities shared with the authors, "Foreign policy is just like the echo of the bell. If the bell is not strong, the echo will be weak. Hence, for a country to have an impactful foreign policy, it must be economically strong." The next chapter provides a detailed analysis of the bilateral cooperation in the economic sphere, which holds the potential of cooperation to scale greater heights. Evidently, prowess in the technological fields must also translate into improved manufacturing capabilities. The two countries must build capacities for innovation which boost employment, raise living standards and maintain financial stability. The urgency to achieve these is not lost during times when the pandemic continues to devastate lives and livelihoods. The next chapter focuses on both the internal economic dimensions and policies of both countries as well as their bilateral economic relations.

References

Bhatia, R. (2019, November 2). *Values in foreign policy' review: At home in the world*. https://www.thehindu.com/books/books-reviews/values-in-foreign-policy-review-at-home-in-the-world/article29862671.ece. Accessed August 26, 2021.

Bình, N. X. (2019). *Điều chỉnh chính sách đối ngoại của Ấn Độ dưới thời Thủ tướng N. Modi*, Nxb. Khoa học xã hội.

Central Office of the Communist Party of Vietnam [Văn phòng Trung ương Đảng Cộng sản Việt Nam]. (2021). *Results of the XIII National Congress of the Communist Party of Vietnam [Kết quả Đại hội Đại biểu Toàn quốc Lần thứ XIII Đảng Cộng sản Việt Nam]*, Tài liệu lưu hành nội bộ *[Confidential Documents], Hà Nội, 02/2021*.

Communist Party of Vietnam. (2016). *Document of the 9th National Party Congress* (p. 120). The Truth & National Political Publishing House.

Full Vietnam-India joint vision statement for peace, prosperity and people. http://news.chinhphu.vn/Home/Full-Viet-NamIndia-Joint-Vision-Statement-for-Peace-Prosperity-and-People/202012/42482.vgp

Ganguly, A. (2018). Ấn Độ - Việt Nam (Tái định hình khu vực Ấn Độ - Thái Bình Dương như một khu vực tự do và rộng mở), Kỷ yếu hội thảo quốc tế "Hợp tác phát triển Việt Nam - Ấn Độ trên lĩnh vực kinh tế, quốc phòng, an ninh trong bối cảnh Ấn Độ Dương – Thái Bình Dương: Tự do và rộng mở", Nxb. Lý luận chính trị, Hà Nội.

---

[30] Kamala Harris calls on Vietnam to join US opposing China bullying. https://www.hindustantimes.com/world-news/kamala-harris-calls-on-vietnam-to-join-us-opposing-china-bullying-101629870665102.html, accessed on August 30, 2021.

Ghoshal, B. (2013). China's perception on India's LEP and its implication. *IDSA Monograph Series,* No. 26, Institute for Defense Studies and Analysis, New Delhi, October 2013.

India–ASEAN strategic cooperation: Impacting security and stability in the Indo–Pacific region. https://www.orfonline.org/expert-speak/india-asean-strategic-cooperation-impacting-sec urity-stability-indo-pacific-region/

India–Vietnam relations: Strong and getting stronger. https://thediplomat.com/2020/08/india-vie tnam-relations-strong-and-getting-stronger/; The Indo–Pacific Oceans initiative: Towards a coherent Indo–Pacific policy for India. https://www.orfonline.org/research/indo-pacific-oceans-initiative-towards-coherent-indo-pacific-policy-india/

Interaction with the Indian Ambassador Pranay Verma at the Institute for Indian and Southwest Asian Studies, Hanoi, September 17, 2019.

Jaishankar, D. *Look east to act east*. xem: Dhruv Katoch (Ed.), *India's foreign policy towards resurgence* (tr. 117). Pentagon Press LLP.

Jha, P. K., & Vinh, V. X. (2020). *India, Vietnam and the Indo-Pacific security architecture*. Routledge India.

Khurana, G. S. (2007). Security of sea lines: Prospects for India-Japan cooperation. *Strategic Analysis, 31*(1), 139–153.

Kumar, A. (2008). Jaswant Singh and Major General S. P. Bhatia. In *Strategic analysis*. Sage.

Loan, H. T. (2018). India in Vietnam's foreign policy in the new context. In *Emerging horizons in India–Vietnam relations*. Pentagon Press.

Loan, H. T., & Tung, N. D. (2021). Vietnam's responses to India's Indo-Pacific Oceans initiatives and opportunities for Vietnam–India maritime cooperation in the South China Sea. *India Quarterly: A Journal of International Affairs*, Sage.

Marwah, R., & Ramanayake, S. S. (2021). *China's Economic footprint in South and Southeast Asia: A futuristic perspective*. World Scientific.

Ministry of Defence of Vietnam, Basic issues of Vietnam's defence policy [Những vấn đề cơ bản của chính sách quốc phòng Việt Nam]. www.bqp.vn

Mukherjee, M. (2020). Chaos as opportunity: The United States and world order ini India's grand strategy. *Contemporary Politics*.

Nga, L. T. H. (2017a). *Quan hệ Ấn Độ - Hoa Kỳ (1947–1991) [India–U.S. relations (1947–1991)]*. Nxb. Chính trị Quốc gia Sự thật, Hanoi.

Nga, L. T. H. (2017b). *Vietnam-India relations since September 2016: From the symbolic to practical results*. Sage.

Nga, L. T. H. (2018). The Truth & National Political Publishing House.

Nga, L. T. H. (2019). Tầm nhìn của Ấn Độ ở khu vực Ấn Độ Dương – Thái Bình Dương (India's vision in the Indo–Pacific region). *Tạp chí Thông tin Khoa học xã hội (Social Sciences Information Review)*, Số 1/2019 (433), pp. 28–36.

Nga, L. T. H., & Quang, T. H. (2021). Public diplomacy in strengthening India–Vietnam relations. *India Quarterly: A Journal of International Affairs*, Sage.

Nga, L. T. H., & Thuong, N. L. T. (2021, January). India–China Competition in South Asia under Prime Minister Narendra Modi. *Journal of Indian and Asian Studies, World Scientific Publishing House, 2*(1), 2150001.

Ngoại giao Việt Nam: 75 năm đồng hành cùng dân tộc, *Nhân Dân*, August 27, 2020. https://nha ndan.com.vn/tin-tuc-su-kien/ngoai-giao-viet-nam-75-nam-dong-hanh-cung-dan-toc--614495/

Nhân Dân, Ngoại giao Việt Nam năm bắt đúng thời cơ, hóa giải nhanh thách thức, August 20, 2005. https://nhandan.com.vn/tin-tuc-su-kien/ngoai-giao-viet-nam-nam-bat-dung-thoi-co-hoa-giai-nhanh-thach-thuc-411173

Nhân dân, Tuyên bố Tầm nhìn chung Việt Nam - Ấn Độ về Hòa bình, Thịnh vượng và người dân, December 21, 2020. https://nhandan.com.vn/tin-tuc-su-kien/tuyen-bo-tam-nhin-chung-viet-nam-an-do-ve-hoa-binh-thinh-vuong-va-nguoi-dan-628960/

Pant, H. V. (2018). *India and Vietnam: A strategic partnership in the making, Policy Brief, RSIS and NTU, Singapore*.

Springer Science and Business Media LLC. (1984). *Asian perspectives on international security*.

Springer Science and Business Media LLC. (2018) *Mainstreaming the Northeast in India's look and act east policy.*

Springer Science and Business Media LLC. (2019) *Annual report on the development of the Indian Ocean region (2018).*

Springer Science and Business Media LLC. (2020). *India and the European Union in a turbulent world.*

Solanki, V. (2021). India–Vietnam defence and security cooperation. *India Quarterly: A Journal of International Affairs, Sage.*

Sundararaman, S. (2021). India Indonesia relations. In E. Sridharan (Ed.), *Eastward Ho? India in the Indo-Pacific* (pp. 386–387). Orient Blackswan Publishers.

Talbott, S. (2006). *Engaging India: Diplomacy, democracy and the bomb.* Brookings Institution Press.

Tellis, A. (2019, March 24). *Modi's three foreign policy wins.* https://carnegieendowment.org/2019/03/24/modi-s-three-foreign-policy-wins-pub-78675.

The Indo–Pacific Oceans initiative: Towards a coherent Indo–Pacific policy for India. https://www.orfonline.org/research/indo-pacific-oceans-initiative-towards-coherent-indo-pacific-policy-india/

Tiến, T. N. (2016). *India with Southeast Asia in the new international context.* The Culture and Art Publishing House.

Tư liệu văn kiện, Đảng Cộng sản [Documents of the Communist Party]. https://tulieuvankien.dangcongsan.vn/van-kien-tu-lieu-ve-dang/hoi-nghi-bch-trung-uong/khoa-vii/nghi-quyet-so-04-nqhntw-hoi-nghi-lan-thu-tu-bchtw-dang-khoa-vii-ve-mot-so-nhiem-vu-van-hoa-van-nghe-nhung-nam-truoc-1129

Tư liệu văn kiện, Đảng Cộng sản [Documents of the Communist Party]. https://tulieuvankien.dangcongsan.vn/van-kien-tu-lieu-ve-dang/hoi-nghi-bch-trung-uong/khoa-xi/nghi-quyet-so-33-nqtw-ngay-962014-hoi-nghi-lan-thu-9-ban-chap-hanh-trung-uong-dang-khoa-xi-ve-xay-dung-va-phat-trien-590

Vinh, V. X. (2019). India in Vietnam's foreign policy. *Strategic Analysis,* 1–14. ISSN: 0970–0161, https://doi.org/10.1080/09700161.2020.1699997

VNMedia. (2018).

VTV News. (2018).

Yasmin, L. (2019). India and China in South Asia: Bangladesh's opportunities and challenges. *Millennial Asia, 10*(3), 322–336. https://doi.org/10.1177/0976399619879864

Chapter 4
India–Vietnam Economic Relations and Development Dynamics

4.1 The Context

This chapter provides a glimpse into the economic profiles of Vietnam and India to contextualize the discussion on the bilateral economic relations through trade and investment. The contemporary development dynamics are also discussed through the two countries' comparative advantages and limitations in attracting foreign investment and as engines of growth for the region.

4.1.1 Macroeconomy of Vietnam

Vietnam's growth has been impressive since the early 1990s. The reforms undertaken under Đổi Mới since 1986 have enabled the country's transformation from a low income to a lower-middle-income country. However, although Vietnam initiated this economic renovation program in 1986, it was not until the early 1990s that the legislative changes incentivizing foreign direct investment, corporate enterprises, and private farming began to spur private entrepreneurship. In 1992, the constitution acknowledged a shift to a multisectoral economy and from central planning to a socialist market economy; however, the structural transformation occurred gradually (Yusuf, 2018: 1).

The structural changes enabled Vietnam to increase its GDP per capita by 2.7 times, reaching over US$2700 in 2019. Given the economy's thrust on export-oriented manufacturing, coupled with burgeoning domestic demand, the economy grew at almost 7% in 2018 and 2019. Between 2002 and 2018, over 45 million people were lifted out of poverty. Poverty rates reduced significantly from over 70% to below 6% (US$3.2/day PPP) (World Bank, 2021). With a population of 96.2 million in 2019, the country has over 55% of its population below the age of 35 years. The middle-class segment is growing and is expected to reach 26% by 2026.

© The Author(s), under exclusive license to Springer Nature Singapore Pte Ltd. 2021
R. Marwah and L. T. Hằng Nga, *India–Vietnam Relations*, Dynamics of Asian Development, https://doi.org/10.1007/978-981-16-7822-6_4

Table 4.1 Vietnam and India: a comparison

Countries	Population (2019)	Annual GDP USD(M) (2018)	GDP per capita USD (2018)	HDI	Debt (2017)	GovtDebt (%GDP) (2017)
India	1370 mn	2,718,732	2010	0.640	1,849,402	68.05
Vietnam	95.54 mn	241,272	2380	0.704	128,356	58.22

Source https://countryeconomy.com/countries/compare/india/vietnam?sc=XE34; accessed on February 3, 2021

Vietnam is one of the most globalized nations in Asia. This is evident with the contribution of exports and imports as a % of GDP, as shown in Table 4.1. Hence, the economy has been affected adversely by the pandemic-led closure of borders and disruption of supply chains. Nevertheless, it is one of the few economies globally to record a positive growth rate of almost 3% in 2020. The rebound in and beyond 2021, is expected to be stronger, with rates of growth reaching pre-pandemic levels, spurred by the 2021 reforms announced during the 13th Party Congress.

While the provision of basic services has improved in the post-reform period, especially in terms of full coverage of electricity, the physical capital investment as a percentage of GDP has been among the lowest in the ASEAN region. Vietnam, with a rank of 89 out of 137 countries for quality of its infrastructure, needs to prioritize this sector. The country's fast-paced growth has required intensive use of fossil fuels for the power sector, resulting in increased greenhouse gas emissions. The country is also affected adversely by air and river water pollution. The government is endeavoring to reduce the country's carbon footprint, with measures for clean energy generation, among others (World Bank, 2020a, b).

Hence, the government's renewed focus on reforms must push for harnessing clean and renewable energy sources and sustainable development, even as it is emerging as a major growth pole in the Asian landscape.

4.1.2 Macroeconomy of India

India, a country of over 1.3 billion people, had a fifth of its population living below the poverty level in 2011. This was reduced to 13.4% in 2015. The Modi government since 2014, has taken several reforms to spur growth levels. These include increasing privatization with the implementation of the Goods and Services Tax to integrate the national market and a series of reforms to ease business conduct. However, demonetization and weak rural incomes coupled with high levels of non-performing assets of the banking sector had resulted in the rate of growth slowing in years just before the pandemic. With the onset of the pandemic, the country went in for a complete lockdown in the last week of March 2020. Although the government was swift to contain the fatalities, the impact of the pandemic has been severe. The pandemic has exacerbated the vulnerabilities for traditionally excluded groups, such as youth and women.

As stated earlier, even prior to the pandemic, the economy was already decelerating, as real GDP growth had moderated from an average of 7.4% in FY16/19 to 4.2% in FY19/ due to several domestic issues and a subdued global economy. Although the government initiated several policies to arrest the slowdown, the pandemic accentuated the downturn. In the fiscal year starting in April 2020, India's economy has contracted by almost 9.6% (World Bank, 2020a, b).

Intending to boost the flailing economy, the government included a series of measures in the budgetary allocation of February 2021. In addition to a thrust on infrastructure development, privatization of public sector entities, and incentives for inward FDI for the Make in India initiative, other initiatives have been undertaken. These include, among others, incentives for micro, small, and medium enterprises, agriculture infrastructure, microfood enterprises, increased public employment outlay, special liquidity window (IBEF Report, 2020).

According to the World Bank, "To build back better, it will be essential for India to continue to keep a strong focus on reducing inequality, as it seeks to implement growth-oriented reforms to get the economy back on track." (World Bank, 2020a, b).

4.1.3 Developing Synergies: India and Vietnam

As stated above, both countries seek to improve their growth rates and enhance their capabilities as engines of growth in the region and globally. Both countries need to attract foreign investors to help them scale up their manufacturing sectors.

India entered the top 50 innovating countries in 2020 since the inception of the Global Innovation Index in 2007, by improving its rank from 81 in 2015 and to 48 in 2020. For India to become an innovation leader, it needs greater thrust on research and development. India's aspiration must be to compete on innovation with the top ten economies. However, a major constraint is that India's gross domestic expenditure on R&D (GERD) is lowest among other largest economies.

The macroeconomic profiles of the countries are incomplete without the indicators presented in Table 4.1.

Table 4.1 is testimony of Vietnam's success in GDP per capita and levels of HDI and government debt as a percent of GDP; these are much better than India's.

Table 4.2 provides further insights into the development levels and trade openness of both countries. It is evident that while the percentage share of agriculture to GDP is the same in both countries, Vietnam's manufacturing sector's contribution and those of exports and imports to GDP are much higher than that of India. In the words of Ambassador Thanh, "Vietnam's overall trade is US$600 bn, which is 3 times of Vietnam's GDP; but India's overall trade is only one-third of it's GDP." Moreover, Vietnam performs better than India in terms of high-tech exports. Its trade balance has

Table 4.2 Development indicators for Vietnam and India in percent (2019)

Indicator	Vietnam	India
Agriculture/GDP	15	15
Manufacturing/GDP	34.5	26
Exports/GDP	106	20
Imports/GDP	102	24
High tech exports/manufactures/exports	41	9
Global competitiveness index (2019)	67	68
FDI inflows (USD) mn	15,500	42,117
Trade balance as % of GDP	2.83%	− 6.82%

Source https://atlas.cid.harvard.edu/countries/239

also been positive compared to India's negative balance, demonstrating the country's competitiveness.

While economic indicators present important insights into the country's level of development, the indicators of polity, electoral processes, and corruption are also significant to gauge a country's ability and transparency in governance. Corruption has been an issue in Vietnam, post the Đổi Mới reforms. According to Vasavakul, "while anti-corruption efforts have curbed petty corruption between state officials, businesses, and citizens, grand corruption has been overlooked. The institutional set up also has limitations, especially in anti-corruption agency independence and its preventive and investigative powers" (Vasavakul, 2020: 4). India also slipped two places in 2019, as compared to 2018.

As shown in Table 4.3, Vietnam has a low score in democracy index, electoral process and pluralism as well as a lower rank in terms of being a fragile state in comparison to India. During his visit to the country in 2001, Kaushik Basu stated

Table 4.3 Country indicators: polity and pluralism

Country	Fragile state rank* 2018	Democracy index-score/10	Rank/	El. process and pluralism/10	Civil liberties/10	Corruption index 2018	CPI* rank/180 countries 2019
India	72	6.90	51	8.67	6.76	41	80
Vietnam	107	3.08	136	0.00	2.65	33	104

Source Democracy Index, Economist Intelligence Unit (2019); http://www.eiu.com/public/thankyou_download.aspx?activity=download&campaignid=democracyindex2019
*The Fragile States Index measures the vulnerability in pre-conflict, active conflict and post-conflict situations. The index has twelve conflict risk indicator. These measure the condition of a state at a specific time. These include security apparatus, factionalized elites, group grievance, economic decline, uneven economic development, human flight and brain drain, state legitimacy, human rights and the rule of law, demographic pressures, refugees and IDPs, external intervention, among others. The higher the value of the index, the more "fragile" the country is. The higher the rank, the more fragile the country is.

that Vietnam presented a strange mixture of socialism and the free market, where there is an equitable distribution of wealth. Although there is poverty, it is not as stark as in India (Basu, 2001). This points to the political will of the Party leaders in ensuring a just and peaceful society.

The above data presented in the tables help us contextualize bilateral economic relations, discussed in the next section.

4.2 India and Vietnam: Trade Relations

This section discusses contemporary bilateral trade relations and focuses on areas in which the two countries can expand engagement.

4.2.1 Bilateral Trade: Slow Growth

Both India and Vietnam are members of the ASEAN–India Free Trade Area (AIFTA), since 2010, according to which tariffs are eliminated for over 80% of goods traded between ASEAN and India. By 2024, Vietnam would be required to reduce or elimi-nate tariffs under all the categories. Despite India's exit from RCEP, (although doors remain open for India's accession into the RCEP agreement. India can make a written request for the same) India and Vietnam are exploring avenues for increasing trade and investment. Vietnam's total merchandise exports grew at an annualized average rate of 18 percent per annum over the 10 years 2009 till 2019, as compared with India's 5%. During the same period, Vietnam attained a trade surplus of US$47 billion, which again significantly improved the trade deficit of US$13 billion in 2010. While Vietnam had a trade surplus, India's trade deficit increased from US$130 billion in 2010 to US$156 billion in 2019 (Mazumdar, 2020).

Tables 4.4 and 4.5 highlight the top items in terms of value, in India's exports to and imports from Vietnam.

4.2.2 India's Key Exports to Vietnam

India's key exports to Vietnam include machinery and equipment, seafood, pharma-ceuticals, cotton, automobiles, textiles and leather accessories, cattle feed ingredient, chemicals, plastic resins, chemicals products, fibers, steel, fabrics, metals, jewelry, and precious stones.

The export data for the top ten high value items exported by India to Vietnam, presented in Table 4.4, clearly shows that in comparison to 2018–19, there has been a decline in exports of most commodities, except in iron and steel as well as vehicles

Table 4.4 India's exports to Vietnam USD mn

S. No.	H.S. code	Commodity	2018–19 (USD Mn)	2019–20 (USD Mn)	Increase/decrease %
2.	02	Meat and edible meat offal	1710.22	1071.70	−37.34
3.	03	Fish and Crustaceans, Molluscs and other aquatic invertebrates	988.04	280.74	−71.59
9.	09	Coffee, tea, mate, and spices	240.33	27.17	−88.69
23.	23	Residues and waste from the food industries; prepared animal fodder	229.20	119.96	−47.66
30.	30	Pharmaceutical products	135.31	126.28	−6.67
51.	52	Cotton	455.12	206.06	−54.72
71.	72	Iron and steel	486.22	1098.14	125.85
82.	84	Nuclear reactors, boilers, machinery and mechanical appliances; parts thereof	245.27	155.24	−36.71
83.	85	Electrical machinery and equipment and parts thereof; sound recorders and reproducers, television image and sound recorders, reproducers and parts	220.30	156.48	−28.97
85.	87	Vehicles other than railway or tramway rolling stock, and parts and accessories thereof	195.90	250.55	27.90
India's total			330,078.09	313,361.04	−5.06
% Share			1.97	1.61	

Source https://tradestat.commerce.gov.in/eidb/ecntcom.asp; accessed on February 7, 2021

Table 4.5 India's imports from Vietnam (USD mn)

No.	H.S. code	India	2018–19	2019–20	Increase/decrease %
8.	09	Coffee, tea, mate, and spices	222.70	210.25	−5.59
6.	28	Inorganic chemicals; organic or inorganic compounds of precious metals, of rare-earth metals, or radi. elem. or of isotopes	527.70	347.38	−34.17
36.	39	Plastic and articles thereof	118.09	125.91	6.62
37.	40	Rubber and articles thereof	208.18	222.36	6.81
9.	54	Man-made filaments	109.96	81.22	−26.14
59.	64	Footwear, gaiters and the like; parts of such articles	124.86	156.39	25.25
67.	72	Iron and steel	227.72	106.05	−53.43
68.	73	Articles of iron or steel	221.39	228.15	3.06
9.	74	Copper and articles thereof	488.81	447.29	−8.50
78.	84	Nuclear reactors, boilers, machinery and mechanical appliances; parts thereof	315.61	368.35	16.71
9.	85	Electrical machinery and equipment and parts thereof; sound recorders and reproducers, television image and sound recorders and reproducers and parts	3679.53	4010.06	8.98
		India	514,078.42	474,709.28	−7.66
				1.3991	1.5343

Source https://tradestat.commerce.gov.in/eidb/ecntcom.asp; accessed on February 7, 2021

and parts. This has resulted in a decline in the share of Vietnam as a source of exports from India to 1.61% from nearly 2% in the previous year.

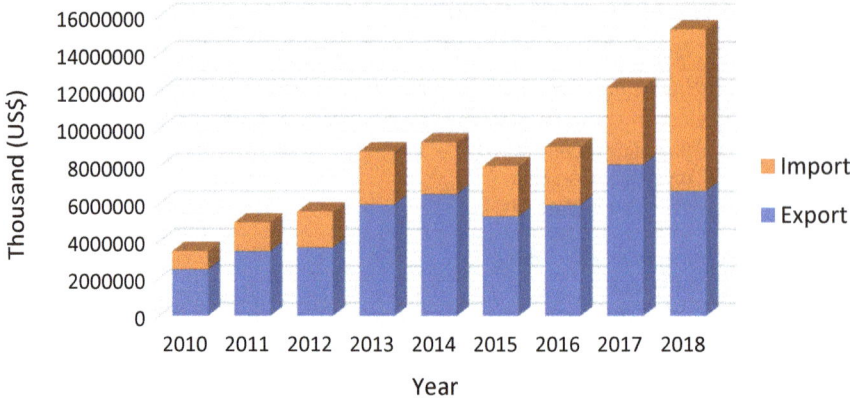

Fig. 4.1   India's bilateral trade with Vietnam (2010–2018). *Sources WITS* (https://wits.worldbank. org/CountryProfile/en/Country/VNM/Year/2017/TradeFlow/EXPIP)

4.2.3   India's Imports from Vietnam

Key imports from Vietnam include mobile phones, computers, electronics hardware, machinery, chemicals, rubber, metals, wood, fibers, pepper, means of transport, steel products, coffee, footwear, chemicals products, polymers, and resins.

4.2.4   Bilateral Trade of India and Vietnam—Exports and Imports

Bilateral trade is also shown in Figs. 4.1 and 4.2, to assess the growing imports from Vietnam over 2010–2018. Total trade has been between US$12 to 14 billion, with India importing more from Vietnam, resulting in a deficit in its bilateral trade.

4.2.5   Export Performance During the Pandemic: Comparing Vietnam and India

The pandemic saw a rise in unemployment, despite government support in the form of tax rebates. There are also concerns of rising public debt and slow disbursement of funds in support packages. Despite these concerns, Vietnam's performance in 2020 demonstrates that it has been able to surmount some challenges.

Vietnam's exports dropped by 6.7% in the first six months of 2020, over the same period in 2019 totaling US$79.8 billion. Despite this, it had an overall positive trade balance of US$4 billion. Moreover, the government is on a fast track to implement

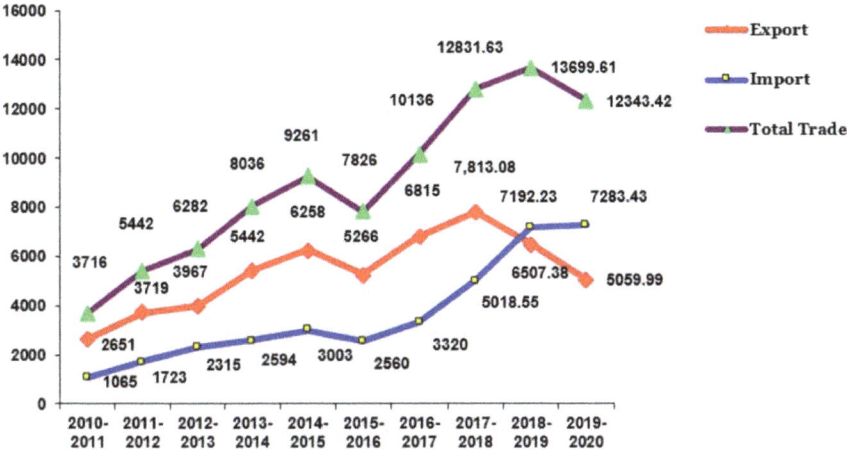

Fig. 4.2 India–Vietnam: exports, imports, total trade, in US$ million (2010–11 to 2018–19). https://www.indembassyhanoi.gov.in/page/economic-andcommercial/#:~ *Source* Indian Embassy, Hanoi; accessed on February 5, 2021

measures to encourage exports, investments, and consumption. The EU-Vietnam Free Trade Agreement and the EU-Vietnam Investment Protection Agreement in 2020 and the country's inclusion in RCEP will help stimulate exports further.

As noted by an HSBC report, Vietnam's economy continues to grow in 2020 and will stand out as the fastest growing economy in 2021 (Vietnam Briefing, July 2020; Dezan Shira & Associates).

In the case of India, overall exports (Merchandise and Services combined) in April–September 2020–21 was estimated to be US$221.86 billion, exhibiting a negative growth of (−)16.66% over the same period in 2019–20. Overall imports in April–September 2020–21 are estimated to be US$204.12 billion, exhibiting a negative growth of (−)35.43% over the same period last year. Given the sharper fall in imports, when merchandise and services are taken together, the overall trade surplus for April–September 2020–21 is estimated at US$17.74 billion compared to the deficit of US$49.91 billion in April–September 2019–20.[1]

The Indian Government's policy of self-reliance, or Atmanirbhar Bharat, is expected to enhance India's export competitiveness further and build some key sector industries like pharmaceuticals, electricals, and plastic goods. The endeavor is also to reduce imports, especially from China.

The next section focuses on areas for India and Vietnam to expand trade relations.

---

[1] Ministry of Commerce and Industry, India, https://pib.gov.in/PressReleasePage.aspx?PRID=1664831, accessed on February 6, 2021.

Table 4.6 India's share of exports to Vietnam as a percent of Vietnam's imports from the world

No.	H.S. code	Vietnam's imports from the world	CAGR (2014–18) %	India's share of Vietnam's imports
1	02	Meat and edible meat	72.35	50.63
2	03	Fish and crustaceans	32.88	26.99
3	07	Edible vegetables	49	0.51
4	10	Cereals	8.15	0.85
5	62	Articles of apparel and accessories	71.82	0.02
6	88	Aircraft	47.92	0.11
7	90	Optical, photo, medical apparatus	26.85	0.28

Authors analysis. *Source* The ITC Trade map https://www.indiantradeportal.in/; accessed on February 6, 2021

4.2.6   Opportunities for Expanding Bilateral Trade Relations

The authors have constructed the table below to understand the opportunities for enhancing bilateral trade. Table 4.6 clearly shows the scope for enhancing India's exports in items 3–7, in which India's share in Vietnam's total imports from the world is less than 1%.

Here, it is also important to note that other opportunities for both countries exist besides the above. India has enormous growth potential to provide I.T. and business services, zinc, steel, and fibers to Vietnam. Vietnam's exports to India can be more robust in cotton, business support, and knitted clothing in addition to an already strong transport, storage, and trade services sector.

Interestingly, Vietnam's share of the global market is fast increasing. From a share of 4.02 in 2015, its share of the world market in textiles increased to 5.05% in 2019, in electronics from 2.62 to 4.07% over the same period. In the agriculture sector, it has plateaued, being 1.48% in 2019, as compared to 1.45 in 2015.

Bilateral Trade Opportunities are presented in Figs. 4.3 and 4.4.

The Standard Chartered report 2021 has estimated that Vietnam could increase high-potential exports to India by US$633 million annually, or 10%. There is scope for increasing goods exports (US$339 million) than services (US$294 million). The top 5 sector export opportunities are wholesale and retail trade services; transportation and storage services; cotton (including sewing thread, yarn, and fabric); office administration and other business support services; and knitted clothing.[2]

---

[2] Standard Chartered Trade Opportunity Report, https://av.sc.com/corp-en/content/docs/Standard-Chartered-Trade-Opportunity-Report.pdf, accessed on February 6, 2021.

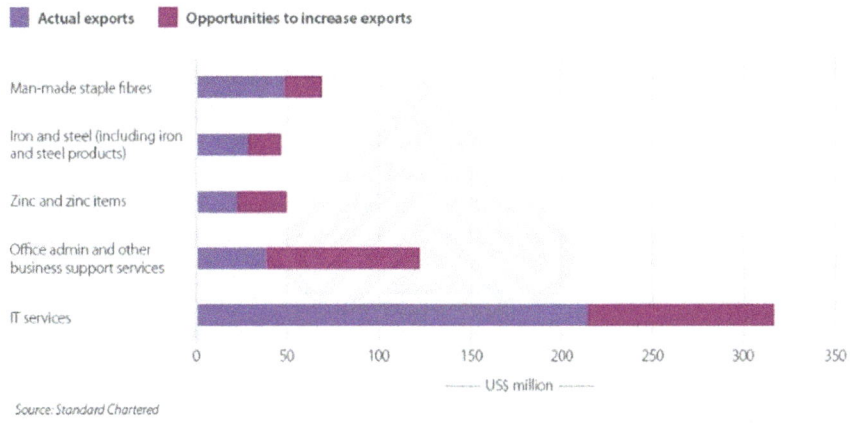

Fig. 4.3 Trade opportunities: India to Vietnam

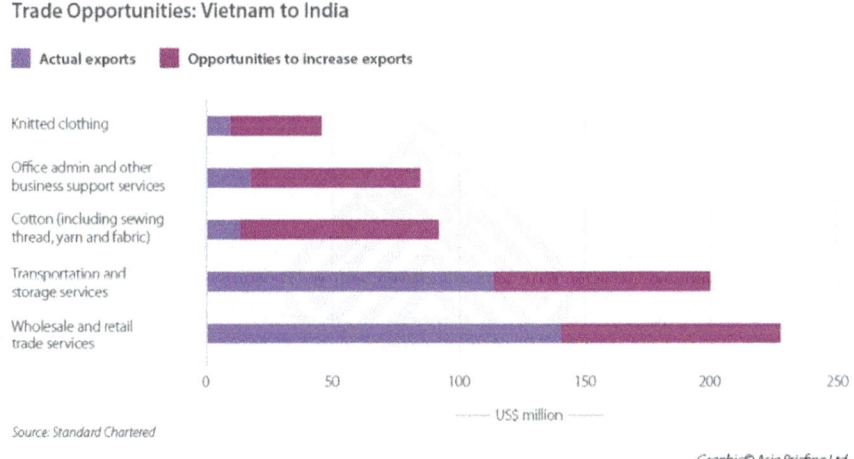

Fig. 4.4 Trade opportunities: Vietnam to India

   Given its current exports, some of the sectors with high potential for diversification in Vietnam are electrical machinery and equipment and industrial machinery. By 2020, both countries expected to achieve trade worth US$15 billion, with trade rising sharply from US$5 billion to US$13.7 billion between 2016 and 2019. The pandemic resulted in a drop in trade, to US$12.4 billion in 2020; this being much lower than the target.

4.3 FDI Flows: India, Vietnam, and China

This section discusses bilateral investment flows. It also compares the footprint of China as an investor of significance. As stated earlier, both India and Vietnam hope to expand levels of growth, by attracting foreign investment. The total FDI equity inflow to India in the fiscal year 2020 was roughly 50 billion U.S. dollars. In 2020, Singapore had the highest FDI equity inflow to India, valued at over 1036 billion Indian rupees, followed by Mauritius valued at over 577 billion Indian rupees. Singapore has been the leading source of foreign direct investment into India, accounting for roughly 30% of total FDI inflows in 2020.

According to the Department for Promotion of Industry and Internal Trade (DIPP), higher inflows of FDI and equity could be attributed to improved ease of doing business and relaxed FDI norms. In F.Y 2020, the service sector received the highest FDI equity inflow, which comprised 17% of the total FDI equity inflows into the country. This was followed by the computer software and hardware sector, while the telecommunications and trading sector's share ranked third and fourth respectively. Table 4.7 presents the data for FDI inflows to India.

- Table 4.7 shows the FDI equity inflow and total FDI inflow. Evidently, equity inflow comprises a significant share of total inflows. Figure 4.5 shows the FDI net inflow and outflow of India. Inflows have been rising fairly consistently since 2012. Outflows declined in 2013, after which there has been some revival. The latest FDI factsheet released by DPIIT shows a positive trend where India has registered a record total FDI of USD 73.45 Bn in F.Y. 2019–20. India has attracted highest ever total FDI inflow of US$81.72 billion during the financial year 2020–21, and it is 10% higher as compared to the last financial year 2019–20 (US$74.39 billion). FDI equity inflow grew by 19% in the F.Y. 2020–21 (US$59.64 billion) compared to the previous year F.Y. 2019–20 (US$49.98 billion) (Ministry of Commerce and Industry, GOI, May 24, 2021) https://pib.gov.in/PressReleasePage.aspx?PRID= 1721268.

Table 4.7 FDI Inflows into India 2014–2019 (amount in US$ billion)

Financial year	FDI equity inflow	Total FDI inflow
2014–15	29.74	45.15
2015–16	40.00	55.56
2016–17	43.48	60.22
2017–18 (P)	44.86	60.97
2018–19 (P)	44.37	62.00

Source DIPP Report, 2021; https://dipp.gov.in/publications/fdi-sta tistics; accessed on February 26, 2021

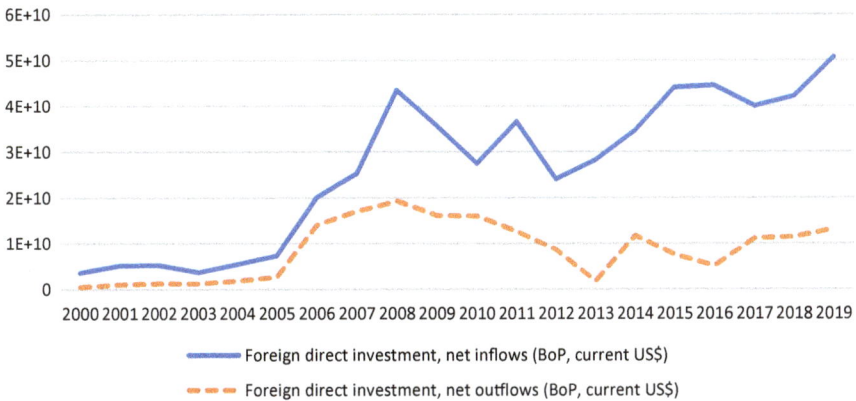

Fig. 4.5 FDI net inflow and outflow of India (2000–2019). *Source* World Bank; World Development Indicators data (2020) (https://databank.worldbank.org/source/world-development-indicators/Type/TABLE/preview/on#)

4.3.1 Indian Investments in Vietnam

Vietnam is considered an important investment destination due to its strong annual growth, of around 6–7%, and the underlying contributing factors, such as a stable political system, a young and dynamic workforce, low wage economy, growing middle class, among others. The Indian Government is expanding business and commercial relations with Vietnam. In 2014, it offered a US$300 million line of credit as an impetus to accelerate bilateral textile trade and investment. In 2017, it approved a Project Development Fund of Rs. 500 crore (US$75 million) for supporting Indian companies to build production and supply chains in Cambodia, Laos, Myanmar, and Vietnam. This will help India's industries in business expansion, maintaining cost-competitive supply chains, and increased integration with global production networks.

India has more than 270 projects in Vietnam with investments amounting close to US$2 billion. In the energy sector, Tata Power is building a US$2.2 billion thermal power project in Soc Trang province. This plant will serve about two percent of Vietnam's power requirements when it is operational by 2030. In 2017, the same group signed a US$54 million pact to build a 49-MW solar park in Vietnam's Southern province of Binh Phuoc. Tata International has an MoU with Agribank in 2017 to support farmers, cooperatives, and plantations with credit support, equipment insurance, and access to a wide range of mechanization solutions in Vietnam. In 2019, Tata Coffee launched its US$50 million freeze-dried coffee plant in the Binh Duong. The Bank of India opened its first branch in Ho Chi Minh City on July 22, 2017, to facilitate investment projects and SMEs.

Figure 4.6 shows the sharp rise in inward FDI to Vietnam; in 2018, this was more than USD 16 billion.

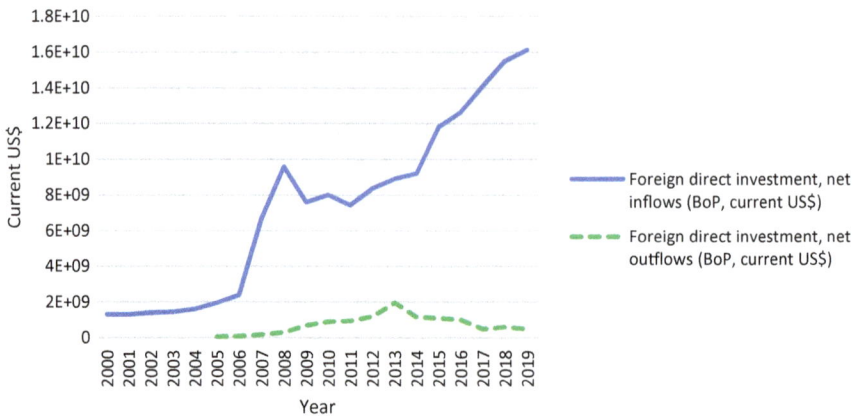

Fig. 4.6 FDI net inflows and outflows in current US$: Vietnam (2001–2019). *Source* World Bank World Development Indicators data; accessed on February 5, 2021; https://databank.worldbank. org/source/world-development-indicators/Type/TABLE/preview/on#

In 2020, the total foreign direct investment (FDI) flow to Vietnam amounted to approximately 28.53 billion U.S. dollars, almost US$10 billion lower than the registered FDI capital from 2019. Asian countries were the major sources of FDI into Vietnam. Singapore, South Korea, China, Japan, and Thailand were the top five investors by revenue, while South Korea, China, Japan, and Singapore were the leading contributors in terms of number of projects.

India remains at the 27th position on the list of foreign investors in Vietnam. As of December 2017, India invested 169 projects in Vietnam with total investment capital of $756 million.[3] While this figure is small compared to countries as South Korea, Japan, Singapore, or the U.S, it is encouraging to note that in 2017 alone, Indian firms invested $187.5 million, equal to 25% of the total FDI from India in the past 30 years. This shows that Indian firms are awakening to Vietnam's potential as an investment destination.

Vietnam's investment in India: According to the DIPP, GOI, the amount of foreign direct investment inflows (FDI inflows) from Vietnam to India are USD 5.28 mn, as of June 2020.

4.3.2   China: A Major Source of Investment for Vietnam and India

It is important to understand the growing levels of investment by China in both India and Vietnam, given that the China factor has propelled bilateral relations.

---

[3] Data from Foreign Investment Agency statistics under the Ministry of Planning and Investment, Vietnam.

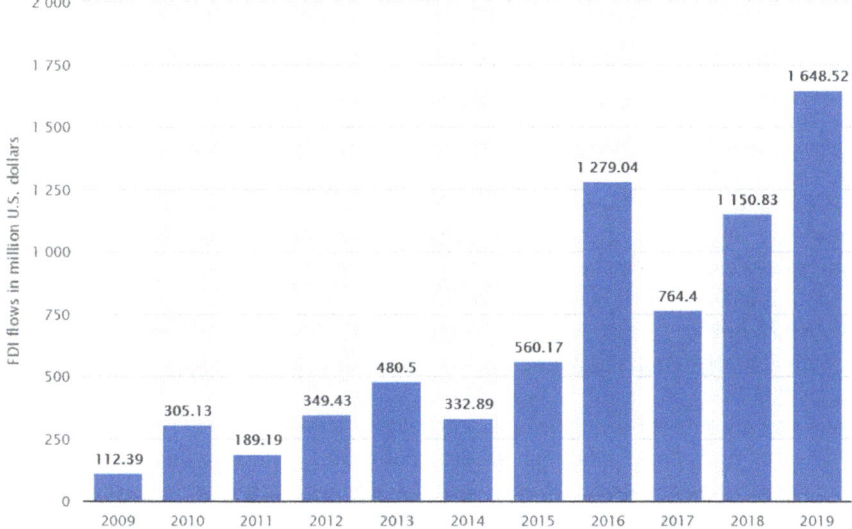

Fig. 4.7 Annual flow of foreign direct investments from China to Vietnam between 2009 and 2019 (in million U.S. dollars). *Source* Statista.com, https://www.statista.com/statistics/720408/china-out ward-fdi-flows-to-vietnam/#

4.3.2.1 China's Investment in Vietnam

In Vietnam, China has grown from being the fourth largest investor in 2019 to the third in terms of total capital and second by the number of projects in 2020. China's total registered FDI in Vietnam was $14.7 billion in 2019, making China the second largest investor in Vietnam, accounting for 15.5% of total registered FDI (Son & Le, 2019). It has also been estimated that almost 80% of all engineering, procurement, and construction (EPC) contracts in Vietnam are awarded to Chinese contractors.[4]

In 2019, the outflow of foreign direct investments from China to Vietnam amounted to around 1.65 billion U.S. dollars (See Fig. 4.7).

U.S. foreign direct investment (FDI) in Vietnam (stock) was $2.6 billion in 2019. While Japan ranks second in cumulative investment, and topped the annual list in 2017 and 2018, it sank to fourth place for 2019. In 2019, with $7.92 billion FDI into Vietnam, South Korea topped all investing 125 countries.

It is well known that some Chinese companies rank low in reputation. Sino-Vietnamese relations are also tense at times; yet in contrast this trend reflects Vietnam's more pragmatic attitude toward attracting much needed private capital and foreign expertise. According to Giang, speaking at an ISEAS-Yusuf webinar on February 8, 2021, the leadership elected during the 13th Party Congress in January

---

[4] Vietnam and China growing economic ties despite strains, https://www.vietnam-briefing. com/news/vietnam-and-china-growing-economic-ties-despite-strains.html/; September 25, 2017; accessed on February 6, 2021.

2021, will continue to keep a lid on anti-Chinese sentiments among the public, even as these sentiments are very real (Giang, 2021).

4.3.2.2   China's Investment in India

China's FDI to India has grown fivefold since 2014. As of December 2019, its cumulative investment in India exceeded $8 billion, out of which almost half has been invested in start-ups, especially in payment portals and other applications. A Brookings India paper pegs the total current and planned Chinese investment in India at over $26 billion.

With a downslide in the political relations, India tightened rules for inward FDI, stating that firms in neighboring countries seeking to invest in Indian companies would first need its approval. A country that shares a land border with India can now invest in its firms "only under the government route." Although this does apply to other neighboring countries as well, this move was seen as a measure to prevent the takeover of Indian companies by Chinese ones.[5]

The next section compares the two economies' ease of doing business rankings to ascertain the future potential of inward FDI and the sectors to which foreign investors would be attracted.

4.4   FDI and Ease of Doing Business: The Way Forward

As shared above, both India and Vietnam are increasingly attractive destinations not only for investment from China, but other countries too. According to the World Investment report, UNCTAD 2020, in SEA, the total number of greenfield projects announced in 2018 and 2019 were 1527 and 1316, respectively. The largest number were in Singapore, followed by Vietnam, which had 290 and 276 projects announced in 2018 and 2019. In India, there were 779 greenfield projects in 2018; in 2019, there were 701 greenfield projects. In all of South Asia, in 2018 and 2019 there were 923 and 786 such projects in all of South Asia.

The World Bank Doing Business Rank Report, 2020 provides a detailed analysis of the indicators of countries in ease of doing business. Table 4.8 provides a comparison of India and Vietnam. While India has improved its overall ranking in 2020 and ranks higher at 63, in comparison to Vietnam at 70, India ranks much lower in registering property, starting a business and enforcing contracts. In contrast, Vietnam ranks lower in protecting minority rights and trading across borders.

---

[5] Prabha Raghavan, https://indianexpress.com/article/explained/why-india-tightened-fdi-rules-and-why-its-china-thats-upset-6374693/; April 23, 2020; accessed on February 7, 2021.

Table 4.8 Ease of doing Business 2020: comparing India and Vietnam

	2020 DBR	Starting a business	Dealing with construction permits	Getting electricity	Registering property	Getting credit	Protecting minority investors	Paying taxes	Trading across borders	Enforcing contracts	Resolving insolvency
India	3	136	27	22	154	5	13	15	2	63	52
Vietnam	0	115	25	27	64	5	97	09	04	8	122

Source DIPP Report, 2019–20; https://dipp.gov.in/sites/default/files/annualReport_English2019-20.pdf; *Source* https://www.doingbusiness.org/content/dam/doingBusiness/country/v/vietnam/VNM.pdf

4.4.1 Prospects for Inward FDI for Vietnam and India

Foreign investors, by registering US$3 billion worth of FDI on average per month kept their confidence in Vietnam in 2019. Hence, there is optimism that Vietnam will continue to attract investors even as the World Bank forecasts a GDP growth of around 6.5% for 2020–22. India, too expects to attract more investments into key areas, including pharmaceuticals, electronics, and insurance being opened up for foreign investors. Both economies are also expanding government spending to boost the fiscal space. India expects debt levels to rise to 90% of GDP. FDI's role in enabling developing countries build a competitive and dynamic private sector is well documented (Moran et al., 2005).

4.4.2 Progress in Improving the Business Environment

While both India and Vietnam have made impressive progress over the past decade, there is scope for improvement. The 2020 Doing Business report ranked India at 63 and Vietnam at 70 out of 190 economies. When the overall rating if further scanned, Vietnam ranks lower than 100th in four subindicators: starting a business, paying taxes, trading across borders, and resolving insolvency. For example, it takes 384 h to pay taxes in Vietnam compared with 64 h in Singapore, 174 h in Malaysia, and 191 h in Indonesia. India ranks below 100 in four subindicators; these are starting a business, registering property, paying taxes and enforcing contracts.

Beyond administrative procedures, private firms in both countries also experience major obstacles, as access to credit, corruption, and lack of skilled labor. In Vietnam, businesses only finance one-third of their investment needs through credit from banks. However, this proportion is over 40% in Malaysia and 50% in OECD countries.

It is important to emphasize that not all firms face these obstacles in the business and a majority of firms being charged penalties are the small and medium ones that do not have the human and financial resources to circumvent those barriers. This is the reason why so many of those small firms opt to operate in the informal sector and why so many of them cannot generate the gains in productivity critical for their success.

4.4.3 Vietnam and India: Attractive Destinations for Inward FDI?

It is important to assess the two countries capabilities as magnets of FDI.

First, while ninety percent of Vietnam's merchandise trade is through seaports, in the case of India, it is not so. Despite having a coastline that is twice as long, India has not been able to take advantage. A key issue is that some of the seaports have dredging issues, unlike in Vietnam which has deep-water ports. Going forward, India needs to undertake a rigorous analysis to compete with its Asian peers, whether in terms of free trade agreements, creating an amicable and stable business environment, financial incentives, creating last-mile connectivity, and, most importantly, low-cost quality labor. It remains to be seen whether India can support global companies set up facilities, when they need it most (Mazumdar, 2020).

Second, key issues to facilitate trade and investment, such as increasing air connectivity and direct containerization, are being prioritized by both governments. These efforts have materialized with direct flights by the Vietnamese carrier, Vietjet Air, (launched by their enterprising businesswoman, Nguyen Thi Phuong Thao) and Indian carrier Indigo, to connect New Delhi and Kolkata with Hanoi and Ho Chi Minh City. Vietnam's recently ratified an FTA with the E.U., signed in August 2020, also signals the country's expanding engagement with non-traditional partners. The FTA is expected to help increase Vietnam's GDP by 4.6% and its exports to the E.U. by 42.7% by 2025. India is also renegotiating a trade agreement with the EU since May 2021 (The negotiations resumed after a gap of 8 years). This signals EU's growing interest in engaging with Asian countries as India and Vietnam.

Third, favorable investment policies have been put in place. In Vietnam, these include preferential corporate income tax rates, import duty exemptions, and privileges awarded to build-operate-transfer (BOT), build-transfer-operate (BTO), and build-transfer (B.T.) projects in special economic zones. The incentives are for the promotion of FDI in the high-tech sector, less-developed regions, labor-intensive industries, and priority sectors such as education and health.

India has set up a Foreign Investment Facilitation Portal, the new online single point interface for investors to facilitate foreign direct investment operationalized by *Department for Promotion of Industry and Internal Trade* (DIPP). Other improvements in trading across borders include a reduction in time and cost to export and import, upgrading equipment on the Nhava Sheva Port in Mumbai and the E Sanchit system, allowing traders to submit all supporting documents with digital signatures. An important development is that 100% FDI under automatic route has been permitted for entities engaged in Single Brand Retail Trading. Mr. Saxena pointed out that shipments from and to Vietnam are routed through the Nhava Sheva port to Ho Chi Minh City and vice versa.

Fourth, large outlays on improvement in infrastructure. Vietnam has over 325 state-supported industrial zones/parks in the country that offer incentives and fewer restrictions. In the next few years, 17 more industrial parks are expected to open. The economic zones, which attract foreign investment in the export-oriented sectors tend to be closer to main roads, ports, and airports for easier movement of goods. India has increased the allocation of funds for the development of highways and ports and plans to spend US$1.4 trillion on infrastructure during 2019–23. While Vietnam was ranked 39, India was ranked 44 out of 167 countries in World Bank's Logistics Performance Index (LPI) 2018. India ranked second in the 2019 Agility Emerging Markets Logistics Index.

Fifth, stable and growing economies. Economic and political reforms under Đổi Mới, launched in 1986, have spurred rapid economic development, transforming

Vietnam into a dynamic emerging economy in the region, with a GDP growth of over 7% in 2019, forecast to be about 3% in 2020 and 6.7% in 2021. Although India registered a negative growth rate in 2020–21, a V-shaped recovery is expected, with an estimated growth rate rising of 11% in 2021–12. Despite uncertainties in the global environment, both economies will help the economic revival in Asia. According to a Forbes report, India has emerged as the country of start-ups, with 54 unicorns (A unicorn is a privately held start-up valued at more than $1 billion).[6] This is an area where Vietnam requires support.

Sixth, rise in global rankings: In terms of ease of doing business, both Vietnam and India have made numerous amendments to their regulations. Hence, their rankings have risen to 70 and 63, respectively, among 190 economies in the World Bank's 2020 Doing Business Report. India has improved its rank in 7 out of 10 indicators during the year and has moved closer to international best practices calculated by a distance to Frontier (DTF) score. India's DTF scores improved from 67.5 in DBR 2019 to 71.0 in DBR 2020. India has been recognized as one of the top 10 improvers for the third time in a row, with an improvement of 67 ranks in three years. India's rank has improved from 142 in 2014 to 63 in 2019, registering an improvement of 79 positions since the start of the initiative (World Bank, 2020a, b). In the Global Innovation Index, Vietnam ranked 42nd among 131 economies and first among the 29 lower-middle-income economies. Its improved business environment and competitiveness have been commended. India ranks 48th among 127 economies, and first in central and Southern Asia.

Seventh, favorable demographics: Both countries have a young population. The median age in Vietnam is 30.5 years, and the workforce is young and skilled, with at least 45% of them in their working age. India's median age was 24.9 according to the 2011 census; however, this is expected to increase to 34.7 in 2036.[7]

Eighth, both governments are placing increasing emphasis on the private sector. The 13th Party Congress is enhancing the role of the private sector in Vietnam. The party's economic goals include: About 1.5 million private companies making up 55% of GDP by 2025, versus 700,000 representing 42% of GDP in 2020. At least 2 million private companies accounting for 60%–65% of GDP by 2030. Average economic growth of 6.5%–7% during 2021–2025 versus 5.9% the previous five years increasing per capita GDP to $4700–$5000 by 2025, from $2750 in 2020 and $1331 in 2010.

However, Vietnam has a paradox. The market is dominated by a few large private groups—Vingroup, Hoang Anh Gia Lai (HAGL), FLC Group—with the rest mainly comprising small and medium-sized enterprises. Several experts warn about the excessive use of financial leverage (borrowing too heavily). For example, HAGL Group is under a huge debt burden, with their core businesses being adversely

---

[6] Sayan Ghosh, https://www.forbes.com/sites/zengernews/2021/08/30/the-next-big-investment-hub-for-unicornsand-its-not-china/?sh=55d30e8d63ec; accessed on September 4, 2021.

[7] Ageing nation and more job seekers by 2036, https://www.telegraphindia.com/india/median-age-of-indias-population-will-rise-to-34-7-from-24-9-in-2011-report/cid/1791498; February 8, 2021; accessed on February 8, 2021.

affected. If a large business group goes bankrupt, the effects on the Vietnamese banking system will be severe. A "too big to fail" attitude is becoming evident in many of these large Vietnamese private sector groups (Vinh & Manh, 2020).

India too is increasingly reliant on the private sector for boosting the economy. Reliance group's Mukesh Ambani, Adani Group's Gautam Adani, the Tatas and Birlas are well established. India's Internet space is one sector that is much sought after. "I suspect the government somewhere is signaling that it is better for multi-national companies to come in with some Indian partner," said Arun Kumar, an economist and the Malcolm Adiseshiah Chair at the Institute of Social Sciences. "So Amazon might decide it is better to cooperate with Reliance than compete against it." Retail is the next frontier for Ambani, whose ambitions include creating a home-grown e-commerce giant like China's Alibaba Group Holding Ltd. (Altstedter & Sanjai, 2020).

Ninth, labor productivity has been improving in both countries. In India, the output per worker at GDP constant 2010 USD, rose from 4030 in 2011 to 6324.4 in 2019, for Vietnam, the increase is from USD 2385.9 in 2011 to USD 3577.9 in 2019 (ILOStat, November 2020). Inward FDI is critically linked to cost and productivity of labor (Barba Navaretti & Venables, 2004).

Tenth, Euromonitor International in its M&A index report rated Vietnam as the market with the most dynamic and potential M&A activity globally just behind the U.S. forecast. Moreover, Vietnam will continue to secure the second place in the top 20 countries with the highest M&A index in 2021. In India, the M&A activity has been high in the years preceding the pandemic and is expected to revive further in 2021 (Euromonitor International, 2020).

Recent Developments

On August 1, 2021, the Vietnamese Embassy in India coordinated with the local authorities in Bangalore city, in the state of Karnataka, India, to organize the Vietnam–India investment and start-up Forum. Speaking at the Forum,[8] Ambassador Pham Sanh Chau emphasized that science and technology are among the important pillars of the Comprehensive Strategic Partnership between the two countries. According to the information at the Forum, Vietnam has developed a project namely, Project to Support Start-up and Innovation Ecosystem up to 2025 (referred to as Project 844). The Project's objective is to support more than 2000 start-ups, of which 600 start-ups have developed into strong enterprises; and turn Vietnam into a start-up and innovation hub of Southeast Asia. With new initiatives and projects, Vietnam hopes to enhance the level of entrepreneurial skills and spirit of its people.

In addition to the state-led improvements in attracting investment into their respective countries, there are sectors in which the two countries can collaborate for mutual benefit. There will be a renewed focus on ensuring that supply chain disruptions caused during the pandemic are made more efficient and smarter. Several auto-mobile manufacturers, including Honda, Toyota, Nissan, and Ford with production

---

[8] Huy Lê, Việt Nam - Ấn Độ đẩy mạnh hợp tác về khởi nghiệp và đổi mới sáng tạo, *Vietnam News Agency*, 19th August 2021. https://www.vietnamplus.vn, accessed on August 20, 2021.

plants in Vietnam, were forced to suspend operations due to the pandemic. Hence, the resilience of supply chains must be ensured.[9] For Vietnam, there will be opportunities to expand exports through the RCEP, once this has been ratified by six ASEAN countries and three non-ASEAN countries.

4.4.4   Bilateral Sector Opportunities

Agriculture: This sector offers several opportunities, especially in rice, coffee, and tea production, which are major country exports. India exported broken rice to Vietnam in early 2021, even as the price of rice rose in the world's third largest exporter of rice. Dwindling supplies and continued Philippine buying have lifted Vietnamese rice export prices to a fresh nine-year high. Vietnam's 5% broken rice is offered around US$500–$505 per ton, significantly higher than Indian prices of $381–$387.[10]

Seafood and Aquaculture: Although Vietnam is also an exporter of seafood, it also imports seafood from India. Herein lies the potential for Indian seafood processing companies to establish a value chain in exploration, processing, and trade units in Vietnam. Indian companies could benefit from the special tax and other concessions available for the fisheries sector in Vietnam. The Indian Government has also requested for training in the rearing of shrimp and catfish.

Information Technology: This sector represents a major opportunity for Indian I.T. companies to expand their footprint in Vietnam through smart technologies, which India has been promoting through Digital India launched in 2015. In October 2020, representatives of the two countries met in Hanoi to discuss the development of smart cities. As stated by the Indian ambassador in Hanoi, "Many Indian I.T. companies have also established their presence in Vietnam to provide I.T. training, solutions, and services, especially in banking, telecoms and cybersecurity." Vietnam can also benefit through technologies in travel and finance.[11] HCL Technologies Ltd, a leading global technology company in India, announced its entry into Vietnam in December 2020. It aims to boost employment, provide resources, and skill local

---

[9] Why Vietnam's outlook for 2021 looks bright, https://www.vietnam-briefing.com/news/why-vietnams-outlook-for-2021-looks-bright.html/; accessed on February 2, 2021.

[10] Read more at: https://economictimes.indiatimes.com/news/economy/foreign-trade/vietnam-the-third-biggest-exporter-of-rice-buys-from-india-for-the-first-time-in-decades/articleshow/80101651.cms?utm_source=contentofinterest&utm_medium=text&utm_campaign=cppst; January 4, 2021; accessed on February 8, 2021.

[11] Vietnamese Indian firms to build smart cities in Vietnam, https://en.vietnamplus.vn/vietnamese-indian-firms-to-build-smart-cities-in-vietnam/188335.vnp; October 9, 2020; accessed on February 8, 2021.

talent to serve its global clients. In 2019, an Indian hotel giant, Oyo had considered USD 50 million investment in Vietnam.[12]

Apple is ramping up the production of iPhones, iPods, Macs, and other products outside of China, in a sign that the tech giant is continuing to accelerate its product diversification.[13]

Apparel Sector: There are several Indian textile companies in Vietnam; notable among these are Saitex, Classic Fashion Apparel, Premco Global, Premier Fashion and some others. K. Srikar Reddy, Indian Consul General in Ho Chi Minh City, had spoken of India's "automatic route" policy, through which overseas investors can invest in India without seeking any approval from the government in advance. He also said that Vietnamese apparel and textile firms could take complete advantage of this policy and the market potential to produce yarns, fabrics and readymade apparel in India.[14]

Infrastructure: With a fast-urbanizing economy, infrastructure needs of Vietnam are on the rise. Indian firms can explore opportunities in projects such as road, energy and vessel-building. Other sectors of interest include hospitality and medical. (Vietnam Briefing, July 2017, updated) There are specific projects that are seeking FDI investment in Vietnam, since 2012. To name a few, these are: Saigon Hi-tech Park (SHTP), Ho Chi Minh City Export Processing and Industrial Zones Authority (HEPZA), Export processing zones (EPZs), and industrial zones (I.Z.s) in Ho Chi Minh City.

A Realistic Assessment: According to Sebastian Bustos, a lead Growth Lab researcher in trade and economic complexity methods, "Asia will continue to head the global growth landscape, driven by gains in diversifying into complex manu-facturing." Even as India and Vietnam target bilateral trade of US$15 billion, post the revival phase, there is a need to strengthen logistics services between the two countries. India can also access many products manufactured in third countries from Vietnam at competitive prices and with lower transportation costs.[15]

Hence, it is evident that both Vietnam and India will continue to attract inward FDI in the post-pandemic phase. Vietnam has been tapped by Japanese firms as the most promising place in Asia to invest in 2020, with India and Southeast Asian countries dominating other top spots, A survey cited by Kyodo News on January 8, 2020, that had been conducted online from November to December 2019 by NNA Japan Co., listed Vietnam as the most promising place to invest in 2020. Vietnam received 42.1% of the 820 valid responses. This was due to it being a growing market and

---

[12] Indian hotel giant OYO eyes $ 50 mln investment in Vietnam, https://e.vnexpress.net/news/business/companies/indian-hotel-giant-oyo-eyes-50-mln-investment-in-vietnam-3947175.html; July 4, 2019; accessed on February 9, 2021.

[13] Apple bolsters production shift to Vietnam, India, 28/01/2021, https://en.vietnamplus.vn/apple-bolsters-production-shift-to-vietnam-india/195460.vnp, accessed on February 2, 2021.

[14] https://apparelresources.com/business-news/sourcing/india-vietnam-building-textile-bond/; 22-December-2018; accessed on February 8, 2021, https://apparelresources.com/business-news/sourcing/india-vietnam-building-textile-bond/; 22-December-2018; accessed on February 8, 2021.

[15] VNA;   https://en.vietnamplus.vn/vietnamese-indian-firms-discuss-trade-investment/158270.vnp; accessed on February 2, 2021.

huge pool of skilled, low-cost labor. India was second at 12.2%, with expectations for its growing market and its potential as a gateway to the Middle East and Africa among the reasons cited. China, ranked lower at fifth place, as it has lost its appeal as an investment location due to concerns about its trade war with the United States and rising labor costs.[16]

The above discussion has been placed in greater focus by Ambassador Chau in his interview to the authors on May 11, 2021. In his words, "The relationship between Vietnam and India has been elevated to the highest level of diplomacy, namely Comprehensive Strategic Partnership. India is one of the only three comprehensive strategic partners Vietnam has had till date. During the most recent summit held on December 21, 2020, the two prime ministers discussed and set forth the Joint Vision for Peace, Prosperity, and People, opening spacious room for the enhancement of bilateral relations in the future. For how it could be further advanced, much has been talked about political, defense, and economic cooperation. There are also other areas where the two sides can cooperate, learn from each other, and bring to full play one's advantages."

There are two prominent examples, among many.

First, medical training, both modern and traditional ones, is a promising field. India is very well known in the world for its pharmaceuticals and rich in herbal medicines. The two countries share the traditions of using herbs and other forms of medical acupuncture. An empirical study highlights the importance of patenting, i.e., investing in R&D for realizing market power for pharma companies in developing countries (Dhanora et al., 2021).

Additionally, demands for medical education in India are high, and Vietnam has some capacity to meet them. The Embassy is working to bring Indian students to Vietnam for undergraduate programs in medical science and practices.

Second, the IT sector shows promise. Vietnam has been emerging as an IT hub in ASEAN. In 2020 the government adopted National Digital Transformation Program by 2025, orientation to 2030, under which digital economy is projected to make up 20% and 30% of the country's GDP by 2025 and 2030, respectively. Vietnam is also set to be among the top three digital governments in ASEAN by 2030 and is working out a plan to roll out its own developed 5G network commercially. Meanwhile, India has also implemented the Digital India Program with a vision to transform the country into a digitally empowered society and knowledge economy. Many cities in India are also in a process of transformation into the world's major technology hubs. "There are plenty of things we can work together and share experiences, including but not limited to information security and safety, smart cities, hospitals, schools, and villages" (Ambassador Chau).

---

[16] Vietnam most promising Asian investment destination in 2020 survey, https://en.vietnamplus.vn/vietnam-most-promising-asian-investment-destination-in-2020-survey/167047.vnp; January 8, 2020, accessed on February 2, 2021.

4.4.5 Challenges in Bilateral Engagement

Despite the two countries seeking to expand economic ties, there are macro and microchallenges.

First, Mergers, and Acquisitions (M&A) as Routes for Investment: For Vietnam, several issues have kept the M&A activity low compared to that of India. Despite M&A's being popular routes for foreign investors to enter the Vietnamese market, the latter have faced some difficulties to get M&A approval from the relevant authorities in the manufacturing industry. Local authorities are scrutinizing documents, and investors have been asked for explanations on several parameters ranging from technology, machinery, labor use, source of input materials, product markets, and environmental protection. These recent developments come as Vietnam becomes more selective in attracting FDI.[17] These include Absence of detailed guidelines for public company M&A, Vietnamese Dong currency exposure for equity investments. Lengthy regulatory approval processes and a lack of reliable publicly available information on target companies and issues of managing accounts in Vietnam remain other challenges. Accordingly, the integration process often involves the foreign investor(s) attempting to introduce international corporate governance rules and practices not familiar to the company and its employees. Hence, foreign investors have been more interested in mergers and acquisitions of domestic firms rather than in greenfield investments for exports.

This was confirmed in an interview by Mr. Amit Saxena, when he said, "Indian investors are only interested in brownfield investment in Vietnam. The paucity of availability of funds for investors restrains them from investing in greenfield projects. Moreover, unless a company has a huge export market from Vietnam, it will be risky to rely only on the domestic Vietnamese market, as the demand for high-tech and luxury products remain low."[18]

Second, the Competition for Inward FDI. There are also concerns in Vietnam about India's break to the top in competition for FDI. In reality, Vietnam and India are rivals in attracting foreign investment. In recent years, by reforming its foreign investment attraction policies, India has become a magnet for foreign investment. After the issuance of the "Make in India" policy, between October 2014 and March 2017, India acquired $99.72 billion in FDI, up 62% compared to the period between April 2012 and September 2014. China has also become concerned about the rising FDI in India, especially in 2015, when India had the first rank in FDI attraction with the total investment capital of $63 billion, exceeding China's $56.6 billion and the U.S.$59.6 billion. Vietnamese economists raised concerns about the competition with India after Apple Inc. released its intentions to manufacture iPhones in India. India is an ideal investment destination for foreign investors as the government issued several policies to attract FDI. In one policy, India permitted foreign airlines to own

---

[17] Challenges in Vietnam's Manufacturing, https://www.aseanbriefing.com/news/challenges-in-vietnams-manufacturing-ma/; December 23, 2020.

[18] Interview to authors on May 4, 2021.

a 49% stake in Indian national carriers, which face financial difficulties. The retail sector is also open for inward investment.

According to Qiao Xinsheng, most of the world's major multinational corporations have established factories or offices in Vietnam. This signifies that the MNCs have much confidence in the future of this country (Xinsheng, 2020).

Besides, India offers low-cost human resources with the labor cost almost 50% lower than in Vietnam. India also has an advantage in the high-tech industry as it is considered the "Silicon Valley" of Asia.[19]

While both countries seek to expand economic cooperation, India has stayed out of RCEP and is undertaking a review of the FTA with ASEAN, which are roadblocks to the engagement. Vietnam, however, continues to expand its intraregional engagement with ASEAN nations.

Third, Lack of State Support for Entrepreneurs

It has been pointed out that, Vietnam has a young generation with great creativity and potential for starting a business, which is clearly shown in various contests about business ideas or events for investment capital. According to statistics of the Ministry of Finance of Vietnam, currently, Vietnam has about 1500 start-ups operating in different fields, and most of the founders of these start-ups are very young, between 25 and 28 years old. However, Vietnam is among the 20 countries with the lowest entrepreneurial skills. The start-ups lack the ability to implement business plans, with only about 3% being considered successful. This shows that there is a huge gap between aspirations and the ability to implement business ideas of the young Vietnamese generation. This also causes difficulties for Vietnamese entrepreneurs to work with Indian partners and utilize the business opportunities from Indian partners. According to Mr. Nguyễn Thanh Đương—CEO of Bistech Vietnam Technology Joint Stock Company, the solution to this difficulty lies in education, that it is important for Vietnam to implement separate master training models in which older generation of entrepreneurs should always be ready to train the younger generation.

Another aspect that prevents Vietnam's entrepreneurs from successfully taking advantages of the business opportunities from India is the language problem. Many Vietnamese laborers show lack of confidence in working with Indian partners because they cannot use English fluently. According to Mr. Amit Saxena and Mr. Nguyen Van Nien in an interview to the authors, for India—Vietnam business cooperation to develop, there is an imperative for investment by the state to provide training in entrepreneurial and English skills for the Vietnamese youth and entrepreneurs. Additionally, the provision of credit by banks could be modeled on the Indian experience of funds provided by banks and financial institutions to start-ups and small and medium business enterprises.

Fourth, the China Factor. China's all-encompassing economic partnership with Vietnam, also impinges on the bilateral economic relationship. According to Nguyen Khac Giang, economic decoupling would be difficult for Vietnam, as the economy

---

[19] Vietnam anticipates wave of FDI from India, https://www.vir.com.vn/vietnam-anticipates-wave-of-fdi-from-india-55916.html; accessed on February 2, 2021.

remains structurally intertwined, in terms of imports for production. There will be moves to balance investment from China by increasing investments from South Korea, Japan and India (ISEAS seminar on February 9, 2021). India, too is diversifying sources of investment and has created barriers for inward investment from China. However, despite policy measures, India's trade with China in the first half of 2021 rose by a record 62.7%—recording the highest increase among China's major trade partners. The two-way trade even surpassed the pre-pandemic levels.[20]

Fifth, Factors Impacting Social Capital. Mr. Nguyen Van Nien pointed out that, at times it is very difficult to work with the Indian partners because of the different ways of doing business among the Vietnamese and Indian people. They often meet at the negotiating table without reaching any conclusion. While it is very easy to conclude a contract with the Chinese counterparts, it is very difficult to finalise a contract with the Indian partners. Some Indian businessmen believe that the business environment in Vietnam is not conducive to doing business as it does not differentiate between long time business partners and new comers. Some Indian businessmen despite being residents in Vietnam for decades, continue to be treated as foreigners. They cannot buy a house and do not have equal access as the local populace to medical treatment. They have to spend huge amounts for medical treatment, as the cost for foreigners is almost ten times that charged from Vietnamese people. This may have discouraged new Indian entrepreneurs to settle in Vietnam to explore business opportunities.

Sixth, Other Aspects. While the ease of doing business has improved in India, the logistics costs continue to be exorbitant. According to a report by Confederation of India Industry (CII) and Arthur D. Little, "the current logistics cost of India is 14% of GDP, while in the US and Europe, it ranges between 8 and 10%. India's supply chain and logistics sector are one of the largest globally, with a logistics industry of $215 billion, growing at a CAGR of 10.5%."[21] This high cost is an obvious impediment to India's ambitions of connecting with Asian and global supply chains. The report also recommended that the cold storage facilities need improvement for India to expand its exports to Vietnam and other ASEAN countries.

4.4.6 The Way Forward

Unless Vietnam accelerates the pace of reforms, it might lose some of its advantages. Vietnam is a trade-dependent economy, and hence, creating a pro-business environment should continue to be the government's priority. While Ho Chi Minh City, has been providing revenue to the government, infrastructure development in the South needs greater focus. Vietnam must also stimulate synergies between small and large

---

[20] Ananth Krishnan, https://www.thehindu.com/business/indias-trade-with-china-soared-62-in-h1/article35310753.ece; accessed on September 4, 2021.

[21] India needs lower logistics cost, https://www.thestatesman.com/business/india-needs-lower-logistics-cost-7-8-gdp-report-1502942310.html; accessed on September 4, 2021.

firms, including foreign ones, and develop innovative start-ups, which are still largely missing. According to the World Bank, while there has been progress in building the hard critical infrastructure—roads, ports, and airports, there is also a need to develop the energy sector through private participation in renewable sources. The private sector's development is critically dependent on credit availability, with ease of access for small and medium firms. Vietnam's integration into the world economy with the conclusion of FTAs as the EVFTA will create an important impetus for Vietnam to accelerate reforms. As stated earlier, the complexity of procedures and rules needs to be simplified through digitalization. Even as Vietnam sets goals for 2045, it will need to improve its business environment by becoming more attractive, cost-effective, transparent, and equitable to all investors (Dione, 2020; World Bank, 2020a, b).

Both India and Vietnam will require a push in digital technology and high-tech products, for an increased contribution to revenue. Although achievements in digital technologies are consistent with the government's desired shift toward high-tech manufacturing, low-tech products such as garments and footwear continue to be Vietnam's top five exports. The development of Industry 4.0 to support innovation continues to be both a priority and a challenge. In the past few years, several major firms established their production and research and development facilities in Vietnam. Ho Chi Minh City proposes to develop an A.I. strategy at a domestic level. Through this three innovation centers will be established. After successfully producing 5G equipment, Vietnam will endeavor to commercialize the technology in the near term. These plans, if well implemented can help the country enhance its competitive advantage.

While India is expected to grow at 5.5% for the next decade, China's growth rate is expected to be higher at 6.1%. According to Ricardo Hausmann, the director of Growth Lab at CID, professor at the Harvard Kennedy School (HKS), and a researcher of The Atlas of Economic Complexity, "India faces more difficult prospects for sustaining its growth, as the country has experienced a remarkable lack of diversification in the past decade." He also said, "Both economies rank in the top 10 globally for the predicted growth in the coming decade as both remain more complex than expected for their income level." India is struggling to reach the level of a US \$5 trillion economy, while China's GDP has crossed the US\$15 trillion level. India's lack of continued entry into new productive sectors has left a widening trade deficit and a narrower policy scope to sustain growth.[22]

India's ability to handle domestic challenges of unemployment and closure of businesses post the pandemic, will also continue to impact its economic engagement with Vietnam, a significant partner for India. This contrasts with the outlook for Vietnam, where growth is being driven by rapid gains in entering sectors, which are drivers for exports.

---

[22] Growth projection, https://atlas.cid.harvard.edu/growth-projections; accessed on March 2, 2021.

4.5 Conclusion

In the ultimate analysis, it is important to analyze whether Vietnam and India can be winners from the USA–China trade war as well as the restrictions placed on the high-tech sector in China. The latter could result in a reduction of wary foreign capital to China and result in its diversion to India and Vietnam. India is already viewing the listing of 160 Initial Public offerings in 2021. Both countries must however improve the ease of doing business parameters to be successful in attracting FDI.

Even as the impact of the pandemic witnesses big budgetary allocations for infrastructure in India, coupled with a rising budget deficit, it is too early to assess any real impact. Although India's share market swung upward, the real economy in terms of jobs, incomes, and growth in productivity is still constrained.

In both countries, the reliance is being placed on the private sector to step in. There is no clear evidence that although Vietnam has emerged as a hub of investment, it is the winner of investment. Relocation is not an easy task for investors and a shortage of skilled and unskilled labor further compounds the complexity. The one-stop window and other government incentives have been provided for investors, including Samsung and few other homegrown companies as the Vin and Sun groups, yet there is a need for greater incentives. Moreover, according to Paul Schuler (ISEAS webinar on February 9, 2021), the large private sector groups have been engaged mainly in real estate and construction. They would need to diversify into other areas and develop innovative products that are competitively priced. That would be the path for boosting exports. In India, the pace of privatization has been given further momentum in the 2021 Budget announced on February 1, 2021. India's rising trade deficit continues to be worrisome as also its overreliance on imports from China. Globalization has led to a rise in increased incidence of mergers and acquisitions, increasing participation in global innovation networks through R&D in FDI, and compliances with WTO, which India has benefitted from (Joseph, 2013). Yet, India is far less integrated globally than Vietnam, though both countries can develop synergies between their private sectors in key areas identified in the chapter.

The panelists at the ISEAS webinar on January 9, 2021 also underlined the fact that private domestic investors should realize opportunities from FTAs; so far, foreign investors have seized greater opportunities than domestic investors. Here, there is a learning for Vietnam from India. The latter encourages inward FDI by foreign countries through its domestic private sector, so that the returns can be equitably shared. In Vietnam, the government and party should prioritize market reforms to permit domestic businesses scale up and diversify their businesses. Moreover, governance procedures need to be more predictable and consistent. The private sector must also be able to bring their issues to the court so that they can compete and get benefits from FTAs and opportunities from the USA–China trade war. However, a dilemma for Vietnam is that although it must rely on the private sector for aiding growth, it would not allow it to challenge the State's authority. The Chinese experience of managing Jack Ma's ambitions provides lessons for the Communist Party of Vietnam, which cannot afford any upheavals.

While India's political leadership is moving closer to the USA, Vietnam must walk the tight rope and balance relationships with the USA and China. The 13th Party Congress key orientation demonstrates this, even as the leadership will engage with other partners as India, Japan and South Korea. Among the economic policies, first, the reforms of state-owned enterprises would continue, similar to India's continuing disinvestment program; second, the preference would be for high-tech sustainable development. Here too, the resonance with policies of the Indian Government is discernible. While Vietnam's South must not be overlooked in sustainable development, India must also focus on balanced, regional development. Finally, both Vietnam and India must take full advantage of emerging opportunities by adjusting the international industrial structure and drawing investors for economic structural transformation.

The next chapter assesses the bilateral partnership in the areas of science, technology, and education; these being viewed by both countries as significant levers of growth and development.

References

Altstedter, A., & Sanjai, P. R. (2020). *Bloomberg.* https://www.business-standard.com/article/com panies/for-big-tech-all-roads-to-india-s-digital-space-seem-to-go-through-ambani-120091200 152_1.html. Accessed September 12, 2020.

Barba Navaretti, B. G., & Venables, A. J. (2004). *Multinational firms in the world economy.* Princeton University Press.

Basu, K. (2001). https://www.indiatoday.in/magazine/guest-column/story/20010903-vietnam-may-be-poorer-than-india-but-it-is-not-as-impoverished-774142-2001-09-03

Dezan Shira, D., & Associates. (2017). *Vietnam briefing.* https://www.vietnam-briefing.com/news/ indian-investments-vietnam-how-to-structure-operations.html

Dezan Shira, D., & Associates. (2020, July). *Vietnam briefing.* https://www.vietnam-briefing.com/ news/tax-accounting-audit-vietnam-2020-new-publication-dezan-shira-associates.html/

Dhanora, M., Sharma, R., & Park, W. G. (2021). Technological innovations and market power: A study of Indian pharmaceutical industry. *Millennial Asia, 12*(1), 5–34. https://doi.org/10.1177/ 0976399620944272

Dione, O. (2020, January 8). *Vietnam: Doing Business 2020, challenges and solutions.* World Bank Country Director for Vietnam, Hanoi, Vietnam. https://www.worldbank.org/en/news/speech/ 2020/01/08/speech-by-ousmane-dione-world-bank-country-director-for-vietnam-at-the-event-vietnam-doing-business-2020-challenges-and-solutions

Euromonitor International. (2020). https://go.euromonitor.com/white-paper-consulting-2020-MA-Investment-Index.html

Giang, N. K. (2021, February 9). *Webinar on Vietnam's 13th party congress: Political significance and implications.* ISEAS Yusof Ishak Institute.

IBEF Report. (2020). https://www.ibef.org/industry/infrastructure-sector-india.aspx. Accessed February 7, 2021.

ILOStat. (November 2020). https://ilostat.ilo.org/topics/labour-costs/

Joseph, K. J. (2013). Has trade been an engine of inclusive growth? India's experience under globalization. *Millennial Asia, 4*(2), 135–157. https://doi.org/10.1177/0976399613506315

Mazumdar, R. (2020, September 2). *The Hindu.* https://www.thehindubusinessline.com/opinion/for get-china-can-india-match-vietnam/article32506729.ece. Accessed February 6, 2021.

Mazumdar, R. (2020, September 2). *Forget China, can India match Vietnam?* https://www.thehin dubusinessline.com/opinion/forget-china-can-india-match-vietnam/article32506729.ece

Ministry of Commerce and Industry, GOI. (2021, May 24). https://pib.gov.in/PressReleasePage. aspx?PRID=1721268. Accessed May 26, 2021.

Moran, T. H., Graham, E. M., & Blomström, M. (2005). *Does foreign direct investment promote development?* Institute for International Economics and Center for Global Development.

Son, M., & Le, H. (2019, December 3). *Chinese investment in Vietnam surges.* https://e.vnexpress. net/news/business/economy/chinese-investment-in-vietnam-surges-4021060.html

Vasavakul, T. (2020). *Vietnam fights corruption: Towards more inclusive initiatives?* ISEAS—Yusof Ishak Institute. Issue: 2020 No. 92; ISSN 2335-6677.

Vinh, V. X., & Manh, C. D. (2020, June 4). *The paradoxes of private sector development in Vietnam.* University of Economics Ho Chi Minh City. https://www.eastasiaforum.org/2020/06/04/the-par adoxes-of-private-sector-development-in-vietnam/. Accessed February 9, 2021.

World Bank. (2020a). *Vietnam overview.* https://www.worldbank.org/en/country/vietnam/ove rview. Accessed October 6, 2020.

World Bank. (2020b, October 08). https://www.worldbank.org/en/country/india/overview

World Bank. (2021). https://www.worldbank.org/en/country/vietnam/overview

World Bank; World Development Indicators Data. https://databank.worldbank.org/source/world-development-indicators/Type/TABLE/preview/on. Accessed February 5, 2021.

Xinsheng, Q. (2020, May 15). https://www.thinkchina.sg/china-should-be-worried-about-political-developments-vietnam-not-economic-rivalry. Accessed February 9, 2021.

Yusuf, S. (2018) East Asian cat or African cat: Which one is the better mouse catcher? *Sage, Global Journal of Emerging Market Economies 10*(1–3).

Chapter 5
India–Vietnam Partnership in Science, Technology, and Innovation

Chapters 1 and 2 delineated the robust historical, civilisational and cultural linkages between our two countries. Despite the fact that India's soft power and cultural traditions, affinity, and affability are well understood in Southeast Asian countries, it is equally true that India is a repository of scientific and technological innovations. Both countries can exchange much knowledge even as they continue to invest in new technologies and in emerging areas of research and development.

While Chap. 3 focused on the foreign policies of both countries, the previous chapter comprised a discussion on both countries' bilateral economic engagement and the potential for expanding the partnership. The scope for synergy between India and Vietnam in science, technology, and innovation is also immense, given the imperative for both countries to improve these capabilities. Both countries' per capita incomes were almost similar, prior to the pandemic disruptions, being just over USD 2000 in 2018–19. While India's English-speaking skills are well known, Vietnam encourages teaching/learning in both English and Vietnamese. India's digital sector's growth and innovation in information technology has been leveraged by several countries in Southeast Asia, especially Vietnam. Both countries also need to invest in new technologies and in the areas of research and development. This assumes even greater priority given the possibilities emerging from the USA–China trade war and the decoupling from China in the post-pandemic phase. Both countries can access opportunities through public–private partnerships.

5.1 India's Science, Technology, and Innovation

Given the fact that even religion is a kind of science, Mahatma Gandhi himself considered truth/religion as a kind of experiment. The scientist Albert Einstein once said: "We owe a lot to the ancient Indians, teaching us how to count, without which most modern scientific discoveries would have been impossible."[1] It is not incorrect to state that science, technology, and innovation are India's strengths.

5.1.1 History of Science, Technology, and Innovation in India

India has early scientific thinking. As beautifully expressed in *thebetterindia.com*, "ancient India was a land of sages and seers as well as a land of scholars and scientists".[2] Research had shown that "from making the best steel in the world to teaching the world to count, India was actively contributing to the field of science and technology centuries before modern laboratories were set up. Many theories and techniques discovered by the ancient Indians have created and strengthened the fundamentals of modern science and technology",[3] for example, the idea of zero, the decimal system, numeral notations, a theory of the atom, plastic surgery, cataract surgery, Ayurveda, and iron-cased rockets.[4]

It is to be noted that, "the first iron-cased rockets were developed in the 1780s by Tipu Sultan of Mysore, who successfully used these rockets against the larger forces of the British East India Company during the Anglo-Mysore Wars. He crafted long iron tubes, filled them with gunpowder, and fastened them to bamboo poles to create the predecessor of the modern rocket. With a range of about 2 km, these rockets were the best in the world at that time and caused as much fear and confusion as damage, with even the British army having suffered one of their worst-ever defeats in India at the hands of Tipu".[5]

Thus, being an ancient civilization, India has a history of achievements in mathematics, logic, astronomy, and medicine handed down over generations. This was interrupted for a few centuries because of repeated invasions, until the British, in some sense, restored a kind of political unity. The country missed the Industrial Revolution, but in the early 1800s, reformers in Calcutta (currently Kolkata) urged Indians to take to English science. This set in motion a process whereby Western scientific thinking soon became accepted. During the British rule, India had two homegrown Nobel laureates including Rabindranath Tagore (1913) in literature and C. V. Raman (1930) in physics. There were many other outstanding scientists such as J. C. Bose of wireless technology and the mathematical genius Ramanujan who was at Cambridge University.

---

[1] Ancient India Science and Technology, https://www.thebetterindia.com/63119/ancient-india-science-technology/, accessed on June 1, 2020.

[2] Ibid.

[3] Ibid.

[4] Ibid.

[5] While some of India's groundbreaking contributions in S&T have been acknowledged, some are still unknown to most people. Many people in Vietnam continue to think that we have to look to the United States, the West for Science & Technology. Nevertheless, in fact, we can look to India, which is much nearer/closer to us.

Since 1947, science and technology have always been the top priority of all ruling governments in India. In the words of Indian President Abdul Kalam, "Science brings two great changes to life. First, science is a way of thinking that transforms people. Second, when science has turned into technology, it can bring about a nation's rapid development. That is why, since 1947, science and technology have always been the top priority of all governments."[6] So far, India has implemented four major science and technology policies/strategies, and they are: the resolution on science policy in 1958, technology policy in 1983, science and technology policy in 2003, and policy of science and technology innovation in 2013 (Sandhya, 2018, pp. 1–16). By the beginning of 2020, India has improved its Innovation Index, with a rank of 52. India has the second largest number of scientists and engineers in the world.[7]

Today, India possesses a vast system of science and technology infrastructure. The country has made significant breakthroughs in space technology, its wide applications in communications, television, weather forecast, natural disaster management, and internationally recognized resources. The number and size of Indian research institutions are no less than any developed countries (Sandhya, 2018, pp. 1–16). The World Economic Forum (WEF) assessed that India plays a crucial role in shaping the Fourth Industrial Revolution.[8]

In the first two decades of the twenty-first century, India has become a world power in some areas of science and technology and has been recognized as the source of a skilled workforce of the world.

As a result of specific policies and orientation in science and technology since Independence, India has brought about major changes in people's lives, creating rapid development for the country. From an economy with serious problems in terms of food security at the time of independence, India has become the world's second largest rice producer, the fourth largest wheat and milk producer (Bình, 2016).[9] India's breakthrough in space technology and its widespread uses in communications, television, weather forecasting, and disaster management among others have received much admiration. India's information technology and software industry has emerged as one of the fastest-growing sectors of the economy, making India "the office of the world". Progress in nuclear technology is also a significant achievement for India. Recently, India has made remarkable achievements in biotechnology, cell phones, steelmaking, and other manufacturing sectors.

India has increased its annual budget for science and technology research in recent years (by 16% in 2017[10]; in 2020: giving another push by increasing 8% compared to the previous year). In the first decade of the twenty-first century, the Government

---

[6] Ấn Độ phát triển kinh tế trên nền tảng khoa học công nghệ, https://tiasang.com.vn/khoa-hoc-cong-nghe/an-do-phat-trien-kinh-te-tren-nen-tang-khcn-993, accessed on June 1, 2020.

[7] Ministry level research project: *India's Comprehensive National Power*, Institute for Indian and Southwest Asian Studies, Vietnam Academy of Social Sciences, 2019–2020.

[8] See Footnote 7.

[9] *Ấn Độ phát triển kinh tế trên nền tảng khoa học công nghệ, (India develops its economy on the basis of science and technology)*, http://tiasang.com.vn/-khoa-hoc-cong-nghe/an-do-phat-trien-kinh-te-tren-nen-tang-khcn-993, accessed on June 1, 2020.

[10] Ibid.

of India has invested in 1280 basic research projects, modernizing the infrastructure of 200 laboratories and 220 universities and building 20 more new research centers. With the right policy in attracting talented people, more than 30,000 Indian scientists and leading experts have returned to their homeland.[11] The Government of India is giving priority to investing in strategic fields such as information technology, biotechnology, space research, nuclear energy for socioeconomic development.

India's S&T strengths are information technology, biotechnology, medical biotechnology, space exploration, and energy science (nuclear and renewable energy).

5.1.2 India's Strengths in Science, Technology, and Innovation

5.1.2.1 Information Technology

It is said that India's future belongs to information technology. Bangalore is known as "the second Silicon Valley" with more than 200 multinational companies. This technology hub contributes 36% of the total software industry output of India.[12] As of 2017, more than 100 countries in the world have to import software from India. The top 25 software companies in India have achieved tremendous results in terms of revenue and market capitalization.[13]

5.1.2.2 Biotechnology

Biotechnology is a strategic area where India has invested in its development with a well-designed biotechnology policy helping poverty alleviation and increased integration. India is among the top 12 biotech destinations globally and ranks second in Asia, after China. The Indian biotech industry is likely to experience significant growth due to increasing economic prosperity, health consciousness, and a billion-plus population base. The sector is divided into five major segments: bio-pharma, bio-services, bio-agri, bio-industrial, and bio-informatics. Vaccines and recombinant therapeutics primarily drive the biotechnology industry's growth in India. India has the potential to become a major producer of transgenic rice and several genetically modified (G.M.) or engineered vegetables. (Embassy of India Hanoi, *India Newsletter*, February, 2021) The Government of India has taken several initiatives, including a biotechnology industry partnership program to develop new technologies and launched a National Rural Healthcare Mission to boost healthcare spending. As

---

[11] Ibid.
[12] Ibid.
[13] Ibid.

per the 12th Five Year Plan, the government aims to spend $3.7 billion on biotechnology compared to $1.1 billion in the 11th Five Year Plan to accelerate the pace of research, innovation and development. Also, the Department of Biotechnology (DBT) has designed the National Biotechnology Development Strategy (NBDS) to strengthen the industry's human resources and infrastructure while promoting growth and trade. Furthermore, the government has allowed 100% foreign direct investment (FDI) through the automatic route for manufacturers of drugs and pharmaceuticals.[14]

India's bio agricultural technology is at the top of the world. Indian policy aims at innovating and applying new technologies in agritech projects. In recent years, the Indian Government has emphasized and commercialized agriculture in various innovative ways. For example, it uses drones for mapping and invests in data collection. The top five agritech projects deployed by the Government of India are: Agri Udaan (it is primarily a six-month programme where shortlisted agritech start-ups are guided in order to enhance stage innovator, entrepreneurs and start-ups in Food and Agribusiness sectors); CropIn (a SaaS-based agritech start-up which utilizes cutting-edge technologies like big data analytics, artificial intelligence, machine language, and remote sensing to enable its clients in order to analyze and interpret data to derive real-time actionable insights on standing crops); Maha AgriTech Project (launched in January 2019 is one of South India's largest producers and marketers of bioproducts and seeds suppliers); SatSure (an innovative prominent area analytics start-up which utilizes advances in satellites, machine learning, and big data analytics to give answers to significant area questions across a number of domains including agriculture, forestry, insurance, irrigation, cities, environment, and Oil and Gas); Thanos (an agritech drone tech start-up established by Pradeep Palelli and Prathyush Akepati in 2016 which use drones to provide innovative solutions to conventional problems).[15]

Also, *India's medical biotechnology* has grown exceptionally fast in recent years. Indian scientists, through R&D, have developed new therapies that minimize the cost of treatment and medication for the people. India has become the world's second largest country in producing child vaccination and exporting to more than 100 countries.[16] India's biotechnology in pharmacy is also very advanced. With around 17,000 kinds of precious herbs, Indian pharmaceutical companies have sold their products in the markets of 125 countries.[17] India's pharmaceutical industry occupies about USD 6 billion in the total assets of USD 550 billion of the global pharmaceutical industry.[18]

---

[14] Indian Biotechnology Industry Analysis, https://www.ibef.org/industry/biotechnology-presentation, accessed on June 1, 2020.

[15] 5 Latest Agritech Projects Deployed by the Government, https://analyticsindiamag.com/5-latest-agritech-projects-deployed-by-the-government/, accessed on June 1, 2020.

[16] See Footnote 6.

[17] Phương Sơn, *Hợp tác phát triển Việt Nam - Ấn Độ nhằm đảm lợi ích chiến lược và sự phát triển bền vững*, http://cis.org.vn/article/204/hop-tac-phat-trien-viet-nam-an-do-nham-dam-bao-loi-ich-chien-luoc-va-su-phat-trien-ben-vung-phan-2.html, accessed on June 1, 2020.

[18] Ibid.

India is the fourth largest market for medical devices in Asia. The medical devices industry in India consists of large multinationals as well as small and medium enterprises (SMEs) growing at an unprecedented scale. The current market size of the medical devices industry in India is estimated to be $11 bn and is expected to reach $50 bn by 2025. India is among the top 20 markets for medical devices in the world.[19] (Embassy of India Hanoi, *India Newsletter*, February, 2021).

During the COVID-19 pandemic, India has also implemented vaccine diplomacy. New Delhi has sent consignments of the COVID-19 vaccine to over 70 countries. Around 36.194 million doses of vaccine vials have been sent to various countries, of which 6.75 million doses have been supplied as grant assistance and 29.444 million doses on a commercial basis. India has offered the COVID-19 vaccine to all U.N. peacekeepers—nearly 95.000 troops in 12 missions worldwide received vaccine doses. India is also proposing to create a regional network with ten neighboring countries to collate, compile and study data about the effectiveness of COVID-19 vaccines, and promote technology-assisted epidemiology to prevent future pandemics.[20]

5.1.2.3 Space Exploration

India is also advancing in terms of space exploration. India continues to develop new shipping vessels and launch more satellites into space to meet the country's key tasks. India had joined the selected group of six countries in 1994 when the PSLV shipping vessel fulfilled its mission by bringing the 800-kg IRS-P2 satellite into orbit. Several other shipping vessels capable of carrying larger satellites into space have also been developed, such as the GSLV shipping vessel, capable of loading a 2000-kg satellite into space. With its remarkable investment in space technology, India is the third largest country in the world to develop its own long-range sensor satellite. In the present time, the gadgets of Indian space technology have been widely applied in scientific research, communications, education, health, environment, defense, resource management, weather forecasting among other and have become the key tool for India's development and integration.

On February 26, 2021, the Indian Space Research Organization (ISRO) successfully launched PSLV C51 with Amazonia1 satellite of Brazil and 18 Co-passenger satellites from Sriharikota. Amazonia1 is the first dedicated commercial mission of New Space India Limited, a Government of India company under the Department of Space. Addressing scientists at the Mission Control Centre after the successful launch of Amazonia1 of Brazil and 18 other satellites, ISRO's Chairman, Mr. K. Sivan informed that ISRO has lined up 14 missions for launch in 2021, including the

---

[19] Embassy of India Hanoi, *India Newsletter*, February 2021.

[20] India has provided over 361 lakh doses of COVID-19 vaccine to other countries so far, https://www.livemint.com/news/india/india-has-provided-over-361-lakh-doses-of-covid-19-vaccine-to-other-countries-so-far-mea-11614303650203.html, accessed on June 1, 2020.

space agency's first uncrewed mission.[21] The Gaganyaan mission envisages sending three Indians to space by 2022.

5.1.2.4   Energy Science (Nuclear and Renewable Energy)

- Nuclear Energy

  Being the first Asian country possessing nuclear power and becoming the 6th member of the world nuclear club, *India is recognized as one of the most advanced countries in nuclear technology.* The key objective of the nuclear energy program is to develop and use nuclear energy for peaceful purposes. India has 15 nuclear power plants in operation nationwide and eight other nuclear power plants under construction to increase nuclear power in the coming years, to gradually reduce energy import. It is estimated that nuclear power is expected to account for about 35% of total electricity consumption in the country by 2050.[22]

- Renewable Energy

  India has a vast supply of renewable resources, and it has one of the most extensive programs in the world for deploying renewable energy products and systems and is the only country in the world to have an exclusive ministry for renewable energy development, the Ministry of New and Renewable Energy (MNRE). The Indian Government has increased the target of renewable energy capacity to 175GW by the year 2022 which includes 100 GW from solar, 60 GW from wind, 10 GW from bio-power, and 5 GW from small hydropower.[23]

5.2   Vietnam's Science, Technology, and Innovation

5.2.1   History of Science, Technology, and Innovation in Vietnam

Since the Đông Sơn cultural period (around the seventh century B.C.—first or second centuries A.D.), Vietnam has made certain achievements in science, technology, and innovation. This is reflected in its achievements in production tools, weapons, jewelry, and musical instruments that archeologists have unearthed in the early years of the twentieth century. Historians believe that, during the Đông Sơn period, the

---

[21] 14 missions lined up for launch in 2021, says ISRO chairman K Sivan, https://www.hindustan times.com/india-news/14-missions-lined-up-for-launch-in-2021-says-isro-chairman-k-sivan-101 614511876421.html, accessed on June 5, 2020.

[22] *Ấn Độ phát triển kinh tế trên nền tảng khoa học công nghệ*, http://tiasang.com.vn/-khoa-hoc-cong-nghe/an-do-phat-trien-kinh-te-tren-nen-tang-khcn-993, accessed on June 5, 2020.

[23] Renewable Energy in India: Current Status and Future Potential, Indiary.org., accessed on June 5, 2020.

Vietnamese people had mastered the materials and technology of brass manufacturing entirely.[24] Đông Sơn drums were the peak achievement of Hùng Vương times and were the intellectual product of the ancient Vietnamese people. The themes decorated on Đông Sơn bronze, culminating in typical bronze drums, including Ngọc Lũ, Sông Đà, Hoàng Hạ, Cổ Loa, reflected the excellent bronze casting skill of the ancient Vietnamese people.

Over the period of one thousand years under Chinese domination, Vietnam did not have favorable conditions to develop science, technology, and innovation. According to sources, there are not many records on the history of science, technology, and innovation in Vietnam before Independence. March 04, 1959, was a landmark day in the history of Vietnamese science, technology, and innovation when the State Department of Science was formally established by Decision No. 016-SL by the President of the Democratic Republic of Vietnam. This Department later became the Ministry of Science and Technology of Vietnam. The establishment of the Department (Ministry of Science and Technology) is a testament to the strategic vision of the party and the state regarding the critical role of science and technology in the development of the nation. However, at that time, Vietnam was still facing many difficulties and hardships due to the wartime situation in South Vietnam and the new independence of the North. During the early years of Independence and in the war situation, many generations of Vietnamese scientists contributed to the development of science, technology, and innovation in Vietnam. Scientists such as Trần Đại Nghĩa, Hồ Đắc Di, Tôn Thất Tùng, Tạ Quang Bửu, Lương Đình Của, and Bùi Huy Đáp are notable for their great contribution to the country's science, technology, and innovation.

After the liberation and reunification of Vietnam in 1975, the scientist's force of the country, along with the people from all sections of the society, tried to heal the wounds of war, restore, and develop the economy in the situation of being embargoed by the U.S. and many other countries. After 1980, all English scientific documents and books were no longer funded. After the collapse of the Soviet Union, the number of scientific journals, books, and documents in Russian has also decreased significantly. Technical facilities, research equipment, and resources were very scarce. It was during these difficult years that a contingent of the scientific and technical staff was mobilized to take part in the task of designing and constructing Vietnam's centennial projects, including the construction of the Hòa Bình Hydropower Plant; reclaiming and improving Đồng Tháp Mười area; building the 500 kW North–South transmission line; exploiting oil and gas in the East Sea; or selecting and creating new plants, to facilitate the development of industry and agriculture in later periods.

From 1986 onwards, Vietnam has promoted industrialization, modernization, and international integration. Science, technology, and innovation have continued to make significant strides in all aspects.

---

[24] Văn hóa Đông Sơn – Phát hiện và nghiên cứu, http://baotanglichsuquocgia.vn/vi/Articles/3099/14397/van-hoa-djong-son-phat-hien-va-nghien-cuu.html, accessed on June 5, 2020.

5.2.2 Vietnam's New Developments in Science, Technology, and Innovation

Although not comparable to India, Vietnam has made new/important developments in S&T in recent years. Vietnam's national S&T potential has grown at a fast pace over the years. In the 1960s, there were only eight research institutes in the North and six universities in the country. In 2019, there are more than 4000 S&T organizations across the country, three national high-tech parks, 13 hi-tech agricultural zones, eight concentrated information technology parks, and nearly 67,000 scientists (researchers). Thus, the level of S&T development in Vietnam has improved markedly over the years. Social sciences and humanities have provided profound consultancy service for policymaking of the Party and the State of Vietnam; natural sciences, technology have contributed positively to improving domestic research capacity, enhancing productivity, quality, and growth of the economy, contributing to creating a new position for the country in the regional and international landscape.

Vietnam's innovation capacity has constantly been rising. When Vietnam celebrated its 60 years of the establishment and development of S&T in 2019, it ranked 42 out of 129 countries and led the group of low–middle income countries. The number of international publications of Vietnamese scientists increases an average of 26% per year and is always at the top of ASEAN countries in mathematics and physics.

In the initial days of 2019, an important event which marked a milestone in the development history of Vietnam's space technology industry was the first time that a satellite designed by Vietnamese engineers flew into space. The satellite, named Micro Dragon, carries Vietnam's scientists' dream of reaching into space and helped catapult Vietnam on the map of world space science.

In 2019, the Ramanujan Prize—a prestigious prize in mathematics, was first awarded to a Vietnamese scientist, Professor Phạm Hoàng Hiệp, Institute of Mathematics—Vietnam Academy of Science and Technology.[25]

In 2019, ST25 Rice of Vietnam was voted "the World's Best Rice" in a contest organized by The Rice Trader in Manila, the Philippines on November 10–13, 2019. Thanks to the application of scientific and technological achievements, Vietnam could produce ST25 rice. This is specialty rice in Sóc Trăng province. This shows that the quality of Vietnam's rice is not inferior to any other country, even with more advantages such as higher productivity and tolerance to the harsh climate. Many crops can be cultivated a year. It is pertinent to add here that although Vietnam was growing rice before independence and had collaboration with the International Rice

---

[25] The prize is given every year to young mathematicians less than 45 years of age who have conducted outstanding research in a developing country in the memory of Srinivasan Ramanujan (1887–1920), a genius in pure mathematics who was essentially self-taught and made spectacular contributions to elliptic functions, continued fractions, infinite series, and analytical theory of numbers. The prize is supported by the Ministry of Science and Technology (India) and Norwegian Academy of Sciences and Letters through the Abel Fund, with the cooperation of the International Mathematical Union (IMU).

Research Institute since 1960, even in the 1980s, it was an importer of rice from India. India helped Vietnam establish its first Rice Institute in the late 1980s, after which Vietnam's production of rice expanded at a fast pace, leading Vietnam to become a global exporter of rice. This was shared by Mr. Amit Saxena in an interview to the authors; he also added, "Vietnamese people are so industrious that in a year's time, their rice production increased substantially."[26]

Since the COVID-19 pandemic broke out in early 2020, Vietnamese science has helped solve the urgent problems associated with the coronavirus. In the context of the pandemic, Vietnamese science has become a vital force by undertaking tasks such as developing and manufacturing a kit for fast detection of coronavirus; designing and manufacturing robots for medical service and care; assessing the efficacy and safety of lopinavir/ritonavir supplementation; vaccine research and development among others. On March 03, 2020, after a period of active research, the research team headed by Associate Professor Đồng Văn Quyền and Associate Professor Đinh Duy Kháng from the Institute of Biotechnology of Vietnam Academy of Science and Technology has successfully manufactured the SARS-CoV-2 Diagnostic Kit. This SARS-CoV-2 Diagnostic Kit has been tested to have a sensitivity and specificity comparable to WHO's RT-PCR Real-Time Kit with 100% specificity, five copies/response insensitivity, and the time of detection procedure is 80 min from receipt of patient's RNA samples.[27] The timely efforts of Vietnamese scientists have contributed to the country's overall success in the fight against the coronavirus.[28]

5.3 The Reality of India–Vietnam Cooperation in Science, Technology, and Innovation

Vietnam–India cooperation in science, technology and innovation are to be studied in the overall context of Vietnam–India relations. Along with the tremendous progress in political-diplomatic, security–defense relations, cooperation in science and technology, and innovation between the two countries have also been strengthened.

---

[26] Interview of Mr. Amit Saxena, (an Indian businessman who has done business in Vietnam for 32 years), on May 4, 2021.

[27] Vietnam Academy of Science and Technology; https://vast.gov.vn/web/vietnam-academy-of-science-and-technology/tin-chi-tiet/-/chi-tiet/introducing-research-results-of-successfully-manufacturing-the-sars-cov-2-virus-diagnostic-kit-of-institute-of-biotechnology-vast-10314-868.html, accessed on June 5, 2020.

[28] Khoa học Việt Nam: Giải quyết được những vấn đề nóng của đất nước, *Khoa học và Phát triển*, 21/05/2020, https://khoahocphattrien.vn/chinh-sach/khoa-hoc-viet-nam-giai-quyet-duoc-nhung-van-de-nong-cua-dat-nuoc/20200521093639381p1c785.htm, accessed on June 5, 2020.

Table 5.1 Agreements between India and Vietnam on Science and Technology cooperation (before 1990)

Year	Name of agreement
1956	Agreement on establishing telegraph line between Republic of India and the Democratic Republic of Vietnam
1968	Agreement on nuclear energy cooperation for peaceful purposes
1978	MOU on cooperation on agricultural science and technology research

5.3.1 Before 1990

Both India and Vietnam recognized the importance of international scientific collaboration in S&T quite early and have signed several S&T agreements. The first milestone in Vietnam–India S&T cooperation was in 1978 when the first bilateral agreement was signed; this was renewed in 1996. Under this agreement, a Joint Committee on Science and Technology was constituted in 1997 to oversee the implementation and process of collaboration (refer Table 5.1). The Joint Committee on Science and Technology meets periodically to review the progress made. Cooperation was established in nuclear energy, agriculture, fisheries, animal husbandry, computer hardware, computer software, pharmaceuticals, remote sensing, water resources, biotechnology, and information technology. India has helped build technology centers and hi-tech parks in Vietnam. India has agreed to set up a high technology laboratory (Indira Gandhi Hightech Cyber Forensic Laboratory), an I.T. Training Center, and a Vietnam–India English Center at Vietnam Defence Academy.

5.3.2 Initiatives Post-1990

Since the 1990s, cooperation in human resource training in science and technology has been given priority and has proved to be one of the most effective cooperation formats between India and Vietnam. Cooperation in education and training has been instrumental in strengthening cooperation in science and technology between the two countries. Annually, the Government of India grants scholarships for Vietnamese students under various programs. Vietnam has been the largest recipient of training programmes under the Indian Technical and Economic Cooperation (ITEC) programme.[29] Since 2013, 150 ITEC slots have been offered to Vietnam every year along with 16 scholarships under the General Cultural Scholarship Scheme (GCSS), 14 scholarships under the Educational Exchange Programme (EEP), and ten scholarships under the Mekong Ganga Cooperation Scholarship Scheme (MGCSS).[30] Between 2018–2019, within the framework of the ITEC programme, nearly 400

---

[29] Bình and Nga (2011, p. 7).

[30] India–Vietnam Relations, http://mea.gov.in/Portal/ForeignRelation/Vietnam_May_2017.pdf, accessed on June 5, 2020.

students who work for the government and non-government organizations and other institutions in Vietnam have benefited from short-term training programs at the leading institutions of higher learning in India. Most of the ITEC beneficiaries have returned to Vietnam with much appreciation for India. In 2017, India also began granting Vietnam four slots of scholarship for Buddhist and Sanskrit studies. Educational fairs have also been organized in Hanoi to introduce the educational system of India to the Vietnamese people to encourage Vietnamese students to go to India for learning and research.

The year 2012 was a turning point in India–Vietnam S&T cooperation. Since 2012, after the visit to India of Vice Prime Minister Nguyen Thien Nhan, Vietnam–India cooperation in science and technology shifted from individual cooperation among scientific institutions to a national approach focusing on critical areas of each country. Previously, a few research institutes in Ho Chi Minh City National University and the Vietnam Academy of Science and Technology had engaged in bilateral cooperation with some Indian partners. However, since 2012, the Ministry of Science and Technology of Vietnam is playing the leading role in promoting scientific and technological cooperation between the two countries.

In 2016, during the visit of Prime Minister Modi to Vietnam, the two sides signed 12 agreements, including Agreement on the Exploration and Uses of Outer Space for Peaceful Purposes, I.T. Cooperation, Cybersecurity, Uses of Atomic Energy for Peaceful Purposes; Memorandum of understanding about I.T. cooperation; MOU on cooperation between VASS and ICWA as well as an Agreement on building information infrastructure for high-quality information technology training (Nga, 2018).[31]

The Implementing Arrangement between the Indian Space Research Organization and Vietnam Ministry of Natural Resources and Environment for Establishment of Satellite Tracking and Telemetry Centre in Vietnam under the India–ASEAN Space Cooperation was signed during the visit of Vietnamese Prime Minister Nguyen Xuan Phuc to Delhi in January 2018.[32] The leaders of the two countries expressed satisfaction at the past three and half decades of bilateral cooperation in the use of atomic energy for peaceful purposes according to the agreement signed by the two countries in 1986.[33]

So far, significant areas of cooperation between the two countries in science and technology are as follows:

(i)   Research and application of nanotechnology in the production of materials and equipment for defense, health care, agriculture, information technology and telecommunications, and chemicals.

---

[31] Tuyên bố chung giữa Việt Nam - Ấn Độ (Joint Statement between Vietnam–India), http://baoquo cte.vn/tuyen-bo-chung-giua-viet-nam-an-do-35432.html, accessed on June 10, 2020.

[32] India–Vietnam relations, https://www.cgihcmc.gov.in/page/bilateral-relation/, accessed on June 10, 2020.

[33] Joint Statement between the Socialist Republic of Vietnam and the Republic of India, September 2–3, 2016. https://www.mea.gov.in/, accessed on June 10, 2020.

(ii)   Biotechnology includes molecular biology, biotechnology in agriculture, biotechnology in medicine, and biotechnology in environmental services.
(iii) Oceanography, including the areas of an earthquake and tsunami warning system, as well as seismic exploration in the ocean are other important areas.

Among these three areas, the most urgent area for Vietnam is biotechnology in agriculture—one of the key determinants of Vietnam's agricultural restructuring. The two countries have exchanged possibilities of cooperation in the exploitation and development of indigenous gene sources, genetically modified plants, salt-tolerant rice varieties; studies on post-harvest losses assessment; using GIS in soil management, water resources, and monitoring of climate change. India has also asked Vietnam to share experience in raising catfish and shrimp.

Major achievements in the S&T cooperation between the two countries include.

(i)   The establishment of the Advanced Resource Centre in Information and Communications Technology (ARC-ICT) worth US$2 million in Hanoi in September 2011. The center has been set up by the Centre for Development of Advanced Computing (CDAC) to train students and government officials in various areas such as Web designing, network systems, Java, GIS applications, and e-governance.
(ii)   High Performance Computer (PARAM-HUST) under the project "Enhancing capacity for High Performance Computing in Vietnam" was inaugurated on 12/11/2013 at the Hanoi University of Science and Technology. The inaugural ceremony was attended by Professor Chan Quang Quy, Vice Minister of Education and Training, Indian Ambassador Preeti Saran (Secretary East, Indian Ministry of External Affairs), and Professor Rajat Moona, Director-General of the Center for Development of Advanced Computing (CDAC). The 16-node cluster with a basic visualization laboratory and a five-node grid computing facility at an estimated cost of Rs. 4.7 crore has been gifted to Vietnam by India. This is the highest configuration of supercomputers ever gifted by the Indian Government to date.
(iii) The signing of MOU on the establishment of Indira Gandhi Hitech Crime Laboratory in November 2013 (refer Table 5.2).
(iv)   The establishment of the Army Software Park at the Telecommunication University in Nha Trang. On August 11, 2021, Ambassador of India to Vietnam, Shri Pranay Verma, handed over a cheque of one million USD to the Deputy Minister of Defence, Senior Lt. Gen. Hoang Xuan Chien at the Ministry of National Defence of Vietnam. This is the first tranche of the US$5 million grant assistance being provided by the Government of India to Vietnam for the establishment of the Army Software Park at the Telecommunication University in Nha Trang.[34] The Army Software Park is an important symbol of hi-tech cooperation under the India–Vietnam defense partnership and will contribute to capacity building of Vietnam defense forces in the IT sector.

---

[34] India in Vietnam, Embassy of India, Hanoi, August 11, 2021. https://www.indembassyhanoi.gov.in, accessed on June 10, 2020.

Table 5.2 Agreements between India and Vietnam on Science and Technology cooperation (2007–2020)

Year	Name of agreement
7/2007	MOU between Vietnam's Science and Technology Ministry and India's Nuclear Energy Ministry to continue with nuclear energy cooperation for peaceful purposes
11/2013	MOU for setting up of the Indira Gandhi Hightech Crime Lab (IGHCL) in Hanoi
11/2013	Agreement on Protection of Classified Information
11/2013	Cooperation Agreement between Hanoi National University and Indian Council for Scientific and Industrial Research
10/2014	MOU on establishing the Centre for English Language and Information Technology Training at the Telecommunications University in Nha Trang
10/2014	MOU on Exchange of Audio-Visual Programmes
9/2016	Framework Agreement on Cooperation in the Exploration and Uses of Outer Space for Peaceful Purposes
9/2016	MOU on cooperation in Information Technology
9/2016	MOU on cooperation between Vietnam Academy of Social Sciences (VASS) and Indian Council of World Affairs (ICWA)
9/2016	MOU on cooperation in cybersecurity
12/2016	Agreement on cooperation between the two governments on the peaceful use of atomic energy
12/2016	MOU between the Vietnam Atomic Energy Institute and India's Global Centre for Nuclear Energy Partnership
12/2020	Agreement for the US$5 million Indian Grant Assistance for Army Software Park at National Telecommunications University, Nha Trang
12/2020	MOU between India's Atomic Energy Regulatory Board and Vietnam Agency for Radiation and Nuclear Safety
12/2020	MOU between National Solar Federation of India and Vietnam Clean Energy Association

Apart from natural sciences, Vietnam and India have also been partners in terms of social sciences. Vietnam Academy of Social Sciences, founded in 1953, is the leading think-tank in Vietnam in promoting social science research collaboration with India. VASS has signed several MOUs with Indian partners, including Indian Council for Social Science Research, Indian Council of World Affairs. The Institute for Indian and Southwest Asian Studies under VASS has also signed 09 MOUs with Indian partners including School of International Studies, Jawaharlal Nehru University, Institute of Chinese Studies, Institute of Defense Studies and Analysis, Maulana Abul Kalam Azad Institute of Asian Studies, Center of South and Southeast Asian Studies, Madras University, Center of Southeast Asia and Pacific Studies, Sri Venkateshwara University, Asian Confluence among others. However, only some of these MOUs have been implemented effectively as a majority remain largely on paper. The collaboration is mainly limited to organizing joint seminars and conferences, publication of books and journals, and exchange of research fellows. There is a need to push forward the collaboration in conducting larger research projects of mutual concern. Both sides should encourage co-authors in writing research articles to be published in journals listed in the Science Citation Index (SCI). The study on the joint publication resulting from India's collaboration with selected Southeast Asian countries points to a lack of co-authored articles by scholars from India and Vietnam in social sciences published in international and refereed journals. Most of the co-authored articles between the two countries are on natural sciences (physics and biology) (Gupta et al., 2002, pp. 69–86).

5.3.3 India–Vietnam Cooperation in Science, Technology, and Innovation at Multilateral Levels

Vietnam–India science and technology cooperation occurs at bilateral and multi-lateral levels (primarily through India–ASEAN partnership). Within the ASEAN framework: India set up the Vietnam–India Center for English Language Training in Đà Nẵng in July 2007; the Vietnam–India Entrepreneurship Development Centre in Hanoi in May 2006 supports the Initiative for ASEAN Integration and provides technical assistance to the Government of Vietnam. It has been decided to start a new Vietnam–India Centre for English Language Training at the National Defence Academy of Vietnam. Both sides have also planned to establish a Vocational Training Centre in Ho Chi Minh City. A Centre for Satellite Tracking and Data Reception and an Imaging facility in Vietnam under the ASEAN–India Cooperation mechanism is soon to be established. India will fully fund the center, and ISRO will be the imple-menting agency. It will utilize data provided by Indian remote sensing satellites and harness it for multiple developmental applications.

5.4 Conclusion

In essence, a Comprehensive Strategic Partnership is the result of a long-term evolu-tion and development of bonds of friendship and amity between the two countries.[35] It is also the outcome of the efforts made by both countries in science, technology, and innovation cooperation. The promotion of Vietnam–India relations requires the active participation of both state and non-state agencies. The support of high-ranking politicians/diplomats/academicians from both sides is essential. There is an imper-ative for more action, to provide fillip to science and technology cooperation to achieve effective coordination among various S&T institutions in the two countries. On a note of optimism, with the new developments in both India and Vietnam's science, technology and innovation as well as the policy shifts, bilateral coopera-tion in these fields will see breakthroughs in the coming years. India has invited the

---

[35] Nga (2017).

CLMV countries to join the India headquartered International Solar Alliance. It is hoped that Vietnam's future participation in the International Solar Alliance "would bring new opportunities for cooperation in large-scale deployment of solar energy."[36]

Technological superiority is a non-negotiable enterprise for both countries. This requires alignment and cooperation with partners in economic, security, and strategic spheres. Hence, the next chapter interrogates the evolution of a pan Asian identity, with a delineation of a few multilateral initiatives of these two countries, as opposed to the hub-and-spokes format. The discussion brings into focus Vietnam's leadership experience and its engagement with major powers including India.

References

14 missions lined up for launch in 2021, says ISRO chairman K Sivan. https://www.hindustantimes. com/india-news/14-missions-lined-up-for-launch-in-2021-says-isro-chairman-k-sivan-101614 511876421.html

Ấn Độ phát triển kinh tế trên nền tảng khoa học công nghệ, (India develops its economy on the basis of science and technology). http://tiasang.com.vn/-khoa-hoc-cong-nghe/an-do-phat-trien-kinh-te-tren-nen-tang-khcn-993

Ancient India Science and Technology. https://www.thebetterindia.com/63119/ancient-india-sci ence-technology/

Embassy of India Hanoi. *India Newsletter*, February 2021.

Gupta, B. M., Lal, K., & Zainab, A. N. (2002). India's collaboration in science and technology with South East Asian Countries. *Malaysian Journal of Library & Information Science, 7*(2), 69–86. http://mea.gov.in/Portal/ForeignRelation/Vietnam_May_2017.pdf

India–Vietnam Relations. https://www.cgihcmc.gov.in/page/bilateral-relation/

India–Vietnam Relations.

India has provided over 361 lakh doses of Covid-19 vaccine to other countries so far. https://www.livemint.com/news/india/india-has-provided-over-361-lakh-doses-of-covid-19-vaccine-to-other-countries-so-far-mea-11614303650203.html

India in Vietnam, Embassy of India, Hanoi, August 11, 2021. https://www.indembassyhanoi.gov. in

Indian Biotechnology Industry Analysis. https://www.ibef.org/industry/biotechnology-presentation

Interview with Mr. Amit Saxena, former Chairman of the Indian Chamber of Commerce in Ho Chi Minh City, and Mr. Nguyen Van Nien, Director of Vinatana Company, Hanoi on 11 August 2021.

Joint Statement between the Socialist Republic of Vietnam and the Republic of India, September 2–3, 2016. https://www.mea.gov.in/

Khoa học Việt Nam: Giải quyết được những vấn đề nóng của đất nước, Khoa học và Phát triển, May 21, 2020. https://khoahocphattrien.vn/chinh-sach/khoa-hoc-viet-nam-giai-quyet-duoc-nhung-van-de-nong-cua-dat-nuoc/20200521093639381p1c785.htm

Latest Agritech Projects Deployed by the Government. https://analyticsindiamag.com/5-latest-agr itech-projects-deployed-by-the-government/

Nga, L. T. H. (2017). "Những phát triển mới trong Quan hệ Đối tác Chiến lược Toàn diện Việt Nam - Ấn Độ", Kỷ yếu hội thảo khoa học quốc tế *"45 Năm Quan hệ Việt Nam - Ấn Độ: Thành tựu và Triển vọng" (45 Years of Vietnam – India relations: Achievements and Prospects)*, Nxb Khoa học xã hội, Hanoi.

---

[36] Udai Bhanu in an interview to Jyoti Kataria, https://www.idsa.in/askanexpert/future-of-india-vie tnam-cooperation; February 19, 2021; accessed on August 29, 2021.

Le Thi, H. N. (2017). *Vietnam–India relations since september 2016: From the symbolic to practical results*. Sage.

Ministry level research project: *India's Comprehensive National Power*, Institute for Indian and Southwest Asian Studies, Vietnam Academy of Social Sciences, 2019–2020.

Bình, N. X., Nga, L. T. H. (2011). Quan hệ Việt Nam - Ấn Độ trong bối cảnh mới [Vietnam – India Relations in the new context], *Tạp chí Nghiên cứu Đông Nam Á (Southeast Asian Studies), 12*(141).

Bình, N. X. (2016). *Vietnam–India Economic Ties*. Sage.

Quế, N.T., Quan hệ Việt Nam - Ấn Độ: Quá khứ, hiện tại và tương lai", Kỷ yếu hội thảo khoa học quốc tế *"Việt Nam - Ấn Độ: 45 Năm Quan hệ Ngoại giao và 10 năm Đối tác Chiến lược*, Nxb. Lý luận Chính trị, Hà Nội.

Sơn, P., *Hợp tác phát triển Việt Nam - Ấn Độ nhằm đảm lợi ích chiến lược và sự phát triển bền vững*. http://cis.org.vn/article/204/hop-tac-phat-trien-viet-nam-an-do-nham-dam-bao-loi-ich-chien-luoc-va-su-phat-trien-ben-vung-phan-2.html. Accessed December 29, 2017.

Sandhya, G. D. (2018). India's science, technology and innovation policy: Choices for course correction with lessons learned from China. *Journal of STI Policy and Management, 3*(1), 2018.

Tuyên bố chung giữa Việt Nam - Ấn Độ [Joint Statement between Vietnam and India]. http://bao quocte.vn/tuyen-bo-chung-giua-viet-nam-an-do-35432.html

Vietnam Academy of Science and Technology. https://vast.gov.vn/web/vietnam-academy-of-sci ence-and-technology/tin-chi-tiet/-/chi-tiet/introducing-research-results-of-successfully-manufa cturing-the-sars-cov-2-virus-diagnostic-kit-of-institute-of-biotechnology-vast-10314-868.html

Xuân, P. Việt Nam cần môi trường chuyên nghiệp rèn luyện tư duy làm chủ cho người trẻ [*Vietnam needs a professional environment to train entrepreneuship thinking for the youth*], Giáo dục Việt Nam, 23 July 2021. https://giaoduc.net.vn

Chapter 6
Multilateral Engagement: Envisioning a Peaceful, Cooperative Multilateral Architecture

The previous chapter delineated opportunities for bilateral cooperation in areas of science and technology. This chapter takes the reader through a few multilateral initiatives to delineate the nuanced multi-alignment imperatives of these two countries, as opposed to the hub-and-spokes format. The first section posits Vietnam as a potential leader of maritime ASEAN states in contemporary times. The second articulates the state of Southeast Asia as detailed in the ISEAS Survey report of 2021. The authors have gleaned relevant information from the survey to understand ASEANs and its member countries concerns, affinities, aspects of governance, and confidence in the major players. It also brings into focus Vietnam's leadership experience and its engagement with major powers including India. The third section positions Vietnam within the ambit of a trilateral grouping with Japan and India, even as it engages with both through bilateral and multilateral forums. The Quad and Indo-Pacific are also discussed in the last sections.

6.1 Vietnam and India: Multilateral Engagement

6.1.1 Vietnam in ASEAN: Leadership Redefined

ASEAN as a grouping has, since 1967, grown to occupy a pivotal position in regional and global affairs. It is ASEAN's unity and centrality which has lent it this eminent positioning. The driving force has been ASEAN's unique normative frameworks which have been embedded in Asia–Pacific regionalism for a long time. This "centrality" serves a major purpose for ASEAN. It allows regional states to set the agenda thereby ensuring that their interests are not overridden by the objectives of major powers. Although ASEAN is considered by China within its immediate sphere of influence, with its historical and contemporary economic, social, and strategic engagement, ASEAN countries individually respond in diverse ways to Chinese influence.

© The Author(s), under exclusive license to Springer Nature Singapore Pte Ltd. 2021
R. Marwah and L. T. Hằng Nga, *India–Vietnam Relations*, Dynamics of Asian Development, https://doi.org/10.1007/978-981-16-7822-6_6

Vietnam has transformed substantively to emerge as a member whose engagement benefits ASEAN itself. This suggests that Hanoi will continue to invest in the strategic relevance of ASEAN and play a leading role in its cooperative process in the near future. India's Act East Policy of 2014 seeks Vietnam in a pivotal role for galvanizing India's engagement with ASEAN, as well as with member countries individually.

6.1.2 Vietnam's Leadership Role in ASEAN: Multilateral Engagement and Activism

Small and medium-sized countries prefer multilateralism when dealing with complex issues that involve a multi-alignment frame. This explains Vietnam's multilateral activism in the present times (Tinh, 2020). According to Emmers and Le Thu, the most significant element of leadership in the evolving and transforming world order is a role in international security. They interrogate ASEAN members' consideration of the candidature of Vietnam as assuming this role, especially as these would be viewed in the context of member country's individual perceived security threats and interests. What Vietnam could achieve for the grouping is to establish a stable and secure environment in tandem with its national interests (Emmers & Thu, 2021). It is well known that Vietnam's international recognition and integration in ASEAN in the 1990s provided it with the radar to re-orient its foreign policy. According to its own assessment, it was Vietnam's entry into ASEAN that transformed the region from being referred to as the "Balkans of Asia," to transforming into a zone of peace (UNSC 8711, 2020). This metamorphosed image of Vietnam now lends the country an aura of benevolence, cohesion, and leadership.

Speaking about the possibility of Vietnam assuming a leadership role in ASEAN maritime states, Prof. Nagao, in an interview to the authors on May 8, 2021, stated, "China has been successful in separating the maritime states in ASEAN from the continental states. Among the maritime states, Vietnam is the most confident, as from historic times, it has shown that it can pushback China."

ASEAN's embrace of Vietnam has enabled the latter to emerge from diplomatic isolation and be recognized as a cooperative and collaborative partner and regional actor, capable of forging unity in the grouping. Vietnam's first chairmanship of ASEAN was in 2010, when in October that year, two important events were convened. These were the 17th ASEAN Summit and the 5th East Asia Summit (EAS). At the EAS Summit, ASEAN extended the invitation of permanent membership to USA and Russia. With both the ADMM+8 newly established and the EAS membership expanded in 2010, Vietnam's efforts through ASEAN to initiate dialog mechanisms bringing in strategic partners were fructified. This was also a time when Hillary Clinton had stated in Hanoi, "The United States has a national interest in freedom of navigation, open access to Asia's maritime commons and respect for international law in the South China Sea." This was perceived as a rebuke to China (Landler,

2010). Ever since, the region has been perceived by regional and global powers as critical to the security and prosperity of the Asia–Pacific region (Kim, 2010).

Here it is essential to underline that the Vietnamese 2009 Defense White Paper states, "Vietnam highly values and actively participates in multilateral cooperation on security issues through international and regional organizations such as the UN, ASEAN, ARF and APEC." Hence, it deserves the credit for initiating ASEAN Plus mechanisms which include the ARF and the ASEAN Defense Ministers Meeting Plus (ADMM+). ASEAN, in turn, has enabled Vietnam to increase its diplomatic bandwidth in bargaining with China.

We now move to the present times to understand Vietnam's interest in assuming the leadership position in ASEAN. Given that Vietnam's economy required all the attention of its leaders, Emmers and Le Thu underline that although Vietnam's role has been critical in taking ASEAN to its present stature, the former has rarely taken the credit for its initiatives.

A few are stated here:

First, Vietnam played a catalytic role in the creation of ASEAN-10; its sterling contribution has manifested in ensuring that the region is nuclear free. This has been achieved through the adoption of the 1995 Southeast Asia Nuclear-Weapon-Free Zone Treaty (SEANWFZ).

Second, the expansion of ASEAN's membership is bringing in external dialogue partners, including the ASEAN plus six (China, India, Japan, S. Korea, Australia, and New Zealand). The inclusion of eight strategic partners (Australia, China, India, Japan, New Zealand, The Republic of Korea, the Russian Federation, and the United States) into the ASEAN Defense Ministers Meeting (ADMM) led to the creation of the ADMM+ that first convened in Hanoi in October 2010. In the multilateral sphere, Vietnam has also engaged partners like the United States, China, Japan, Australia, and others in various groupings.

Third, Vietnam deserves the credit for the internationalization of the South China Sea (SCS) dispute to reduce the asymmetry of power with China as well as to enforce a peaceful and rules-based resolution of the conflict. Given that ASEAN member countries have failed to speak in one voice on the dispute, it is Vietnam that has to maintain its pitch within ASEAN. For Vietnam, the SCS is known as the "East Sea," or "Bien Dong."

Vietnam has steered the diplomatic negotiations on the Code of Conduct and rejected compromises and a watering down of the common ASEAN position on the South China Sea issue. For example, Le Thi Thu Hang, a spokeswoman at the Vietnam Foreign Ministry, said: "negotiations on the CoC had made some progress with Vietnam actively participating and other countries are showing their constructive and cooperative spirit … Vietnam wishes related countries to continue their efforts and make a positive contribution to the negotiation process in order to achieve a substantive and effective CoC." (Talmadge, 2019).

Fourth, Vietnam's centrality in ASEAN has played a foundational role in ASEAN's present-day centrality in the Indo-Pacific, even as it engages with all major powers from a position of strength, without compromising on its principles of sovereignty and unity. Despite the complex interdependence that pervades equations and alliances across the Indo-Pacific, sovereign actors as Vietnam are seeking new hues of strategic networks, rooted in institutionalized cooperation.

Fifth is the positive trajectory of Vietnam's macroeconomic development. Since 1995, when Vietnam joined ASEAN, it had been placed within a grouping of "low income" or the "CLMV countries," including Cambodia, Laos, and Myanmar. Given that a predictable economic situation is a prerequisite for a position of sectoral leadership even in security matters, Vietnam has been, through a process of ongoing reforms demonstrated economic performance, comparable to other countries in ASEAN. Vietnam acknowledges that without international organizations' support as the Food and Agriculture Organization to UN Development Program, the World Bank, and the International Monetary Fund, Vietnam could not have achieved its lower-middle-income status.

Sixth, Vietnam's activism in the multilateral sphere is evident through the fact that it is now party to 16 free trade agreements of high standards such as the Comprehensive and Progressive Agreement for Trans-Pacific Partnership (CPTPP) and EU-Vietnam Free Trade Agreement (EVFTA) (Tinh, 2020).

Seventh, Vietnam is at ease with ASEAN's traditional norms and principles and discards any form of outside interference in its internal matters. Hanoi has on multiple occasions opposed proposals to alter this cardinal principle of ASEAN and continues to view its membership as the route to strengthen state sovereignty.

With an understanding that Vietnam's active participation in multilateral forums has imbued Hanoi with confidence to emerge as a leader within ASEAN, it is also important to articulate that ASEAN's embrace of Vietnam has been a win–win for both. According to historian Guan (1988), "Vietnam's best and perhaps only solution in order to pre-empt a fait accompli in the Spratlys is to depend on ASEAN support and to 'internationalize' the issue as much as it possibly can." This objective was partially realized when the foreign ministers of ASEAN and China's Vice Foreign Minister, Wang Yi, signed a Declaration on the Conduct of Parties (DoC) in the South China Sea on the sidelines of the ASEAN summit in Phnom Penh in 2002. ASEAN has, in turn, provided Vietnam with an institutional vehicle to internationalize its territorial dispute over the SCS with Beijing (Ang, 2001).

Eighth, as the chair of ASEAN in 2020, Vietnam worked with partners and members to preserve the unity of ASEAN on a range of issues, including overcoming the challenges posed by the pandemic. It also ensured that China's moves to engage ASEAN members bilaterally on the South China Sea issue could not push this security issue into oblivion.

Ninth, at the United Nations Security Council (UNSC), as a non-permanent member, Vietnam has sought the implementation of the Ruling of the Permanent Court of Arbitration (PCA). Both Malaysia and Indonesia followed Vietnam, which is now being viewed as the bellwether within maritime ASEAN and external powers. According to Prof. Reddy, "Vietnam is the only country which has maintained a consistent approach towards the SCS dispute."

Regarding the requirement of filing another case by Vietnam at the International Tribunal, Renato De Castro (speaking at the Association of Asia Scholars webinar on April 20, 2021), stated, "There is no requirement to take the case for arbitration. The

Philippines had already filed it in January 2013. The Permanent Court of Arbitration had invalidated China's historical claims in 2016. Unfortunately, President Duterte, despite the big win for the Philippines, only acknowledged it in 2020, even as China aims to deprive our country of 85% of its exclusive economic zone."

Hence, given that since 2020, Vietnam's capabilities as the chair of ASEAN in a leadership role have been well acknowledged and as maritime prowess becomes the order of the day, there is a rationale to assume greater responsibility in protecting the larger interests and unity of ASEAN. According to Emmers and Thu, despite being successful with the China-ASEAN Single Draft Negotiating Text of the Code of Conduct (CoC) in the South China Sea in 2018, Vietnam is conscious of not simply pushing for a less than substantive CoC for the South China Sea. Vietnam remains clear-minded about the substance of the CoC and is unwilling to make compromises for the sake of a premature diplomatic announcement. This could become a critical issue if Beijing succeeds in convincing some ASEAN states to settle on a less mean-ingful document. Moreover, China and ASEAN entered into discussions in 2017; ever since the struggle continues. When in 2019, Malaysia invoked international law, particularly the U.N. Convention on the Law of the Sea (UNCLOS), against China's expansive claims to the South China Sea, it was joined by other ASEAN countries including Vietnam and Indonesia. As expected, this was met with a firm rebuttal by China.

While in 2017, the two sides announced a draft Framework COC, and in 2018, a Single Draft Negotiating Text (SDNT), was prepared, the stalemate continues, due to differences in the scope of the CoC itself. According to Hoang, quoting an expert from a prominent Singapore think tank, "the two sides were only holding discussions on "how to resume the negotiations, not the negotiation itself." Technically, the SNDT is viewed as a document for discussions; however, questions remain unanswered. Given China's rigid stance on historical claims and rights, it is evident that the inclusion of territories as even the Paracel Islands, as Vietnam would like, would continue to be debated (Hoang, The Diplomat 2020). The path to a mutually agreed upon CoC is long and winding.

According to Vietnam Law Magazine, Vietnam, as proved by historical evidence, has been the first state having administration over the Spratly and Paracel Islands at least since the seventeenth century.[1]

When the authors spoke to Ambassador Chau about the issue of ASEAN unity with respect to the SCS disputes, his response was, "We all know that sovereign nations have different concerns, different interests, and different priorities. So, upholding unity among them is not an easy task at all. This is an issue faced by all intergov-ernmental organizations, not just ASEAN. Furthermore, as a grouping of small and medium-sized powers, ASEAN has been affected by its external powers and the

---

[1] Only until 1909, did China take interest in the Paracel Islands. In 1932, China claimed Paracels as the southern terminus of its land. China was also the last country to put its foot on the Spratly Islands in 1988 after having used force to shoot down three Vietnamese logistic ships and brutally massacred 64 Vietnamese military civil engineers without any weapon in their hands.

https://vietnamlawmagazine.vn/the-truth-about-who-is-the-biggest-aggressor-in-the-south-china-sea-3796.html; August 3, 2015; accessed on May 23, 2021.

calculations of each member have been influenced by uncertainties in the environment. The past few years witnessed increased uncertainties and instabilities. Tension in the South China Sea is on a rise and the disputes become very destabilizing due to great power politics. China unlawfully claimed the waters within the 9-dash line which accounts for 80% of the sea. It reclaimed and militarized the insular features, put equipment and weapons there, keeps sending vessels to its neighbors' waters under UNCLOS and blocks lawful oil and gas activities. The intensified competition between China and the USA also seeds division among ASEAN members. And we have seen over the past more than a year the Covid-19 pandemic which presents a huge, unprecedented challenge and crisis to every country and every person in the world. ASEAN is not an exception. Yet, ASEAN unity has also been strengthened as its members understood that ASEAN is a long-term project which could bolster their regional autonomy. Given those challenges that will continue, what is important is that ASEAN members are realistic and are able to identify issues of mutual concerns and mutual interests, discuss, and then come to agreeable points. Moreover, ASEAN has shown a great degree of coordination in coping with the pandemic and respond to the arising issue such as the political crisis in Myanmar. Though it has not been up to the expectations of many observers, I believe the grouping will continue to be strengthened." (Ambassador Chau).[2]

6.2 ISEAS Survey: Setting the Context for Trilateral and Multilateral Cooperation

To further take forward this discussion of ASEAN's responses to the prevailing geopolitical paradigms and specifically, Vietnam's position on the turbulent relations between the major powers and the level of confidence in the multilateral architecture, the authors have excerpted responses from the ISEAS-Yusof Ishak Institute Survey 2021. The state of Southeast Asia, the annual survey report *has been considered as a reliable source for understanding the position of ASEAN's ten countries on key issues as a collective grouping as well as in understanding the member countries' concerns and affinities. Interestingly, in 2021, 17% of the survey respondents were from Vietnam. ISEAS-Yusof Ishak Institute Survey Report (2021) A few questions and responses are provided in* Table 6.1.

The below survey results as depicted in Table 6.1 clearly point to the following:

(a) China's aggressiveness has become an increasing source of concern for ASEAN countries, with over a third of respondents voicing this. In the case of Vietnam, this figure is 98%.

(b) ASEAN countries, especially the lower riparian countries, are increasingly aware of the dangers posed by Chinese dams on the Mekong River and its

---

[2] H.E. Chau, Vietnam's ambassador to India, in an interview to the authors on May 11, 2021.

Table 6.1 State of Southeast Asia: Responses from the ISEAS Survey, 2021

	Key questions; only "yes" responses are provided	ASEAN	Vietnam
1	ASEAN is becoming an arena of major power competition and its members may become proxies of a major power	69.1	81.1
2	The region's anxiety over Beijing's growing strategic clout has increased	76.3	97.7
3	China's militarization and assertive actions in the SCS is a major concern	62.4	84.6
4	ASEAN should "take a principled stand that upholds international law, including UNCLOS and respect for the 2016 arbitral tribunal's ruling"; 70.4% urge ASEAN to conclude a code of conduct (COC) for the SCS with China as early as possible	84.6	
5	China is overwhelmingly regarded as the most influential economic power	76.3	
6	ASEAN should include Mekong River issues in its agenda". The preference for ASEAN to pay greater attention to the Mekong River is most pronounced in its downstream riparian states, Thailand (87.8%) and Cambodia (73.0%) & Vietnam	72.2	92.6
7	ASEAN countries welcome USA's strategic clout	63.1	91.7
8	Country considered as capable of providing leadership in championing free trade, it was the US which was the top choice for Vietnam (40.0%), Japan for Myanmar (28.2%) and China for Laos (27.5%)	USA Japan China	USA (First)
9	Country/regional grouping which can help to maintain rules-based order and fill the global leadership vacuum (preference in order) 6 ASEAN countries favor EU	1 EU 2 USA 3 ASEAN 4 Japan	Vietnam supports USA as number one

(continued)

Table 6.1 (continued)

	Key questions; only "yes" responses are provided	ASEAN	Vietnam
10	"ASEAN needs to articulate its ASEAN Outlook on the Indo-Pacific (AOIP) more clearly in order to stay relevant"	40.3	
11	Preference to "deepen cooperation with like-minded multilateralist partners beyond ASEAN"		62.3
12	The "threat of "decoupling" will divide Southeast Asia into two exclusive blocs led by China and the US. Vietnam (59.4%) believe the trade war will benefit their country	56.3	58.3
13	(a) Support for USA: 7 out of 10 members (b) Support for China: 3 out of 10 members (c) Support for EU (d) Support for Japan: Vietnam places Japan as number 1	61.5 38.5 40.8 39.3	
14	China is a revisionist power and SEA is in its sphere of influence according to 7 countries	46.3	65.1
15	ASEAN countries bilateral relations with China will worsen	Mostly status quo	25.7
16	China's economic and military power could be used to threaten their country's interest and sovereignty	51.8	
17	INDIA: Little or no confidence due to two reasons: "India is distracted with its internal and sub-continental affairs and thus cannot focus on global concerns and issues"; Others opine—"India does not have the capacity or political will for global leadership"	50.3	31.4 support India

Source Constructed by Authors from the ISEAS-Yusof Ishak Institute Survey on State of SEA, Singapore, 2021 adverse impacts on communities dependent on it. Yet, hesitation in calling out China and fence-sitting by most members of ASEAN are evident.

(c) The USA under the leadership of Joe Biden receives the support of seven ASEAN countries, with China receiving support from only three. These include Myanmar, Laos, and Cambodia. In Myanmar, there has been a significant pushback to China, with several Chinese factories and offices having been burnt down by anti-coup protestors. China is perceived to be supporting the Tatmadaw.

(d) Japan remains the most trusted major power in the region with the overall trust level increasing from 61.2% in 2020 to 67.1% in 2021. Vietnam considers Japan as the number one country for support.

(e) Vietnam is the only country in ASEAN in which almost a third of respondents believe that India has the political will for global leadership. Hence, India–Vietnam relations continue to be deepened; yet this remains a work in progress.

Hence, Vietnam's sectoral leadership role is critically dependent on whether it is proficient to effectively exercise influence in ASEAN amid the rising tension between the United States and China. "This tension," according to Andrew Nathan, speaking at an ICS lecture on April 28, 2021, "will continue under the Biden administration, as it has continued the Trump Administration's declaratory policy identifying China as a strategic competitor. It has retained Trump's tariffs, the "Quad," and other policies and it will pursue its key interests with allies especially in the South China Sea." Given that the US Navy will continue to traverse the waters of the SCS, securing Taiwan for securing its own role as a global security provider, Vietnam will continue to be sought as a strategic partner (Nathan, 2021).

Hence, while relations between USA and China have become more competitive, ASEAN has found itself constrained to restrict their involvement and interference in Southeast Asian affairs. India's growing stature in the Quad grouping and its inclusive vision for the Indo-Pacific converge with Vietnam's leadership in ASEAN and its willingness to assume the role of a middle power in the region. This is succinctly articulated by Harsh V. Pant, when he writes about the pushback of China, as, "The BRI is confronted with multiple fault lines; the Indo-Pacific geography is now more well-established than ever; the Quad has been resurrected; and various regional players are beginning to engage with each other much more cohesively." Such an engagement also refers to the trilateral partnership between Japan, India, and Vietnam (Pant, 2021).

6.3 Japan–Vietnam–India: A Trilateral Partnership: Possibilities and Challenges

The fact that Japan and India are both trusted partners of Vietnam, the trilateral partnership holds much weight. In an interview of Prof. Binh, Ambassador Thanh and Prof. Reddy, by the authors on April 15, 2021, this idea was unanimously welcomed.

Prof. Binh remarked, "Japan, India and Vietnam have excellent relations. Whenever any problem arises, the source is China. China may voice good things, but they cannot be trusted to do the right thing." (Authors interviews on April 15, 2021).

Prof. Reddy also echoed the same sentiment when he said, "India and Vietnam can develop bilateral relations to any extent and trilateral partnership with Japan—no punctuation; it is our wish and will to continue—no third-party issue which we need to consider." He also added, "A trilateral partnership would serve the three countries well; Japan as the investor, India as a market and Vietnam as the host country for investment."

Ever since Vietnam and Japan established an extensive strategic partnership for peace and prosperity in Asia in March 2014, regular visits by leaders and contacts at important forums have been maintained. While the former PM of Japan, Mr. Abe visited Vietnam four times, Mr. Suga also chose Vietnam as the first country he visited after assuming office. Vietnamese Prime Minister Nguyen Xuan Phuc also visited Japan in October 2019. Pursuing substantive progress in its strategic partnership with Vietnam, Japan has increased defense cooperation in research, development of infrastructure, supply of vessels for boosting maritime security, and much more. While the two countries have age-old ties, having exchanged the Most Favored Nation (MFN) status with each other in 1991, the continued emphasis is intended to ramp up relations with countries that could in turn help balance against China (Basu, 2020). It is also important to note that Japan is the largest ODA provider to Vietnam, in addition to ranking second in terms of FDI, this being USD 59.87 billion by September 2020. For India, Japan is even more than a development partner, with the two bidding for joint projects in other Asian countries. They also share common concerns about China and are partners in the Quad with a common vision for the Indo-Pacific and a rules-based international order.

Hence, Japan has been a key development partner for both Vietnam and India. Both countries also prefer Japan to visualize a trilateral comprehensive partnership, given the convergences as elucidated below. This was also echoed by Prof. Saturo Nagao, in an interview to the authors when he said, "Japan and India as well as Japan and Vietnam have a deep economic partnership. However, while Japan seeks to strengthen partnerships in Asia, it is reluctant to build infrastructure which may be for dual purposes. Hence, Japanese investment will always be for civilian purposes, soft and need based." This amplifies the fact that Japan's investments will be transparent and demand-driven, unlike those of the Chinese whose motives are veiled in secrecy and opaqueness. In this geopolitical matrix, Japan has economic and strategic interests in both countries and has been investing in India and Vietnam. "Given the fact that China's economic trajectory might face challenges in terms of costs and real wages, Japan's reduced investment to China, because of tensions on the East China Sea, would adversely impact Chinese industries." (Jha & Vinh, 2020, p. 151).

Ambassador Chau, in the interview to the authors, also highlighted the high level of trust reposed in Japan, when he said, "Japan is the important partner of both India and Vietnam. For Vietnam, it is the largest ODA donor, the second-largest investor, the third-largest tourist partner, and the fourth-largest trade partner. Japan is also an important partner for India. Good bilateral partnerships would constitute a firm foundation for larger cooperation, perhaps tripartite ones. What we are talking quite frequently recently in the context of the pandemic is supply change and supply chain resilience. So, if the three can talk, work on and foster it, it would be very good. Another example I can see is that both India and Japan are conducting development projects in Vietnam. Why can't we think of trilateral development projects in the future. In terms of infrastructural development, I am thinking of Japanese funding for East West corridor which could start from India and link up various parts of Southeast Asia to Vietnam. Of course, this linkage is huge and would take a very long time to materialize." (H.E. Ambassador Chau's interview to authors on May 11, 2021).

6.4 AEP and Japan's FOIP: The Bulwark for Connectivity with Vietnam

As is well known, Japan's economic rise was also matched by its commitment to investing in Asian economies, during the 1980s and 1990s, through various kinds of support programs. Ever since, Japan has been considered as a development partner by Asian nations.

In the 1980s and 1990s, India bolstered its defense and military cooperation with Vietnam. This has further been deepened in the twenty-first century. Japan, however, (according to Saturo Nagao in an interview to the authors on May 8, 2021), steadily improved its economic relations with South and Southeast Asia, building mainly civilian infrastructure. Hence, when Japan committed to developing infrastructure in India's Northeast region, this converged with its own vision for a free and open Indo-Pacific and the latter's alignment with India's Act East policy. Japan has decided to be the lead country in the connectivity pillar of IPOI. Ambassador Suzuki on March 18, 2021, reiterated that "connectivity should be captured in a broad perspective," and the unique case of India–Japan cooperation in India's North East and Bangladesh highlights the partnership capability and prospects to increase both land and sea connectivity mutually (Embassy of Japan, 2021: 2–3).

Japan's interest in infrastructure in Asia is not new. In fact, as articulated by Dr. Panda at a seminar on May 8, 2021, "The idea of the Silk Road connecting to Central Asia was that of Japan. When China overtook Japan in this subregion of Asia, Japan focused on building economic partnership with South and South east Asia." (Panda, 2021).

Japan has also initiated the Partnership for Quality Infrastructure (PQI) and the Asia Africa Growth Corridor (AAGC), as well as through its trilateral partnership with Australia and the United States.[3] Japan is committed for investments on energy,

---

[3] This initiative by the Japanese Government, in collaboration with the Asian Development Bank, other international organizations, and other countries, aims to provide approximately US$110 billion for "quality infrastructure investment" in Asia from 2016 to 2020. For details, refer https://www.gica.global/initiative/partnership-quality-infrastructure-pqi#; accessed on May 24, 2021.

transportation, tourism, and technology infrastructure. This is Japan's own response to China's Belt and Road Initiative (Brînză, A. 2018).

India's AEP and Japan's vision for a FOIP are also witnessing resonance with Bangladesh. During the visit of India's Prime Minister Modi to Bangladesh on March 26, 2021, his counterpart PM Sheikh Hasina expressed the country's interest in joining the India–Myanmar–Thailand trilateral highway project. Bangladesh is keen to enhance its connectivity with and beyond the immediate neighborhood. The trilateral project, conceived in 2002, is a 1360 km transnational highway connecting Moreh in India, Bagan in Myanmar, and Mae Sot in Thailand. Though there have been delays in execution, the project, which is expected to boost trade and people-to-people connectivity, is likely to be completed by 2022. This highway has the potential to ultimately connect landlocked Bhutan with Da Nang in Vietnam. The key to this massive undertaking is the 19.2 km Dhubri-Phulbari Bridge over the Brahmaputra. The joint foray is a fusion of India's "Act East policy and Japan's Free and Open Indo-Pacific" strategy.

With Mae Sot as the junction, the 1450 km EWEC route passes through Thailand's Province of the Mukhandan—the gateway to Laos, which is connected by the 1.6-km-long Second Thai-Lao Friendship Bridge over the Mekong—built with Japanese assistance. From Savannakhet in Laos, the corridor will lead to the East toward Da Nang, 486 km away. On the way, the Japanese has also been involved in constructing the 6.28 km "Hai Van Tunnel"—the longest in Southeast Asia. It links Hue—a city in Central Vietnam—with Da Nang. Hence, this gigantic effort will merge two parallel initiatives—the New Delhi-led India–Myanmar–Thailand trilateral highway and the "East–West Economic Corridor" (EWEC)—marshalled by Japan in partnership with Thailand, Laos, and Vietnam (The Sentinel Assam, 2021).

If connectivity projects are successfully implemented, (sans the volatile situation in neighboring Myanmar since the military coup post-January 2021), there is every possibility for the Supply Chain Resilience Initiative of India, Japan, and Australia to be strengthened. Vietnam should be a welcome partner!

6.5 Supply Chain Resilience Initiative (SCRI) and RCEP: Issues of Competitiveness and Decoupling

The India, Japan, and Australia value chain was formally launched on April 27, 2021, in a virtual trilateral meeting of trade ministers, with the primary objective of enabling countries to diversify their supply chains. Initially, SCRI's focus was limited to organizing events for investment promotion as well as sharing best practices on supply chain resilience (Mishra, 2021). Indian competitiveness holds the key to forge this initiative. Moreover, plans with Japan for improved auto components, electronics, food processing, medical devices, logistics, digital partnership, and trade facilitation will dictate the extent to which India can be included in the regional value chains (Suneja, 2021). Hence, the FDI into India may or may not follow a relocation or

China + 1 strategy for now. The focus will continue to be on realizing the FDI plans of existing companies.

When questioned about Japan's relocation of factories away from China, Prof. Nagao stated, "Japan has started the process of shifting some manufacturing out of China. As it does so, over a period of time, the most important destinations that are considered are Vietnam and India." If the competitiveness of Indian companies improves, then their mainstreaming into RVCs and GVCs will be easier. Radar technology and robotics for HADR operations are potential areas for joint manufacture. While Japan has indicated that it would prefer to bring ASEAN countries into this initiative, India's reluctance stems from its suspicion of Chinese direct influence creeping into the SCRI, through ASEAN. However, given Vietnam's geoeconomic positioning, all three SCRI partners can jointly bring in Vietnam. What is certain is that Indian companies must become more competitive if they envision being mainstreamed into resilient supply chains in the Indo-Pacific.

Here a discussion on RCEP is pertinent. India's reluctance to join the Regional Comprehensive Economic Partnership and its final exit in November 2019, evidently because of the China challenge, was not conducive to its seeking a robust Act East Policy. Japan and Vietnam among other ASEAN countries were disappointed, when after seven years of negotiations, India opted out of RCEP (Priya & Ghosh, 2020). Although in 2020, India's ease of doing business ranking has moved up to 63 among 190 countries, it lags behind several peer developing countries in terms of expenditure on R&D and global competitiveness index. There are several reasons for this, viz. cost and quality of power, high logistics cost (14–15% of GDP compared to the 9% global benchmark), low labor productivity, and low R&D expenditure (0.7% compared to 2–4% globally). Singh has shown that RCEP may not bring much export opportunity for India in general as well as in food and agribusiness sector (Singh, 2019: 316).

Whether India will or can benefit from companies decoupling from China will again be critically dependent on the improvement in competitiveness of Indian companies. In an interview to the authors, Mr. Amit Saxena, an Indian businessman in Ho Chi Minh City, affirmed this when he said, "From 1989 till 2004, India was the largest supplier of pharmaceuticals to Vietnam with 70% market share; however, this has reduced to a mere 10% in 2021. This is because other countries have overtaken India in the pharmaceuticals sector."

Mr. Saxena also explained that there is tremendous scope for Indian investment in Vietnam in the manufacture of battery-operated vehicles. In his words, "While there are several opportunities for Indian businesses, it has been perceived that without Government support, many big companies have failed. Moreover, Indian entrepreneurs seek quick returns on their investments in Vietnam. This is a deterrent, especially as funding from local banks or government agencies is not forthcoming." In Mr. Saxena's opinion, companies from Taiwan, South Korea, and Japan have been able to benefit by relocating to Vietnam as they already have large export markets. He added, "Vietnam, by itself has a low consumption base and has low demand for high-tech products. Unlike India, these countries have huge money power and relocating to Vietnam, implies a reduction in manufacturing costs."

A possibility for a trilateral partnership in the electric vehicles sector could be foreseen and considered by India and Vietnam. During the tenure of former Japanese PM, Mr. Abe, several companies had announced plans for investment in India. Suzuki is expected to invest Rs. 3800 crore in a new car plant and with Toshiba and Denso and Rs. 1150 crore in a lithium battery plant. Nippon Telegraph and Telephone, (NTT), a telecom company had announced a $2-billion FDI in data centers. With Japan and Vietnam, India can be fulsome partner in the region. Moreover, despite India's absence from RCEP and CPTPP, Japan is committed to engaging India robustly with a strategic intent.[4] For India, while there could be possibilities for partnering with Japan and Vietnam in the areas of auto components, steel and its products among others in addition to sectors as pharmaceuticals, medical devices, marine products, tourism and travel services, financial services, information technology, and skill development, the solution lies in the political will coupled with confidence in manufacturing and service competitiveness.

Eyeing a shift to Vietnam, Nidec, a Japanese company, which aims for a market share of 40–45% of the global market has set up operations in China, given the huge size of its market. "It is my policy to do different things and ahead of other people," said Nidec Chairman and CEO Shigenobu Nagamori. He predicts China will become the company's biggest market but added that it is also eyeing expansion in countries near China, such as Vietnam. "I started doing business in Vietnam before the diplomatic normalization between the U.S. and Vietnam" in 1995, he said. "I was able to develop a strong business base because I went in when nobody else did." (Mitsuru, 2021).

Indian businesses were also the first to do business and counter trading operations during the 1980s and 1990s in Vietnam when other countries were absent. To a question pertaining to the future of India–Vietnam commercial relations, Mr. Saxena said, "Indian businesses will take a few more years to develop industries in Vietnam. Our Indian banks as State Bank of India failed. Bank of India is also struggling. The most important requisite for Indian entrepreneurs is finance, which is not easily available. I too had obtained a government license for the manufacture of tyres in Vietnam, but was unable to do so due to the lack of financial support." (Interview of Mr. Amit Saxena).

Moreover, Asian countries, especially India, are increasingly depending on home-grown supply chains. Japan's logic for staying in RCEP was to balance the China-led grouping from overwhelming the trade and investment alliance. The alliance of India and Japan in the Quad and Indo-Pacific is also to ensure that the region is not economically subsumed by China. With Xi Jinping's Belt and Road Initiative providing the much-needed infrastructure boost to developing Asia, China has reinforced its erstwhile tributary system with small countries.

Given Vietnam's economic interdependence with China as also that of all Southeast Asian economies, and with their coming together under the mega-deal of RCEP, it is unlikely that ASEAN will join the SCRI of Japan, Australia, and India. Most

---

[4] Gurjit Singh, https://www.tribuneindia.com/news/comment/strategic-option-of-quad-to-boost-trade-ties-222983; March 10, 2021; accessed on May 24, 2021.

importantly, India's palpable reluctance to bring ASEAN into the SCRI draws a parallel with its exit from the RCEP.

In response to the authors' question on the possible impact of the US–China trade war on India–Vietnam bilateral relations, Ambassador Chau responded, "Since the trade war between the US and China intensified, there have been reports and analyses saying that Vietnam would be the greatest beneficiary of the frictions. Companies are reported to shift their productions and purchases from China to other countries including Vietnam. Yes, many investors have done that. However, the shifting of production is a natural process. Business tends to run for profits. When they encounter mounting difficulties in China due to increased competition of Chinese businesses, rising labour costs and stricter policy environment, they would flock to other places. They must have also eyed markets elsewhere, not only Vietnam. India is only one place in the world which witnesses increase in foreign direct investments during the pandemic. One issue I think we should be clear in our mind is that USA and China are the two biggest economies of the world. Any frictions between them would be detrimental to everyone, in one way or another as supplies are organized in chains. Vietnam is not an exception. Those negative implications are far bigger and more profound than the opportunities it can bring about. We have faced many disruptions, suspicions of trans-shipments threats from both sides though Vietnam did nothing to induce such shifts. Of course, in any situation like this, we must make every effort to minimize challenges." (Amb. Chau in an interview to the authors).

The best thing is to continue to improve and reform ourselves, our own market, and business environment, including improvement of infrastructure, particularly logistics, to make it strong and attractive to investors. Second, we need to diversify both supply chains and export markets to help mitigate economic risks arising from external economic turbulences. In this regard, Vietnam and India could and should work together to make full use of their domestic markets and manufacturing potentials, growing the cake by allowing greater market access to each other's businesses. Vietnam's former Ambassador to India, Mr. Thanh speaking about the China challenge in RCEP (to the authors on April 15, 2021), said, "There are also big challenges in the region, especially from China both from the economic and strategic fronts. In the economic domain, if China tries to dominate the entire market, then all neighboring countries will become dependent on it. Moreover, there are negative effects of Chinese investment. In terms of RCEP, the balance will be in favor of China if India is not there; this is not good for ASEAN, because ASEAN will be in very difficult situation and it is not easy to compete with cheap products from China. ASEAN and Vietnam would like very much to have India in RCEP and India should rethink. You should try to open and challenge—improve yourself and get the benefits of RCEP." (Amb. Ton Sinh Thanh to authors on April 15, 2021).

Prof. Reddy in an interview to the authors on April 20, 2021, spoke of the RCEP in a different vein. Concurring that ASEAN countries would prefer to include India in RCEP, yet given India's well-established trade alliances, RCEP would not bring great benefit. Referring to the China factor, he said, "RCEP for China it is nothing but a replacement for ASEAN countries to be appeased and is a strategy to divert ASEAN's attention from SCS and to make them forget about sovereign rights. Second, as a result of its trade war, China will be deprived of huge markets of USA and EU; hence to balance, the neighborhood market is very important. A third reason is that the other allies of USA viz. Australia, Japan, South Korea are in RCEP. Hence, their presence will ensure that China does not monopolize RCEP." He further justified India's stance in RCEP. Given India's burgeoning trade deficits, there is not much value for India in joining RCEP, he affirmed.

6.6   The Quad and Japan's EPQI

Interestingly, when the Quad or the Quadrilateral Security Dialogue was first envisioned by Japan's Shinzo Abe, initially in 2007, India, Australia, and the United States were hesitant to align with the idea. It was the China factor which, then a deterrent, became a catalyst a decade later. Soon after the onset of the pandemic in 2020 with China's increasing belligerence, Quad 2.0 evolved. Infrastructure outreach in Asia was also embedded in Quad 2.0 by Japan's EPQI and USA's Blue Dot Network (BDN), as tangible alternatives to China's BRI.

Evidently, its attractiveness and rationale increased for the four "like-minded" democracies. Despite Abe's departure from political leadership, his successor, Suga's complete endorsement of his predecessor's vision for the Quad and the Indo-Pacific reassured allies. In fact, he chose Vietnam as his first destination outside Japan, to articulate enduring economic and political interests in the country. It is well known that Japan is one of the largest investors in both India and Vietnam, as well as other ASEAN countries.

Quad is moving beyond being a security dialogue to affirming commitment for building infrastructure, addressing the requirement for vaccines in Asia, among other initiatives. Quad has plans to invest in, as Harris (2019) puts it, as "quality infrastructure" projects in the countries of the Indian Ocean Region, which evolved even before the initiation of the Quad 2.0. Japan took the lead role by invoking its wider infrastructural role in the Indo-Pacific region since 2015 when it announced its "Partnership for Quality Infrastructure and the Expanded Partnership for Quality Infrastructure" in 2016 (This has been referred to earlier).

The EPQI evolved as Abe's brainchild–Asia-centric infrastructure diplomacy that stood out as a direct response of China's BRI, which emphasizes quality and sustainability as the main goals and strategizes security-driven initiatives (Panda, 2020). Japan is also widening its connection to both Quad and non-Quad members by aligning with their infrastructure development projects—such as India, Vietnam, The Philippines, and Bangladesh, to name a few (Ministry of Foreign Affairs, ND). The Ministry of Foreign Affairs (MoFA) of Japan has outlined four pillars of Partnership for Quality Infrastructure:

1. Expansion and Acceleration of Assistance through The Japan International Cooperation Agency (JICA).
2. Collaboration with Asian Development Bank (ADB) on infrastructure projects.

3. Measures to increase the supply of funding for projects with relatively high-risk profiles through Japan Bank for International Cooperation (***JBIC***).
4. Promoting the Importance of Quality Infrastructure Investment Globally in the process of Developing Relevant International Standards.

USA, Japan, and Australia have already initiated their trilateral infrastructural projects in the Indo-Pacific region. While the Indo-Pacific Business Forum was initiated in Washington DC in July 2018 with America contributing $130 million as seed money, the trilateral forum expanded its activities in the Indo-Pacific region under the framework of a Free and Open Indo-Pacific (FOIP) to counter China's influence in the region. Within the FOIP umbrella, Japan, India, and Australia advance their wider networks and connections in their proximate regions (Bajpai, 2019). FOIP has provided the Quad a fresh option to connect Quad non-members with infrastructural issues more than defense issues, as argued by Brewster (2018). The senior officials of the Foreign Ministries of the Quad also unequivocally discussed in 2020 the "ongoing and proposed practical cooperation in the areas of connectivity and infrastructure development" along with the vital recognition of inclusivity and the centrality of the Association of Southeast Asian Nations (ASEAN) (Lakshman, 2020). With the first Quad Summit having been held in the virtual platform on March 19, 2021, the grouping seems to be on track with addressing issues of global commons and the push for vaccines for the Indo-Pacific countries. Whether Quad will evolve into an Asian NATO will largely depend on whether China plays by the rule book? Another key question is if Vietnam will join the Quad Plus grouping. While Vietnam is not averse to joining any grouping for addressing issues of common concern, any collective perceived as anti-China, would certainly keep Vietnam away!

6.7 Vietnam and India: Indo-Pacific Oceans Initiative and ASEAN's Indo-Pacific Outlook

It was on June 1, 2018, when India's Prime Minister Narendra Modi, during the Shangri La Dialogue in Singapore, outlined India's vision for the Indo-Pacific region. As has been stated earlier as well, India has underlined the centrality of ASEAN, even as it has called for a free, open and inclusive order in the Indo-Pacific. The tenets include respect for sovereignty and territorial integrity of all nations, peaceful resolution of disputes through dialogue and adherence to international rules and laws, including freedom of navigation and overflight for the seas.

Even prior to this vision for the Indo-Pacific, India had launched the initiative of SAGAR, which is Security and Growth for All in the region in 2015. PM Modi had highlighted the importance of coastal security as well as security in the maritime waters in proximity to India. On November 4, 2019, India launched the Indo-Pacific Oceans Initiative. While the IP Outlook of ASEAN defines the core areas where

ASEAN seeks to collaborate with other regional partners, areas as maritime cooperation, connectivity, and UN Sustainable Development Goals 2030 are in line with the seven pillars of the IPOI.

At the 17th Meeting of the India–Vietnam Joint Commission on Trade, Economic, Scientific and Technological Cooperation held in August 2020, India and Vietnam agreed to enhance their bilateral cooperation in synchronization with India's IPOI and the ASEAN Outlook on Indo-Pacific. The aim is to achieve shared security, prosperity, and growth for all in the region. India invited Vietnam to collaborate on one of the seven pillars of the IPOI. Here again, it is the China factor, which is in a way, forging the synergy between the ASEAN Outlook on the IP and India's Indo-Pacific Oceans Initiative (IPOI), (MEA, Govt. of India, 2020).

The IPOI focuses on seven central pillars. These are maritime security; maritime ecology; maritime resources; capacity building and resource sharing; disaster risk reduction and management; science, technology, and academic cooperation; and trade connectivity and maritime transport.

When India mooted this important idea, the vision was that each pillar be strengthened through a cooperative and transparent mechanism. For taking a leadership position, the key spheres for India are maritime security, (which would encompass even illegal, unreported, and unlicensed fishing) and disaster risk management. India has been making progress in beefing up its capabilities in these areas.

According to Saha and Mishra (2020), discussion on the SCS would yield more cogent outcomes, if Quad countries utilize multilateral platforms like the ASEAN or the EAS. Moreover, it needs to engage on issues outside those of hard security, viz. connectivity, blue economy, and capacity building, among others. These include maritime workshops, academic exchanges, Sagarmala, BDN, the EPQI, AAGC, among others. Another critical area for India to engage with Vietnam and other countries in SEA is the building of disaster-resilient infrastructure through the Coalition for Disaster Resilient Infrastructure (CDRI). The technically superior Navies of the four Quad countries can conduct workshops to provide training to the navies of the Southeast Asian countries, and workshops with the coast guards can also be organized. All four countries of the Quad need to work together to strengthen their influence in Southeast Asia.

Responding to a question on the convergence of India's IPOI and the ASEAN Outlook on Indo-Pacific adopted in 2019, Ambassador Chau said, "The AOIP is a fundamental paper, which defined the position of ASEAN as how the Indo-Pacific would be. We understand that the Indian position as communicated by PM Modi is very close. We both stress on ASEAN's centrality and the upholding of peace, security, and rule of law in the region. There are ways the two can benefit from the convergence of the positions on Indo-Pacific. The most prominent area is defense which is defined as an important pillar of our comprehensive partnership. In this pillar, we had identified a list of things to be done. And out of that list, we focus a lot on service personnel training in different fields including language. We also discussed the purchase of equipment and implementation of two important credit lines, provided by India to Vietnam. So that is very important, and it reflects the trust between two countries. In the maritime area, we can explore new collaborations to build capacities in maritime security and safety, and blue economy. Indian companies are involved in energy projects in Vietnam. We have created and will continuously create favourable conditions for them to operate there. That investment I think is profitable for both of us." (Ambassador Chau).

Even as India and Vietnam agreed to be partners in one of the seven pillars, the IPOI and ASEAN Outlook on Indo-Pacific to achieve shared security, prosperity, and growth for all in the region are aligned for joint supportive actions.

6.8 India and Vietnam: Deepening Security Cooperation!

According to Brewster, India's caution in aligning with other powers in the realm of defense and security cooperation has been a tenable fact. Before the United States became a global power, it had endeavored to steer clear of what it called "foreign entanglements." However, while the USA could unilaterally dominate the areas in its vicinity, the present situation in the Indo-Pacific, both for India and the USA, requires local partners. Security cooperation is now understood to be a way of expanding strategic influence, not restricting it (Brewster, 2013).

Speaking about the Sino-India standoff in the Himalayas in 2020, Prof. Reddy, in an interview to the authors on April 15, 2020, said, "China initiated the border confrontation to keep India out of Quad; earlier India never responded with such aggressiveness. It was only after China had continuously tested India's position that it finally took the decision of disengagement after almost nine months."

Post the June 2020 clashes with the Chinese PLA troops in the Himalayas, the Indian Navy deployed one of its frontline warships in the South China Sea. Additionally, frontline vessels were also dispatched to the Malacca Straits near the Andaman and Nicobar Islands. India's naval exercises have been held with several countries, including Vietnam, Singapore, Indonesia, and Japan. The increased presence of the Chinese naval forces in the Indian Ocean Region has also merited this shift in policy stance; the hesitancy in joining alliances as the Quadrilateral Security Dialogue and expanding that to a Quad Plus structure has been vanquished.

According to Indian Naval official, "There are four to six Chinese research vessels operating in the IOR beyond India's EEZ in addition to over 600 Chinese fishing vessels that are in the IOR beyond India's EEZ for every year since 2015–2019." Hence, issue-based alliances with significant partners in the Indo-Pacific region are coalescing to work toward a peaceful global order. Even as middle power coalitions are emerging as those of India, Australia, and Indonesia, there is every potential for an India, Japan, and Vietnam trilateral, not only to secure the East China Sea and the SCS, but also the Indian Ocean.

India and Vietnam agreed to establish in 2018, an Indian Space Research Organisation (ISRO) satellite tracking and satellite imagery receiving station to be located in Ho Chi Minh City in Vietnam. The station, called a Data Reception and Tracking and Telemetry Station (DRTTS), will enable ISR to track and receive telemetry from its launch vehicles after they have been launched from India, track its own satellites as they pass over Southeast Asia, and also allow Vietnam and its partner states in the Association of Southeast Asian Nations (ASEAN) to receive timely satellite imagery from Indian Earth observation satellites for the purposes of ocean surveillance, resource management, environmental monitoring, and disaster response and management. Although the DRTTS was first discussed in 2016, the two countries did not move ahead with the system, as China voiced strong opposition to this (Space Watch, 2018). The urgency of this initiative is not lost on either country.

Based on their strong convergence of views on many global and regional issues, both sides have also agreed also to coordinate closely at multilateral forums, including at the UN Security Council, where both India and Vietnam will serve concurrently as non-permanent members in 2021 (Gurung, 2020).

6.9   Conclusion

When China seeks to build a Community of Common Destiny with ASEAN nations, its objective is to keep the USA out of Asia, both in terms of its economic and strategic influence. It is not without reason that China considers the countries of Southeast Asia as being within its immediate sphere of influence, or "backyard." Vietnam too is entangled with China at the levels of party, people, and projects. Although Vietnam–China economic ties are age-old, the relationship has had several knots in recent times. The relations have progressed in terms of "cooperating while struggling." Both India and Vietnam have close economic linkages with China. Although India did not join the BRI, due to issues that impinged on its territorial sovereignty, Vietnam's strategies toward China and its BRI, according to Vu et al. (2021) are in fact a hedging strategy which is a flexible combination of both bandwagoning and balancing strategies (Vu et al., 2021, 56–68). Hence, Japan, India, USA, and the EU will remain important partners for Vietnam in the strategic and economic strata of the Indo-Pacific.

The transforming dynamics of the Asian region imply that both Vietnam and India must leverage each other's strengths to adapt to the "new normal," which will only witness a greater contestation in the maritime space in their vicinity. While ASEAN will continue to be divided in its attitudes and affinities, with states hedging and balancing their relations with the USA, China, the EU, Japan, India and Australia, it will remain intact as a grouping. However, Vietnam, despite its paternal and economic connections with China, has continued to consistently respond to Chinese aggressiveness. In the strategic domain, it has comprehensive partnerships with both India and Japan, which provides it with opportunities to negotiate with China from a position of greater heft.

Given India's reluctance to join the RCEP, the economic possibilities of its multilateral cooperation with ASEAN countries remain limited. However, minilateralism and multilateralism will be significant in the shaping of Vietnam's foreign policy. Hence, while its engagement with India and Japan will continue to be robust and multifaceted, the possibility of joining a Quad Plus formulation cannot be ruled out.

The Indo-Pacific vision cannot be realized without a rules-based regional architecture with ASEAN nations at the center. Vietnam occupies a unique and central position within the realm of ASEAN's geocommercial and geopolitical stature.

The complexities of the South China Sea disputes notwithstanding, there are other pressing non-traditional security challenges, such as pandemics, climate change, cybersecurity, relief and rescue operations, which point to opportunities for collaboration. Vietnam's leadership has been revealed through multiple successes; from the hosting of the second USA–North Korea Summit in 2019, to its handling of the pandemic as well as its roles within the UNSC and ASEAN. However, as articulated by Tinh, "whether Vietnam will succeed with its new foreign policy depends not on Vietnam's efforts alone, but also on the support and collaboration of its network of friends and partners." (Tinh & Lai Anh, 2021).

The China challenge for India cannot be surmounted unilaterally. This is despite the fact that India's ability to withstand China's aggression on multiple fronts has given other countries greater confidence in their ability to shape China's behavior (Pant, The Pushback against China, 2021). With the irony that China cannot be isolated and predicated on economic interdependence and joint initiatives for addressing global challenges, India has an inclusive Indo-Pacific vision for which it seeks a united ASEAN, and a confident Vietnam, as partners. When India's External Affairs Minister S Jaishankar reiterated that the Indo-Pacific is a seamless world which has been historically present in the form of Indian–Arab economic trading ties and cultural influences from ASEAN nations like Vietnam and the East coast of China, the vision for Indo-Pacific is in fact, " a return to history" and "is actually the overcoming of the Cold War and not reinforcing it." (Sibal, 2021).

On the question of the role of the US and China in India–Vietnam relations, Ambassador Chau stated, "they (US and China) are two biggest economies and two strongest military powers, which wield substantial influence to affect the world's security and development. India and Vietnam's national security and development are by a larger extent influenced by their behaviors. Still, our relations are developed with lesser impacts of outer world, including both great powers. In the last 2000 years we have never fought each other, we have never had enmity. We always supported each other. One of our prime ministers portrayed the relationship between India and Vietnam "as clear as a blue sky without a single cloud." I believe the India-Vietnam relationship has its own independence." The China factor will continue to impact the alignments of major powers and middle powers, both through economic and security partnerships.

The turbulent waters of the SCS will dominate the encirclement game in the twenty-first century!

The next chapter discusses how the players in the game will surmount the China challenge.

References

Ang, C. G. (2001). *Vietnam-China relations since the end of the Cold War*. RSIS Working Paper, No. 98. Nanyang Technological University.

Bajpai, K. (2019). "India and the Free and Open Indo-Pacific (FOIP)," Presentation at International Workshop, "The New International Relations Template and Japan's Indo-Pacific Vision" organized by Hiroshima Peace Institute and Konrad-Adenauer-Stiftung (KAS), Japan Office, January 24–25.

Basu, P. (2020, October 21). ORFOnline, https://www.orfonline.org/expert-speak/the-rising-prominence-of-vietnam-for-the-indo-pacific/. Accessed on May 5, 2021.

Brewster, D. (2013, November 5). India: Regional net security provider. *Gateway House*. https://www.gatewayhouse.in/india-regional-net-security-provider/

Brewster, D. (2018, March 7). A "free and open Indo-Pacific" and what it means for Australia. *The Interpreter*, Lowy Institute. https://www.lowyinstitute.org/the-interpreter/free-and-open-indo-pacific-and-what-it-means-australia

Brînză, A. (2018). The Diplomat. https://thediplomat.com/2018/11/japans-belt-and-road-balancing-act/, Nov 18, 2018.

De Castro, R. C., Professor in the International Studies Department, De La Salle University, Manila, speaking at the 41st webinar of the Association of Asia Scholars, April 21, 2021, hosted by the author, Reena Marwah.

Dr. Satoru Nagao, fellow (non-resident) at Hudson Institute, based in Tokyo, Japan, by Dr. Reena Marwah on May 8, 2021, hosted by the author, Reena Marwah.

Embassy of Japan March 18 2021: 2–3. https://www.in.emb-japan.go.jp/Japan-India-Relations/20210318-Ambassador_Suzuki_Inaugual_Address_for_IPOI_Seminar.pdf

Emmers, R., & Thu Le, H. (2021). Vietnam and the search for security leadership in ASEAN. *Asian Security, 17*(1), 64–78. https://doi.org/10.1080/14799855.2020.1769068

Guan, A. C. (1988). *Vietnam China relations since the end of the cold war*, IDSS working paper No. 1 p. 28, Singapore. Institute of Defence and Strategic Studies.

Gurung, S. K. (2020). Alarm over Chinese research ships in Indian Ocean Region. *Economic Times*. https://economictimes.indiatimes.com/news/defence/alarm-over-chinese-research-ships-in-indian-ocean-region/articleshow/73755293.cms?utm_source=contentofinterest&utm_medium=text&utm_campaign=cppst. 2020, January 30, accessed on April 25, 2021.

Harris, T. (2019, April 9). 'Quality infrastructure': Japan's robust challenge to China's belt and road. *War on the Rocks*. https://warontherocks.com/2019/04/quality-infrastructure-japans-robust-challenge-to-chinas-belt-and-road/

Hoang, V. (2020, September 28). The code of conduct for the South China Sea: A long and Bumpy Road. *The Diplomat*. https://thediplomat.com/2020/09/the-code-of-conduct-for-the-south-china-sea-a-long-and-bumpy-road/

India pushes for trilateral highway via Bangladesh. (2021, April 1). *The Sentinel*. https://www.sentinelassam.com/topheadlines/india-pushes-for-trilateral-highway-via-bangladesh-531491

ISEAS-Yusof Ishak Institute Survey Report. (2021). *The state of Southeast Asia*. https://www.iseas.edu.sg/wp-content/uploads/2021/01/The-State-of-SEA-2021-v2.pdf

Jha, P. K., & Vinh, V. X. (2020). India, Vietnam and the Indo-Pacific security architecture, Routledge India.

Kim, N. B. (2010). Vietnam hosts final summit as ASEAN Chair. *The Asia Foundation*. https://asiafoundation.org/2010/10/27/vietnam-hosts-final-summit-as-asean-chair/. October 27, 2010. Accessed on April 4, 2021.

Lakshman, S. (2020, September 25). Quad discusses 5G, Indo-Pacific infrastructure. *The Hindu*. https://www.thehindu.com/news/national/quad-discusses-5g-indo-pacific-infrastructure/article32699021.ece

Landler, M. (2010). Offering to aid talks, U.S. challenges China on disputed Islands. *The New York Times*. https://www.nytimes.com/2010/07/24/world/asia/24diplo.html. Accessed on April 19, 2021.

Mishra, A. R. (2021). Live Mint, April 28, 2021; https://www.livemint.com/news/world/india-japan-australia-launch-supply-chain-initiative-to-counter-china-11619532624451.html. Accessed on April 29, 2021.

Ministry of Foreign Affairs (ND), Japan, *Partnership for Quality Infrastructure*. https://www.mofa.go.jp/files/000117998.pdf

Ministry of External Affairs, Government of India. (2020, February). *Indo-Pacific Division Briefs*. https://mea.gov.in/Portal/ForeignRelation/Indo_Feb_07_2020.pdf

Mitsuru, O. (2021). Nikkei staff writer, February 10, 2021. https://asia.nikkei.com/Spotlight/The-Big-Story/Decoupling-denied-Japan-Inc.-lays-its-bets-on-China. Accessed on May 8, 2021.

Nathan, A. (2021). Speaking at a lecture titled, Biden's China Policy: Old Wine in New Bottles? Organised by the Institute of Chinese Studies on April 28, 2021, hosted by the author, Reena Marwah.

Panda, J. (2020, July 31). Shinzo Abe's infrastructure diplomacy. *Asia Times*. https://asiatimes.com/2020/07/shinzo-abes-infrastructure-diplomacy/

Panda, J. Speaking at a seminar on India-Japan relations and the Indo-Pacific, organised by Tillotama Foundation, May 8, 2021, hosted by the author, Reena Marwah.

Pant, H. V. (April 24, 2021). The pushback against China. *Times of India*. https://timesofindia.indiatimes.com/blogs/toi-edit-page/the-pushback-against-china-now-the-european-union-has-released-its-own-indo-pacific-strategy-too/

Priya, P., & Ghosh, A. (2020, December 15). India out of RCEP: What's next for the country and free trade? *The Diplomat*. https://thediplomat.com/2020/12/indias-out-of-rcep-whats-next-for-the-country-and-free-trade/

Saha, P., & Mishra, A. (2020, December 23). The Indo-Pacific oceans initiative: Towards a coherent Indo-Pacific policy for India. ORF Occasional Paper No. 292, December 2020. *Observer Research Foundation*. https://www.orfonline.org/research/indo-pacific-oceans-initiative-towards-coherent-indo-pacific-policy-india/. Accessed on April 25, 2021.

Sibal, K. (2021, April 17). In strongest defence of Indo-Pacific concept, India invokes history—And it's the right move. *News 18*. https://www.news18.com/news/opinion/in-strongest-defence-of-indo-pacific-concept-india-invokes-history-and-its-the-right-move-3650516.html

Singh, S. (2019). Examining global competitiveness of Indian agribusiness in the twenty-first-century Asian context: Opportunities and challenges. *Millennial Asia, 10*(3), 299–321. https://doi.org/10.1177/0976399619879889

Space Watch. (2018). https://spacewatch.global/2018/01/india-establishing-satellite-tracking-station-vietnam/. Accessed on May 24, 2021.

Suneja, K. (2021, March 29). India against Asean in supply chain trilateral. *Economic Times*. https://economictimes.indiatimes.com/news/economy/foreign-trade/india-against-asean-in-supply-chain-trilateral/articleshow/81739784.cms?utm_source=contentofinterest&utm_medium=text&utm_campaign=cppst

Talmadge, E. (2019). On summit sidelines, North Koreans study Vietnam's economy. *AP News*. https://apnews.com/eb50d09b6fa94e2e8166098be7dedc5c. Accessed on April 4, 2021.

Tinh, L. D. (2020, May 18). Why Vietnam embraces multilateralism at this uncertain time. *Lowy Institute*. https://www.lowyinstitute.org/the-interpreter/why-vietnam-embraces-multilateralism-uncertain-time. Accessed on April 24, 2021.

Tinh, L. D., & Tu, L. A. (2021, March 10). Vietnam should be more proactive in Global Governance. *The Diplomat*. https://thediplomat.com/2021/03/vietnam-should-be-more-proactive-in-global-governance/. Accessed on April 25, 2021.

United Nations Security Council (UNSC 8711, 2020). *Overview of Security Council Meeting Reports UNSC*. 8711 Security Council Meeting, January 30, 2020. https://www.un.org/press/en/2020/sc14093.doc.htm;UN. Accessed on April 4, 2021.

Vu, V.-H., Soong, J.-J., & Nguyen, K.-N. (2021). Vietnam's perceptions and strategies toward China's belt and road initiative expansion: Hedging with resisting. *The Chinese Economy, 54*(1), 56–68. https://doi.org/10.1080/10971475.2020.1809818

Chapter 7
The China Challenge: Strategic and Security Cooperation

The China factor in India–Vietnam bilateral and multilateral relations has been discussed in previous chapters. This chapter straddles through the logic of strategic and security cooperation among these two civilizational neighbors.

7.1 The Context: India and Vietnam: Strategic Alignment

The year 2020 witnessed the world grappling with the COVID-19 pandemic, with countries big and small encountering mammoth economic and political challenges. Amid the internal tensions and economic disequilibria, the external difficulties became even more formidable. While China sought to present itself as the aggrieved nation, facing the brunt of the coronavirus, it did not fail to demonstrate that its time had come! Chinese aggressiveness both on the mainland and in the maritime spheres accelerated from April 2020, from the East China Sea, to the Himalayan border with India. According to Sridharan, the rising angst is largely due to the naval rivalries all around China, and apart from the tension over Taiwan, China has now asserted itself aero-navally in the East China Sea over the Diaoyu/Senkaku islands, has made sweeping maritime territorial claims in the South China Sea over the Paracel and Spratly islands, and has asserted that its vital national interests extend to the second Pacific island chain, bringing it into conflict with Vietnam, Philippines, Malaysia, Indonesia, and Brunei (Sridharan, 2014: 131). China's rise has created anxieties in other nations who worry that China's growing economic power and increasing military capabilities might threaten their interests (Hollihan & Zhang, 2016).

While the US–China trade war continued relentlessly, China's wolf warrior diplomacy also unleashed heightened tensions in countries worldwide, from Australia to Norway. However, the countries most directly impacted through visible Chinese altercation and upping the ante were India and Vietnam (Nguyen, 2019).

© The Author(s), under exclusive license to Springer Nature Singapore Pte Ltd. 2021
R. Marwah and L. T. Hằng Nga, *India–Vietnam Relations*, Dynamics of Asian Development, https://doi.org/10.1007/978-981-16-7822-6_7

7.2   Neighbors: The Woes of Proximity

Both Vietnam and India share borders with China. Vietnam is an elongated, almost S-shaped country with a North-to-South distance of 1650 km and only 50 km wide at the narrowest point. It has a 1300 km land border with China. Vietnam borders the Gulf of Tonkin, Gulf of Thailand, and Pacific Ocean, along with China, Laos, and Cambodia. The coastline is 3260 km, excluding islands, running from Mong Cai in the North to Ha Tien in the southwest. There is also a group of around 3000 islets in the Tonkin Gulf. It also has islands in the Spratly and Paracel archipelagos. It is of significance that about 80% of its population lives within 160 km from the SCS coast. Millions of its fishermen live from this body of water. Its 86% trade with the world outside passes through this sea.[1] As Howard French asserts, China invaded Vietnam numerous times during two thousand years, even as it sought to absorb smaller societies; this continues to resonate powerfully in their relationship in the present times (French, 2017: 17–22). Today, as in the past, the ideals of the Tian Xia system are being manifested in various forms. This means building up a dependency on China among its far smaller neighbors, the better to dominate them peacefully, as much as possible (French, 2017: 71).

Hence, with China laying complete claim to the South China Sea, the two countries continue to have an unenviable diplomatic history. In January 1950, the People's Republic of China became the first country to recognize the Socialist Republic of Vietnam formally. The two sides formalized neighborly relations under the principles of "friendly Sino-Vietnam relations for peace, stability and prosperity." While interactions between the two countries go back millennia, 2020 marked the seventieth anniversary of official diplomatic ties (Le Thu, 2020).

Even as the neighboring countries held celebrations to commemorate 70 years of diplomatic relations in 2020, the undercurrents of tensions have mounted. Competition and contestation have marred the thin veil of camaraderie.

India, which had acquired the status of a rising Asian power at the turn of this century, had improved relations with China in the late 1980s. The two countries continued to engage diplomatically, with deepening economic ties until the ascendancy of Xi Jinping. As a result of the problematic boundary issue, several skirmishes have been seen since the 1962 war along the 2200 mile border.

It is important to contextualize this discussion. After India's independence from the British in 1947 and with the beginning of the Cold War post-World War II, USA's interest in South Asia grew. South Asia, it must be stressed, has been one of the most critical regions for China's international relations and foreign policy. Ali (1999) notes that the US policy toward South Asia during the 1950s was based on the perception that China and the Soviet Union posed a united Communist threat to American influence in the region. Hence, although India preferred to remain non-aligned, USA was keen to develop partnerships with India and Pakistan to prevent

---

[1] **SD Pradhan** in Chanakya Code, World, TOI. https://timesofindia.indiatimes.com/blogs/Chanak yaCode/vietnams-strategic-interests-in-the-south-china-sea-challenges-and-options June 27, 2021; accessed on August 21, 2021.

the spread of Communism. Moreover, the China–India border issue hinged on the Mc Mohan Line, which was rejected by the Chinese due to the Tibetans' issue.

The fleeing of His Holiness Dalai Lama in 1959, along with thousands of followers, and the boundary issue, resulted in the 1962 Sino-India war. The war meant a breakdown of the Panchsheel Agreement, post which bilateral relations nosedived for over two decades. In the 1980s, Sino-Indian links received a fillip with the visit of Rajiv Gandhi in 1988, after which engagement between the two countries increased. At this time, the South Asian Association for Regional Cooperation (SAARC) was launched in 1985. SAARC was viewed as an India-centric regional grouping comprising the eight countries of Afghanistan (included in 2007), Bangladesh, Bhutan, India, the Maldives, Nepal, Pakistan, and Sri Lanka (Ahmed, 2012: 286).

The raison d'etre for China to engage countries in South Asia has shifted from a mere Sino-Pakistan axis, underlining the Kautilya dictim, "my enemy's enemy is my friend," to reigning in India's ambitions. For China, its accumulated surpluses and deep pockets have replaced Maoism as the tool for gaining global influence. There is no other country where this strategic tool has been better deployed, uniquely as it engineered to keep India, a rising neighbor, in check (Marwah & Ramanayake, 2021: 55). A prime factor has been the India-led SAARC grouping's slow progress, held hostage by the complex India–Pakistan relations (Lama, 2017). In South Asia, the China–Pakistan axis and its growing interface with all countries in India's neighborhood have meant India's distrust of China continues. This is even though China's economic relations with India had been growing (Deshpande, 2010).

Xi Jinping's BRI initiatives in India's neighborhood have continued to contest India's sovereignty. The June 15, 2020, incident when Chinese troops killed 20 Indian soldiers has altered India's foreign policy. The Indian Government has undertaken deliberate measures to reduce its economic dependence on China. It has also expanded its external engagement with countries like the USA, Japan, Australia, and Vietnam.

7.3 India and Vietnam Strategic Alignment: Motivations, Manifestations, and the Restraints of Managing China

The India–Vietnam relationship is one of the most significant bilateral relationships in Asia. Ever since the establishment of diplomatic relations between the two on January 7, 1972, and post-India's Look East Policy, bilateral ties have assumed greater vitality, encompassing culture, economic, strategic, and defense areas.

The ties have been further cemented with India's invigorated Act East Policy of 2014, with more significant exchanges between leaders, think tank representatives, and people-to-people connections. As stated earlier, the bilateral relationship was elevated to a "Comprehensive Strategic Partnership," during Prime Minister, Narendra Modi's visit to Hanoi in September 2016 (Panda, 2017). The discussion below provides good raison d'etre for India and Vietnam to forge a robust strategic partnership. The China shadow looms overwhelmingly in the bilateral relations.

The China challenge, resulting in strategic alignment, is discussed through three sections here:

(a)   Motivations for closer alignment.
(b)   Manifestations of this alignment, in terms of the robust bilateral engagement.
(c)   Restraints in the engagement.

7.3.1 Motivations

7.3.1.1 Territorial Sovereignty

China is involved in multiple disputes with Vietnam and other ASEAN countries, over ownership of territory in the South China Sea. Since 1974, China has laid claims on the Paracels Islands and has steadily asserted its power in the South China Sea. There have been multiple actions of aggressiveness, from detaining Vietnamese fishing boats in the Spratlys, firing on fishing boats, and injuring Vietnamese fishermen. One of the most severe military confrontations occurred on March 14, 1988, when the Chinese navy sank three Vietnamese vessels, killing seventy-four sailors. The incident occurred after Beijing, established a physical presence on Fiery Cross Reef in the Spratlys in January 1987 (Wong, 2010). In June 2011, Vietnam protested China's alleged harassment of its oil exploration ships even as Vietnam worked with multinational corporations, including ExxonMobil and Chevron, to develop hydrocarbon assets.

In June 2012, Vietnam passed the Maritime Law, asserting its jurisdiction over the Spratly and Paracel Islands, demanding notification from any foreign naval ships passing through the area. China issued a strong response, announcing the establishment of a city, Sansha, on the Paracels that would administer the Paracels, Spratlys, and Macclesfield Bank. China also established a new administrative region with authority over the Paracel and Spratly Islands. These developments exacerbated the Vietnamese public's long-simmering antagonism toward China—particularly Chinese hostility in the South China Sea—and led the Vietnamese government to authorize the first protest.

Xi Jinping's China has further consolidated control of features in the SCS, antagonizing maritime Southeast Asian nations. Among Southeast Asian countries, Vietnam's position is vulnerable as it is subject to constant interventionist strategies. Hanoi also protested when China landed a plane on Fiery Cross Reef in 2016. Vietnam also issued official statements opposing China's infringing upon Vietnam's sovereignty after Chinese bombers appeared in the Paracel Islands in May 2018. Undeterred, China began construction on a new building in the Paracel Islands in November 2018. The same year, Hanoi also asked Beijing to remove its military equipment from the South China Sea (Hoang, 2019: 21).

Image 7.1 South China sea: Paracel and Spratly Islands. Wikimediacommons; File:75,967 South China Sea-1.jpg; [File: Vietnam claims Paracel and Spratly islands.JPG|Vietnam_claims_Paracel_and_Spratly_islands]

Speaking about Vietnam's claims in the SCS, Vietnam's Ambassador in India, H. E. Chau, in an interview on October 16, 2020, stated, "Vietnam has sufficient historical and legal evidence for its claim over Paracel Islands. Before 1956, the Paracel Islands was of Vietnam. In 1956, as we were busy recovering the country from France, the Chinese PLA sent its troops and took half of the Paracel Islands. And for the second half, Chinese sent the troops and used force to take it in 1974, when we were busy fighting America. So, China took it from us, illegally, so it's clear the whole world knows. We asked China to give it back to us, so this is the issue between China and Vietnam. We don't need any other countries to do arbitration. Now China has to give it back according to the law. The second issue is the Spratly Island, claimed by six parties but five countries. By six parties I mean- Vietnam, Philippines, Malaysia, Brunei, China and Taiwan. In terms of these claims, we believe that the six parties have to sit down and discuss."[2] Refer Images 7.1 and 7.2.

The strategic partnership of India and Vietnam implies that India must deliver on Vietnam's balancing. India has, time and again, affirmed its support for a rules-based order and adherence of the principles of UNCLOS, both by international-izing the issue and by lending active support to the Vietnamese defense forces. In

---

[2] Manish Kumar Jha, Business World, http://www.businessworld.in/article/We-Are-Determined-To-Protect-Our-Sovereignty-On-The-Sea-As-China-Transgressed-Into-Our-Area-Vietnam-Amb assador-Pham-Sanh-Chau/16-10-2020-332394/; October 16, 2020, accessed on May 19, 2021.

Image 7.2   East sea/South China Sea and the nine dash line. By Trung Nguyen. https://www.voa news.com/east-asia/vietnams-communists-urged-sue-china; July 29, 2014

a recent initiative, i.e., on August 18, 2021, the Indian Navy carried out joint drills with the Vietnamese Navy in the South China Sea. The sea phase included surface warfare exercises, weapon firing drills, and helicopter operations. Regular interactions between the two navies over the years have enhanced their interoperability and adaptability. According to an Indian naval officer, "This has ensured a quantum jump in the complexity and scale of professional exchanges. This visit also holds special importance as Indian Naval ships celebrated the country's 75th Independence Day in Vietnam," he said.[3] Moreover, although India is not a claimant to the South China Sea, its economic interests require to be safeguarded. Moreover, the SCS waters are significant for India's trade flows with ASEAN countries and Japan, Taiwan, South Korea, and Australia.

The Indian Ocean too has not been spared. China's building of ports in the periphery of India, especially in Gwadar in Pakistan, Hambantota in Sri Lanka, the reclaiming of 269 ha of land for the Colombo Port city project, has helped China increase visits by its ships. This has become a security issue for India, which has beefed up its maritime surveillance and coast guard operations in the Andaman Sea and the Indian Ocean and has also forged defense detente with Vietnam and IOR countries.

The issue of territorial sovereignty also looms large for India on its Northern Himalayan borders, with China having upped the ante since April 2020. Its troops continue to occupy several parts of the Sino-India buffer zone. China's outreach through its BRI initiatives in all neighboring countries of India has exacerbated tensions. India's rejection of the BRI is also a "sovereignty issue," the result of

---

[3] Abhishek   Bhalla,   https://www.indiatoday.in/india/story/india-vietnam-naval-exercise-south-china-sea-1842437-2021-08-18; accessed on August 19, 2021.

China's CPEC corridor, which passes through an India–Pakistan disputed territory. China is also planning railway lines to India's border with Nepal, challenging India in every way.

In an interview to the authors, Tillotama Mukherjee, on April 15, 2021, reiterated that the most important decisions between India and Vietnam have been influenced by China. In her words, "Vietnam and India both have outstanding disputes; Vietnam has always stood by India on the territorial dispute and has always condemned incursions by China into Indian territory. Vietnam understands the reasons for India's reluctance in joining the BRI. Vietnam also has concerns of hydro politics in the Mekong region and seeks greater cooperation among lower riparian countries."

7.3.1.2 India and Vietnam—Convergence of Views on a Rules-Based Order

China's claims over 90% of the South China Sea also see a convergence of views by India and Vietnam. Both countries are concerned with China's disregard of the rules-based international order, contributing to rising tension in the region. Hanoi has objected to Chinese vessels ramming—and in one case sinking—Vietnamese fishing boats in the South China Sea (SCS). In July 2019, a Chinese vessel stayed for months in Vietnam's EEZ, while a Chinese survey ship, Haiyang Dizhi 8, and escort ships entered Vietnam's exclusive economic zone (EEZ) near an offshore oil block. China has often attempted to prevent Vietnam from drilling in the region through ship patrols and threatening maritime maneuvers. After Vietnamese officials demanded that China removes the ships, the survey ship left after four months. Again, in April 2020, Hanoi complained about China's actions after a Chinese vessel rammed and sank a Vietnamese fishing boat near the Paracels. Soon after, Beijing established two administrative districts that would take control of the Paracel and Spratly Islands. The Philippines and Vietnam denounced the move.[4]

For India, the Code of Conduct related to the SCS must be signed at the earliest as a rules-based order is vital for ensuring peace and stability in the Asian region (Panda, 2017: 58). India prefers to engage with a China that also considers its sensitivities and affirms its position as a rising power with benign intentions. China's penchant for creating its own rules and coercing other countries to follow its directives has resulted in Vietnam and other ASEAN countries to engage more with India. This is because India has no historical baggage or bilateral disputes with any ASEAN country. The even more obvious motivation is that India, which has always underlined the imperative for a rules-based order can be expected to play a more significant role in the region.

The International Court of Justice at the Hague brought out a ruling on July 12, 2016. It rejected China's claims of having any historical basis of this claimed ownership of almost 90% of the SCS, as defined by its nine-dash line. It was the

---

[4] China's Maritime Disputes 1895–2020, https://www.cfr.org/timeline/chinas-maritime-disputes; accessed on January 9, 2021.

Philippines that had taken the issue to the ICJ. Despite the ruling, China refused to budge on its stance. Ever since China's aggressive activities have continued to increase.

Nationalistic Chinese interpretations of the UN Convention on the Law of the Sea and the "constitution of the oceans" are now incompatible with any official understanding of the law. Hence, they pose a threat to the very meaning of state sovereignty and to the order itself. China's principles are an instrument for enforcing its imperial power, which is anathema to a rules-based order. The systemic implications are perhaps finally being recognized, with the USA recently announcing the reversal of "eight years of cheek-turning concerning international law in the South China Sea." China's rhetorical deference to international law masks the more subversive consequence of its actions: redrawing the boundaries between law and politics in a way that overturns foundational parts of the global order from within. The future viability of international law's authority will lie with the fate of the rules-based order, which will define the structure of power within which legally binding rules can operate (Jorgensen, 2020).

7.3.1.3   Synergy in the Indo-Pacific

India's External Affairs Ministry has taken forward its goals in the Southeast Asian region, specifically the South China Sea, through a new Oceania division. This region, being the backyard of India's fellow Quad nations (USA, Japan, and Australia), India intends to build confidence among them by giving decisive shape to its engagements with Indo-Pacific countries. India's aim is not only to portray itself as a counter to China, rather, as an Asian power that can work with like-minded nations in the region to ensure regional stability.[5] Given that India cannot afford to confront China unilaterally, the option is to make soft alliances in the Indo-Pacific and to counter Chinese behavior with their help (Kumar, 2021).

Vietnam in 2020, when it was ASEAN's chair, also commemorated the 25th anniversary of its relations with ASEAN and served a two-year term (2020–2021) as a non-permanent member of the United Nations Security Council (UNSC). India on January 2021 also joined as a non-permanent member for one year. As the chair of the UNSC for the month of August 2021, India was successful in enlisting the support of members for an outcome document which underlines the importance of a rules-based order in the SCS and affirms the relevance of UNCLOS. Vietnam had also endeavored to highlight the significance of maritime security in April 2021, but without success. Vietnam wholly supported India during the process steered successfully by the latter.

It is in the interest of both the growing economies to make the best out of the strategic partnership, increase and sustain this economic growth and work on sectoral convergences to promote and institutionalize the Indo-Pacific construct. Through

---

[5] Harsh V. Pantnikunj Singh, https://www.orfonline.org/expert-speak/indian-foreign-policy-and-its-aspirations/, December 16, 2020; accessed on January 9, 2021.

joint adoption of policies and strategies conducive to building a safe and secure rules-based Indo-Pacific region, India and Vietnam can promote an inclusive and open policy perspective on the Indo-Pacific (Sarma, 2020: 3).

In an interview with H.E. Pham Sanh Chau, Ambassador of Vietnam to India, published by India Foundation on December 26, 2020, he stated.

> Regarding the Indo-Pacific, I have seen key factors shared by both India's Indo-Pacific Ocean's Initiative and ASEAN's Indo-Pacific Outlook. First, every country has to have respect for international laws, most importantly the UN Charter and UNCLOS 1982. Second, both India and Vietnam shared the view that ASEAN will occupy the central role in any evolving security structure in the region. Third, it is necessary to stick to dialogues, conflict prevention, and peaceful settlements in case of any altercation. With all these shared values and interests, I believe that cooperation between the two countries will be further enhanced in years to come and will be an important factor to the peace, stability and prosperity in the region.[6]

7.3.1.4 Mekong Ganga Cooperation

Both India and Vietnam have shared interests in the Mekong region. While India initiated the Mekong Ganga Cooperation in 2000 with mainland nations of SEA, China initiated the Lancang Mekong Cooperation in 2015. India's initiative has been embedded in cultural and civilizational linkages while China seeks to increasingly exploit the rich resources of the Mekong River by building dams and generating energy. The exploitation of waters of the river has also resulted in the displacement of communities dependent on it for their survival. The Lower Mekong has been affected by climate change and China's stocking up of water in recent years. China did not join the MRC and hence is not obliged to be transparent on issues of water levels. A study by Eye on Earth released in April 2020 has stated that the 11 Chinese dams have stored a high volume of water over the past three decades. Chinese dam construction on the Upper Mekong is having devastating impacts on downstream communities, as dozens of dams are either planned, under construction or built within the Lower Mekong Basin. This rapid expansion of hydropower threatens all countries that share the Lower Mekong Basin, with downstream Cambodia and Vietnam at the greatest risk.[7]

To cooperate to develop the Mekong River Basin, the Mekong River Commission was established in 1995, by Thailand, Laos, Cambodia, and Vietnam. In 2002, Beijing joined as a "Dialogue Partner" and vowed to help the MRC by sharing data on water levels from two monitoring stations on the Lancang (Mekong River is known as Lancang in China) only. However, China has never been transparent about the extent of water it withheld or released from its reservoirs since it started

---

[6] India–Vietnam relations: Convergence of interests—An interview with H.E. Pham Sanh Chau, Ambassador of Vietnam to India, https://indiafoundation.in/articles-and-commentaries/india-vietnam-relations-convergence-of-interests-an-interview-with-h-e-pham-sanh-chau-ambassador-of-vietnam-to-india/; accessed on January 12, 2021.

[7] Linh Pham, http://hanoitimes.vn/vietnam-calls-for-responsible-hydrological-resource-sharing-on-mekong-lancang-313970.html, August 25, 2020; accessed on January 10, 2021.

building dams on the Lancang in the 1990s. The prevailing view of the LMC is that it is intended to exploit MRC weaknesses and entrench China's regional standing as Beijing disperses aid and gains influence over development projects along the waterway. According to Brahma Chellaney, China seeks control of Asia's water map, owing to its annexation of ethnic minority homelands, such as the water-rich Tibetan Plateau and Xinjiang. China's territorial aggrandizement in the South China Sea and the Himalayas, notwithstanding, has not hesitated to use its hydro hegemony against neighboring downstream countries.[8]

India also shares concerns of Vietnam and MGC partners, with which it has been engaged for 20 years. A few aspects of sustainable water management include: water harvesting, water data collection, climate change adaptation and mitigation, integrated water resources management, groundwater management, transboundary basin management, water quality monitoring, flood and drought management and disaster reduction, etc.[9]

These sentiments were echoed by Vietnam's ambassador to India too, when he said, *"The two countries are also key stakeholders in the Mekong-Ganga Cooperation. This will be an opportunity for us to strengthen our cooperation and coordination in global and regional issues of mutual concern and bolster ASEAN's centrality."*[10]

7.3.1.5 Joint Harnessing of Resources in SCS

The strategic significance of the SCS is well known. This busy waterway is also of very critical importance to India as almost 50% of its trade passes through this region of the sea. India's ONGC is engaged in oil exploration operations in Vietnam-claimed areas of the sea and is an important stakeholder in these waters.

Since India's ONGC Videsh Limited (OVL) has already been given five extensions since 2006 for deep sea exploration of Block 128, the license having been renewed in 2017 till June 2019, reflects Vietnam's keenness to engage India in these strategic waters. This has not been without turning a deaf ear to China's repeated threats to both Vietnam and India. Years ago, in 2011, OVL was warned by China against continued exploration in this area. Moreover, Vietnam, already China's partner in its Belt and Road Initiative, risks becoming overdependent on China for its energy needs as well.

---

[8] Will China turn off Asia's Tap? https://www.project-syndicate.org/commentary/china-dam-bra hmaputra-yarlung-zangbo-water-scarcity-asia-by-brahma-chellaney-2020-12; accessed on January 12, 2021.

[9] Mekong—Ganga Cooperation (MGC) Plan of Action (2019–2022), https://mea.gov.in/bilateral documents.htm?dtl/31712/Mekong+Ganga+Cooperation+MGC+Plan+of+Action+20,192,022.

[10] India–Vietnam relations: Convergence of interests—An interview with H.E. Pham Sanh Chau, Ambassador of Vietnam to India, https://indiafoundation.in/articles-and-commentaries/india-vie tnam-relations-convergence-of-interests-an-interview-with-h-e-pham-sanh-chau-ambassador-of-vietnam-to-india/; accessed on January 12, 2021.

However, for several years, China continued its efforts to prevent the Vietnam-based companies from developing oil and gas resources in the area. Given the need for securitization of Vietnam's energy resources, there is an imperative that offshore exploration is not only continued but enhanced further. However, to appease China, Vietnam decided to suspend the joint Repsol project with Spain in the South China Sea in March 2018.Though of moderate size, this Red Emperor Block was a crucial asset in contributing to Vietnam's much-needed energy resources (Marwah, 2018).

Amid the growing Chinese movement in SCS, Vietnam paid nearly a billion dollars to two international companies after canceling their drilling operations following pressure from Beijing, The Diplomat reported, to maintain its presence in the South China Sea region. Citing a well-placed oil industry source, Bill Hayton, author of the article, said, "Vietnam's state-owned energy company PetroVietnam will pay the money to Repsol of Spain and Mubadala of the UAE in 'termination' and 'compensation arrangements."[11]

A secure China whose unmatched supremacy is well understood by its neighbors would do well to project its "peaceful rise" image.

7.3.1.6 Major Powers: Ambiguous Intentions

The Presidency of Mr. Trump in USA, since 2017, altered Asian perceptions of the role of the USA as a trade and security partner. When Trump walked out of the Trans-Pacific Partnership and reduced funding for the World Health Organization (WHO), among other policy directions, the signal sent to allies was that the United States was no longer willing to assume global responsibilities. According to Mahbubani, Trump has single handedly done more to reduce America's prestige and influence in the world than any other American leader. America was generally perceived to be a reliable partner by its closest allies. This sense of trust in America has diminished considerably (Mahbubani, 2020: 48). This is also reflected in the ISEAS survey 2020 results. Almost 62% of Vietnamese respondents of the ISEAS Survey 2020 believed that ASEAN needed to build its resilience and not be dependent on either the United States or China (ISEAS Survey, 2020).

The United States and Vietnam are natural or all-encompassing partners; however, their relationship is not without its warts either (Stauch, 1994). The US trade imbalance remained a thorn in Trump's side, and he appeared to view Hanoi as just as much a part of the problem as Beijing. He called Vietnam "the single worst trade abuser of everybody" and had warned of it being targeted with tariffs.[12] The Biden Presidency, however, recognizes the importance of Vietnam in its relations with ASEAN.

---

[11] China pressurises Vietnam to cancel, compensate offshore firms operating in South China Sea, https://energy.economictimes.indiatimes.com/news/oil-and-gas/china-pressurises-vietnam-to-cancel-compensate-offshore-firms-operating-in-south-china-sea/77189060; accessed on January 15, 2021.

[12] Huong Le Thu, https://carnegieendowment.org/2020/09/30/rough-waters-ahead-for-vietnam-china-relations-pub-82826, September 30, 2020; accessed on January 15, 2021.

Both New Delhi and Hanoi remain invested in encouraging Washington to stay attentive to South and Southeast Asia issues. Vietnam had some success in attracting Trump's attention—it is the only Southeast Asian country that he has visited twice in his first term, since he attended the 2017 Asia–Pacific Economic Cooperation (APEC) Summit in Da Nang and held his second summit with Kim Jong Un in Hanoi in 2019. With India too, the United States has increased its engagement. The signing of the Basic Exchange and Cooperation (BECA) agreement in October 2020, as indicated in the joint statement from the defense chiefs of India and the USA, would give the former access to USA's geospatial intelligence, potentially improving the accuracy of Indian weapons systems along the frontier.[13]

The USA has also condemned China for initiating the border standoff with India since April 2020. The Quad countries, in a tactical move, also held the maritime exercises in Indian waters in late 2020. The 24th edition of the MALABAR naval exercise has been held in two phases in November 2020.[14]

Given Biden's bipartisan approach toward China, both India and Vietnam are hopeful that the USA will continue its freedom of navigation operations and military exercises (revived by the Trump administration) with the Quad alliance.

Biden has appointed officials familiar in Asian capitals who can coordinate Washington's efforts with Southeast Asian states. Regional alliances like the Association of Southeast Asian Nations will become more of a priority for Biden than for Trump, who failed to attend the ASEAN summit two years in a row. According to Trang Pham Ngoc Minh, a lecturer at the Vietnam National University, "We may also see more USA appearances in ASEAN meetings. I think the approach of the Biden administration will be more of 'neo-institutionalism,' which is different from the former President's realist approach" (Le Hong 2020). A high-level US presence will give ASEAN a better chance to air their concerns about being forced to take sides. Brunei, Malaysia, the Philippines, and Vietnam, which have claims in the South China Sea, do count China as a key trading partner and fear economic retribution.[15]

Questions are being raised regarding the capability of the Quad to neutralize the China threat in the Indian Ocean and the South China Sea, as the ultimate vision of China is to ensure that the United States turns its gaze away from China's backyard. However, the Biden administration is determined to continue Trumpism in terms of making China "play by international rules." A strong and growing economic and military bilateral relationship between India and the USA could concern China (Fickling, 2020). Concurrently, China–USA relations will have their fallout for all economies.

---

[13] James Griffiths, CNN, https://edition.cnn.com/2020/10/27/asia/us-india-defense-china-intl-hnk/index.html;October 27, 2020; accessed on January 13, 2021.

[14] Phase 1 of the Exercise MALABAR 20 involved the participation by Indian Navy (IN), United States Navy (USN), Japan Maritime Self Defence Force (JMSDF), and Royal Australian Navy (RAN); this commenced off Visakhapatnam in the Bay of Bengal from 03 to November 6 2020. Phase 2 of MALABAR 20 has been conducted in the Arabian Sea in mid-November 2020.

[15] Cliff Venzon, Kentaro Iwamoto, and Francesca Regalado, Nikkei staff writers. November 12, 2020, https://asia.nikkei.com/Politics/US-elections-2020/Three-ways-Biden-will-immediately-shift-US-policy-on-Asia; accessed on January 9, 2021.

Washington has long strived not to take sides in the South China Sea disputes. However, with the current intensifying USA's competition with China, this is also changing. The United States State Department has repeatedly criticized Beijing's behavior vis-à-vis Vietnam in the South China Sea, while acknowledging Hanoi's legal right to use resources in its EEZ. The US State Department has significantly updated the country's position by explicitly rejecting China's claims and supporting Southeast Asian claimants' rights to exploit offshore resources. This has been an important development for Vietnam, which had been politically and economically impacted by China's possession of these maritime resources.

The China challenge for India and Vietnam has not been assuaged by Trump's vilification of China and the trade war. Joe Biden, while not ruling out cooperation with China on issues of common concern, seeks to regain the trust of allies through greater emphasis on Quad, military deployment in the South China Sea, and upgrading the protocol status of Taiwan.

7.3.2 Manifestations

7.3.2.1 Aligning with Extra-Regional Powers

Vietnam is one among several countries that is worried about China's international conduct under the present regime of Xi Jinping. There is a rising tide of interrogation that relates to China's present path of establishing a Sino-centric order. China's penchant for asserting its perceived rights and place of prominence in the international system is not lost on anyone.

On Vietnam's strengthening relations with extra-regional powers, the following recent engagement merits attention. Ever since the 2014 oil rig crisis and ensuing protests, Vietnam has strengthened its relationship with the United States, which it views as necessary to balance China's increasing security and economic clout in the Indo-Pacific (Nguyen & Truong, 2018). In 2015, Nguyen Phu Trong became the first CPV General Secretary to visit the White House to discuss shared security concerns. Another milestone in bilateral relations occurred in 2016 when the United States lifted its lethal weapons embargo on Vietnam. In 2018, a US aircraft carrier, the USS Carl Vinson, visited Vietnam. According to Derek Grossman, the mention of UNCLOS, the East and South China Sea, in the Quad summit's statement on March 13, 2021, was appreciated by Vietnam. However, Biden can do more to reassure this key ally in the Indo-Pacific, by inviting General Secretary Trong for a visit to the White House.[16]

In addition, Japan and India are key security partners for Vietnam. Given that Shinzo Abe, Japan's former Prime Minister, had adopted more assertive security and foreign policy for Japan, Hanoi has procured maritime and other defense equipment

---

[16] Derek Grossman, https://www.rand.org/blog/2021/03/vietnam-must-be-pleased-with-the-biden-administration.html; accessed on May 26, 2021.

from Tokyo to bolster its capabilities in the South China Sea. His successor, Suga, visited Vietnam and Indonesia (in October 2020) and the USA (in April 2021).

Hanoi's reconciliation with Washington and improving relations with other powers are essential steps toward dealing with China. Hanoi's continued security and economic outreach with external partners and institutions demonstrates the second paradigm of international integration.

As stated earlier, security ties between New Delhi and Hanoi are being strengthened, including increased personnel training, equipment procurement, and other defense- and maritime-related cooperation (Parameswaran, 2018). India's partnerships with other powers, especially, but not only, with the United States also merit attention. India signed the BECA with the United States in October 2020 as well as the Logistics Exchange Memorandum of Agreement (LEMOA) and the Communications Compatibility and Security Agreement (COMCASA). This finalizes a troika of "foundational pacts" for deep military cooperation.[17] The US support to the cause of the Tibetans, in the form of America's Tibetan Policy and Support Act (TPSA), which became law recently, could provide a lever for India. Passed with bipartisan support, TPSA establishes a US policy that the selection of Tibetan religious leaders, including the Dalai Lama's successor, is a decision to be made only by Tibetans, free from Beijing's interference. It mandates sanctions against Chinese officials interfering in such processes Tibet.[18]

The boundary crisis has also resulted in India doubling down on partnerships with like-minded countries. They help India (1) enhance its own capabilities, (2) balance and deter China, and (3) ensure that a rules-based and multipolar order prevails in the region. India is moving forward with deepening ties with Quad partners, viz. USA, Australia, and Japan. Bilaterally, Delhi has been in close touch with Washington during the crisis and has seen the USA as helpful both as a source of diplomatic support, military equipment, and intelligence sharing which also cemented ties through the US–India 2 + 2 Ministerial Dialogue, held in October 2020 in New Delhi. Delhi signed the military logistics agreement with Japan in September 2020. It has signed one with Canberra, upgraded its 2 + 2 Dialogue with Australia to the ministerial level, and signed an agreement to cooperate on cyberaffairs and critical technology. India has already signed mutual logistics support agreements with the USA, France, and Singapore. Beyond the bilateral dynamics, concerns about dependence on China have also led India, along with Australia and Japan, to launch the Supply Chain Resilience Initiative. Indeed, India can be expected to participate in other such issue or interest-based coalitions as well. For instance, the D10 (G7 + Australia, India, South Korea, Britain proposed dealing with concerns related to

---

[17] Shubhajit Roy, Nov.3, 2020; https://indianexpress.com/article/explained/beca-india-us-trade-agr eements-rajnath-singh-mike-pompeo-6906637/; accessed on May 26, 2021.

[18] The Indo-Tibetan border was largely peaceful throughout history until China occupied the buffer Tibet in 1951, imposing itself as India's neighbour and then waging war 11 years later. Brahma Chellaney, https://timesofindia.indiatimes.com/blogs/toi-edit-page/wake-up-call-on-tibet-americas-tibet-law-should-spur-new-delhi-to-reclaim-lost-leverage-on-china/; January 13, 2021; accessed on January 14, 2021.

reliance on China for 5G and other technologies) or the global partnership on artificial intelligence. Delhi has also taken the lead in forming other such initiatives such as the International Solar Alliance and the Global Coalition for Disaster-Resilient Infrastructure (China is not a member of any one of these) (Madan, 2020).

7.3.2.2 Vietnam as ASEAN Chair 2020 and Engagement in the Multilateral Forums

Vietnam, as a rising Asian economy, is being courted by several countries, including Western powers. Vietnam has held the rotating ASEAN chair in 2020 and organized the ASEAN Defense Ministers Meeting (ADMM) and ADMM-Plus. The successful outcome of its tenure has ensured ASEAN's unity and centrality for regional groupings. This makes it a partner of significance in regional and multilateral institutions.

The 37th ASEAN summit chairman's statement stressed that there was a need for rising above regional impediments so as to sustain growth. It also acknowledged a need to recognize the dividend of peace, security, stability, and neutrality for the region, and an imperative for synergy among the ASEAN-led mechanisms. This would impart a cohesive outlook towards the Indo-Pacific architecture. Vietnam, as the chair, underlined the necessity for concluding a Code of Conduct (COC) in the South China Sea in the mutually agreed timeframe, in consonance with United Nations Convention on the Law of Sea (UNCLOS) 1982 and which adheres to international law. Concerns were also raised regarding reclamation activities and serious incidents in the SCS. These hold the potential for escalation of maritime disputes. Eschewing of militarization activities in SCS also found a mention. Such an articulation on SCS by the chair was unambiguous and forthright as compared to many such statements made by the previous chairs and especially so in July 2012 when Cambodia was the chair and when no joint communiqué of the ASEAN Foreign Ministers summit could be issued (Anand, 2020).

Vietnam also holds a new non-permanent seat on the United Nations Security Council and participates in UN peacekeeping missions. The country's relations with both the USA and Europe are also vibrant. The European Union also concluded an FTA with Vietnam, strengthening the latter's position as a key trading partner, with the potential of being a critical node in global supply chains. The United States has also launched the Mekong–USA Partnership, (building on the success of the Lower Mekong Initiative) on September 11, 2020. On January 13, 2021, India was also invited for the first "Friends of the Mekong Policy Dialogue: Towards a resilient and connected the Mekong."[19]

The United States seeks to expand engagement with Mainland SEA to limit China's footprint in the region. China's Global Times has reacted sharply to this

---

[19] Towards a resilient and connected Mekong, https://www.state.gov/towards-a-resilient-and-con nected-mekong/; January 12, 2021; accessed on January 16, 2021.

maneuvering by the United States and asserts that, "the USA is desperately looking for a new agenda to suppress China around the world."[20]

India joined the United Nations Security Council (UNSC) as a non-permanent member on January 4, 2021, beginning a two-year tenure. But New Delhi hopes that this time, its presence in the UNSC will help move the organization toward the ultimate reform: a permanent seat on the UNSC for India. Vietnam is also being viewed as a potential member of the Quad Plus expansion by the four Quad countries, especially India. The reasons for this are several. Here again, it is China's intruding footprint which countries must surmount collectively; either as minilateral groupings or groupings of like-minded countries.[21]

7.3.2.3 Comprehensive Strategic Partnership

The India–Vietnam Comprehensive Strategic Partnership has assumed new dimensions. This has also been discussed in the preceding chapter. The joint naval exercise in the South China Sea was conducted on December 26–27, 2020. This followed two significant virtual meetings between Indian Prime Minister, Narendra Modi, and his Vietnamese counterpart, Nguyen Xuan Phuc, on December 21; and another meeting between Defense Minister Rajnath Singh and his Vietnamese counterpart General Ngo Xuan Lich, in November 2020. At the virtual summit, India and Vietnam agreed to enhance their defense and security partnership by stepping up "military-to-military exchanges, training, and capacity building programs across the three services and coast guards" and to "intensify their defense industry collaboration building on India's defense credit lines extended to Vietnam." In the November 2020 meeting, India and Vietnam signed an implementation agreement on hydrography.[22]

7.3.2.4 Defense Cooperation and Arms Deals

India has strengthened its defense engagement by rendering training and capacity building of the Vietnamese Armed Forces as well as efficient modernization of its security forces. The 12 agreements signed during Modi's visit to Vietnam in 2016 covering cybersecurity, ship building, UN peacekeeping operations, and naval information sharing are within the framework of the joint partnership agreement. There are several strands of teamwork which have been firmed up between the Army, Air Force, Navies, and Coast Guards of the two countries. There will be an exchange of strategic maritime data, joint defense production, as well as training and capacity building. The

---

[20] Hu Yuwei Source: Global Times Published: 2020/9/15. https://www.globaltimes.cn/content/120 0997.shtml; accessed on January 13, 2021.

[21] Mohammed Zeeshan, https://thediplomat.com/2021/01/indias-effort-to-reform-the-united-nat ions-security-council-demands-a-new-mindset/; January 5, 2021; accessed on January 10, 2021.

[22] K. Yhome, https://www.orfonline.org/expert-speak/strengthening-india-strategic-ties-mekong-subregion/; January 5, 2021; accessed on January 13, 2021.

two countries are in discussions over the selling of the supersonic BrahMos missile by India to Vietnam. India has also made the offer of Akash surface-to-air missile systems. The missiles have an interception range of 25 km against hostile aircraft, helicopters, and drones. The significance of the timing of endeavors is important because both countries are strengthening bilateral military ties. New Delhi's offering of a Line of Credit of US$100 to build high-speed patrol vessels has been highly appreciated by Hanoi (Sarma, 2020).

According to the Stockholm International Peace Research Institute's (SIPRI), there has been a 700% surge in Vietnam's defense procurements since 2015. Vietnam's discreet military buildup, designed as a deterrent, is aimed to secure its 200 nautical mile exclusive economic zone (EEZ). The China factor is one of the reasons Vietnam is shopping for fighter jets and more advanced missile systems. It has added six kilo-class submarines too, purchased from Russia (Panda, 2017: 68).

7.3.2.5 Vietnam and India: Position on SCS Disputes

As Chair of ASEAN in 2020, Vietnam has consolidated the ASEAN position on regional issues including the fight against COVID-19 and balancing the grouping's relationship with the U.S. and China. On the South China Sea (East Sea in Vietnam), Vietnam's chairpersonship has been able to place emphasis on the relevance of UNCLOS. Vietnam's success as the ASEAN chair saw the bloc strongly emphasizing its principled stand on the South China Sea. This was achieved due to dynamism displayed by Vietnam in managing the bloc's relationship with the two powers. ASEAN's resolve against China's claims was visible in 2020 (under Vietnam's chairmanship), as the 10-nation bloc affirmed that UNCLOS should be the basis of sovereign rights and entitlements in the South China Sea.

India has been concerned over China's aggressive moves in the South China Sea, including building defense-related infrastructures in the disputed waters, and China's stated plan to create an Air Defense Identification Zone (ADIZ) covering the disputed Pratas, Paracel, and Spratly Islands. India has continued to express concern about such actions and incidents. Therefore, it is prudent that India plays an active role in ensuring freedom of navigation and freedom of flying in the SCS region. Delhi may even consider playing a role in settling disagreements in SCS.[23]

During the virtual meeting of Modi and his counterpart Nguyen Xuan Phuc, both leaders spoke of the importance of a "rules-based order in the region, including upholding international law, especially the UNCLOS (the United Nations Convention for the Law of the Sea)." The leaders also stated that a "peaceful, stable, secure, free, open, inclusive and rules-based region is in the common interest of all countries." Prime Minister Modi stressed that the Code of Conduct negotiations on the South China Sea should not prejudice the interest of other countries in the region. The Indian

---

[23] Read more at: https://economictimes.indiatimes.com/news/politics-and-nation/vietnam-key-par tner-in-delhis-indo-pacific-vision-key-pillar-of-act-east-policy/articleshow/79850863.cms?utm_ source=contentofinterest&utm_medium=text&utm_campaign=cppst.

position was also underlined in the bilateral document—"India–Vietnam Joint Vision for Peace, Prosperity and People"—released after the December 2020 summit. "Both leaders further called for the full and effective implementation of the Declaration on the Conduct of Parties in the South China Sea (DOC) in its entirety and the substantive negotiations towards the early conclusion of a substantive and effective Code of Conduct in the South China Sea (COC) in accordance with international law, especially UNCLOS, that does not prejudice the legitimate rights and interests of all nations including those not party to these negotiations," it stated.[24]

7.3.2.6 Enhanced Economic Cooperation and Connectivity

India–Vietnam economic ties can be traced to 1978 when the bilateral trade agreement was signed. By 1982, the India–Vietnam joint commission was set up for economic, technical, and scientific cooperation. The initial years saw limited trade between the two countries whereby India facilitated a line of credit worth $400 million to Vietnam. India's first investment came from OVL in 1989 off the coast of Vung Tau, near Ho Chi Minh City. Bilateral trade in the early years suffered due to the 1997 Asian financial crisis, which was marked by a slowdown in Vietnam's economy. By 1999, Indian exports had contributed to 90% of the total bilateral trade of $150 million with Indian private sector companies like Ranbaxy and Godrej expanding their footprint in Vietnam.

Bilateral trade touched $1 billion in 2006, crossed the $2 billion mark in 2009, reached $7.8 billion in 2016 and $12 billion before the pandemic. A major impetus to economic ties came with signing the India—ASEAN Free Trade Agreement in August 2009. India began exporting pharmaceuticals, plastics, chemicals, and metals to Vietnam, while Vietnam exported steel, rubber, and electronic items to India. The two countries expanded cooperation in areas such as space exploration and cybersecurity, as well as in the exploration of Outer Space for Peaceful Purposes.

India has also set up a satellite tracking facility in Ho Chi Minh City. Although visualized as a civilian facility, this could be of strategic relevance, especially in tracking Chinese movement in the sea. It has been planned and implemented by the Indian Space Research Organisation (Harsh Pant, Policy Brief, 2018).

7.3.3 Managing China: The Restraints

After discussing the motivations and manifestations of the robust comprehensive partnership between India and Vietnam, it is important to articulate the restraining factors in the relationship.

---

[24] South China Sea Code of Conduct Negotiations shouldn't discriminate: India to Vietnam, https://thewire.in/diplomacy/south-china-sea-code-of-conduct-negotiations-shouldnt-dis criminate-india-to-vietnam; December 22, 2020, accessed on January 13, 2021.

7.3.3.1 Vietnam and India: Ideologies and Policies

After the end of the Cold War, Vietnam has consistently pursued both internal and external balancing against China. Hanoi began to update its naval and air capabilities in the 1990s and accelerated its modernization efforts in the 2000s (Le Hong, 2013). Over the period 2000 to 2017, there was a huge arms acquisition by Hanoi. These included 36 Su-30MK multirole jet fighters, 4 Gepard guided-missile frigates with at least 500 anti-ship missiles, and 6 kilo-class submarines—all of which improved Vietnam's ability to monitor its maritime zones and occupy features in the South China Sea (Stockholm International Peace Research Institute, 2018). In addition to these internal balancing efforts, Vietnam has also pursued multipolar external balancing by establishing strategic partnerships with five major powers: China, India, Japan, Russia, and the United States (Hoang, 2019: 4; Thayer, 2017). However, to avoid becoming entangled in great power rivalries—especially between Beijing and Washington—Hanoi has maintained a national defense policy, which dates back to its first Defense Paper in 1988, viz. of 'Three Nos': **no** to joining any military alliance; **no** to permitting foreign military bases on Vietnamese soil; and **no** to allowing a foreign country to use Vietnamese soil to carry out military activities against other countries (Le Hong, 2013). The national defense policy of Vietnam contributes to demonstrating openness, diversification, and multilateralization of external relations, without aligning with one country against another and without adopting a confrontational stance against any country. The "Three Nos" spirit was reiterated in Vietnam's next two Defense White Papers of 2004 and 2009.

Vietnam's Defense White Paper published in late 2012 states: "Vietnam has consistently advocated neither joining any military alliances, siding with one country against another, giving any other countries permission to set up military bases or use its territory to carry out military activities against other countries nor using force or threatening to use force in international relations. Vietnam also promotes defense collaboration with countries to improve its capabilities to protect the country and address common security concerns."

Asia is facing major geopolitical risks due to China's rise in power and its escalation of territorial claims in the South China Sea, the nuclear arms race, cyberthreats, and the promotion of terrorism. During the uncertain times, when the regional situation turned complicated and unpredictable, especially with US–China dissension, Vietnam considered developing a defense strategy that could adapt to the transforming situation.

The country's latest Defense White Paper announced in 2019 was categorized into three parts: the strategic context and national defense policy, building the all-people national defense, and the development of the Vietnam People's Army. Vietnam seeks "more friends and less enemies," and that phrase is reflected in its continuous Three Nos defense policy, to which a new "no"—"not using force or threatening the use of force in international relations"—has been included. Despite the additional "no," it is expected that Vietnam's overall defense position will not change. Vietnam's Deputy Minister of national defense, Colonel General Vinh Chi Nguyen, explained that Vietnam launched this new Defense White Paper for all Vietnamese to understand the current national defense strategy. Hence, Vietnamese strategists no longer talk about the long-standing "three nos" policy, but instead a transformed "four nos and one depend." This means no military alliances, no taking sides with one country against another, no foreign military bases, and no using force or threatening to use force in international relations; but, "depending on circumstances and specific conditions, Vietnam will consider developing necessary, appropriate defense and military relations with other countries."[25]

In an interview to the authors, Prof. Do Thu Ha shared that Vietnam manages the China threat with its own unique approach. In her words, Vietnam government understands that "Action is bigger than words. The party leadership is very skillful in adapting to the environment and in de-escalating any difficult situation. We believe in quiet negotiations coupled with fierce action." Elucidating on the subject, she added, "During the border war in 1979 with China, the students were very angry and wanted to demonstrate. However, the government prevented the demonstrations against China. This even invited criticism from within and outside the country. When, over one and a half months, two million Chinese tried to enter Vietnamese territory, but they could not proceed beyond 10 km. The Vietnamese military were successful in the pushback." Prof. Ha also shared another incident of defusing a difficult situation differently from that by other nations. In her words, "It was in 2013 when a Chinese battleship entered Vietnamese waters. China had also sent battleships to Japan and America. While America caught the ship near a port in Alaska and chained it with 400 sailors on it and Japan also reacted fiercely, all that Vietnam did was to make a video clip of the ship and invite 300 foreign journalists to view from a distance how Chinese ships attacked Vietnamese fishermen. Given that China is conscious of its 'image', Vietnam leveraged a soft approach to internationalize and publicize Chinese actions. We have both soft and hard skills and we use subtle but effective action, because we understand China well." When questioned on India's approach, she articulated, "India prefers to employ diplomatic tools and non-violent methods and retaliates only when the situation is out of control. However, in Vietnam, everyone is trained in military action—I can fight and shoot. Everyone has to undergo compulsory military training from the age of 16. Everyone here is a soldier and Vietnam uses military action when required."[26]

Hence, it is well known that Sino-Vietnam relations are neither one of contestation nor overly friendly. Yet, Vietnam must keep its options open to engaging with other countries. Integration of China into global capitalism increased economic interdependence in East Asia but also intensified political tensions (Pakhamov, 2021: 70). For Vietnam too, China is a neighbor of increasing global influence. China has also increased its soft power in terms of economic and cultural relations in Southeast Asia, including with Vietnam. Vietnam has also initiated 'shuttle diplomacy' and promoted cooperation at three different levels: "Large neighbor" diplomacy toward

---

[25] Nguyen The Phuong|December 17, 2019; https://amti.csis.org/vietnams-2019-defense-white-paper-preparing-for-a-fragile-future; accessed on January 13, 2021.

[26] Interview of Prof. Do Thu Ha to the authors on August 13, 2021.

China; 'neighborhood' diplomacy with countries of strategic importance, such as Laos and Cambodia; and diplomacy with 'major powers' such as the United States and Russia.

As far as India is concerned, experts agree that Sino-India relations had been for the decades of the 1960s, 70s, and 80s tied to the narrative of a "betrayal," and it is this belief that took root post-1962 (Jaishankar, 2020: 76). It is also true that post-1962, the demonization of China stood in the way of an objective analysis of India–China relations until the 1990s. Ever since and up to April 2020, the bilateral ties had strengthened through increasing economic interdependence, accentuation of people-to-people ties, and a narrative which underlined the important role of the two Asian giants for world peace and prosperity. India had continued to maintain a policy of non-alignment throughout the Cold War period and beyond. She had always been sensitive to China's core interests relating to Tibet and also kept its engagement with Taiwan at a minimal level. However, under Xi Jinping's regime, China's encirclement of India again resulted in India adopting a cautious foreign policy approach. Post the 2020 border standoff, India has also channelized its priorities to strengthening alliances with the United States, Japan, Australia, and Vietnam on strategic matters.

7.3.3.2 Civilizational and Historical Linkages

China and India share civilizational and cultural linkages over several centuries. Sino-Indian trading relations between the seventh and twentieth centuries transformed from Buddhist-dominated exchanges to market-centered commercial transactions, resulting in interactions among communities on both sides, development of urban settlements of migrants, and a shared resistance to British imperialist designs and hostilities (Marwah, 2018: 3–23). Buddhism was indeed important in both the Indian subcontinent and China for approximately one millennium, and there were exchanges as Indian translators went to China and Chinese pilgrims traveled to India. Given this shared Buddhist setting, great stories have been generated by both countries of intimate Sino-Indian relations in the past, which are mooted as an example for present and future interstate relations (Scott, 2016).

According to Wang Gungwu, in Vietnam, as in parts of Southwest China like the Nan Zhao kingdom in Yunnan, the Buddhism that took root had been impacted by the Tang Chinese classical and literary education and creative arts (including music and dance, painting and calligraphy, architecture and the plastic arts). This was most visible among the aristocracy and official classes. Chinese influence continues to be pervasive in societal attitudes and behavior. The rise of China did have cultural implications in what is exported (Wang, 2004).

In an interview to the authors, Ambassador Thanh stated, "In Vietnam our morning starts with Chinese tea and noodles; the people-to-people connections are strong; the influence of China is in our day to day life; hence for us to come out of her clutches, there needs to be 24 × 7 engagement of other partner countries."

7.3.3.3 The Economic Compulsions

Given the large quantum of Chinese investment in Indian businesses and India's increasing trade dependency on China, experts question the viability of immediate decoupling from China. China accounted for over 5% of India's total exports in 2019–20 and more than 14% of imports. India runs a huge trade deficit with China, the biggest exporter to India. Chinese exports to India comprise smartphones, electrical appliances, power plant inputs, fertilizers, auto components, finished steel products, and capital goods like power plants, telecom equipment, metro rail coaches, iron and steel products, pharmaceutical ingredients, chemicals and plastics, and engineering goods, among other things. According to invest in India, India's imports from China jumped 45 times since 2000 to reach over $70 billion in 2018–19. Foreign direct investments from China have been received in several sectors, including, among others, renewable energy (solar panels), electrical equipment, automotive, and chemicals. India's commerce ministry pegged the inward FDI from China at $8 billion for 2018–19. There are almost 75 manufacturing facilities for smartphones, consumer appliances, automobiles, optical fiber, and chemicals. Oppo, Vivo, Fosun International, Haier, SAIC, and Midea are some of India's largest Chinese brands and manufacturers. Chinese tech investors have put an estimated $4 billion into Indian start-ups. As of March 2020, 18 of India's 30 unicorns were Chinese funded. India's pharmaceutical industry is the third-largest in the world in volume and ranks 14 by value; however, it imports two-thirds of its active pharmaceutical ingredients, or critical ingredients of drugs, from China.[27]

Vietnam too has a robust economic engagement with China. The two-way trade grew rapidly over the period 2000–17; in fact, this increased by almost 30 times, from USD 3 billion in 2000 to almost USD 88 billion in 2017 (Le Hong, 2019). In 2020, bilateral trade was $103 billion, with imports comprising almost two-thirds.

7.3.3.4 Existential Challenges

Sears writes about the growing disjuncture (or "contradiction") between the material context of anthropogenic existential threats ("forces of destruction"); and the security practices of war, the use of military force, and the balance-of-power ("modes of protection"); the political units of nation states and structure of international anarchy ("political superstructure"); and the primacy of "national security" and doctrines of "self-help" and "power politics" in international politics ("security ideologies"). The centrality of national security and survival in international politics is ever significant, and in an age of existential threats, "security" is better understood as about the survival of humanity (Sears, 2020).

The pandemic has further fueled China's aggressive postures, territorial ambitions, and belligerent tone. This has created intense fears among countries, viz. fears about

---

[27] Read more at https://www.bloombergquint.com/economy-finance/six-things-to-know-about-india-china-economic-relations.

the loss of sovereignty, territory, and political independence. Policies of balancing, hedging, and bandwagoning or a combination of these seem to be the only option for countries like India and Vietnam. Both have witnessed Chinese encroachment on their territory on the mainland and maritime space, respectively.

It does not help that at the start of 2021, Xi Jinping, who is also Chairman of the Central Military Commission (CMC), said the armed forces must devise strategies for the new era and take on responsibilities for preparing and waging war. *A former director of Intelligence and Information Operations for the US Pacific Fleet, predicts that,* "Given the PLA Navy's operational and naval construction trajectory, the PRC's overall economic strength, the PLA Navy's decade long experience operating in the far seas, and its established track record of intimidating neighbours to forfeit their coastal state rights to China, we can also assess the PRC is on track to able to achieve sea control in the global maritime commons as early as 2030, and potentially even sea superiority by 2049, and it will use its power for the expansion of China's interests at the expense of others. A global PLA Navy will increasingly threaten US, India and allied interests abroad, increasing, not decreasing the risk of major powers war."[28]

In his words, "People's Liberation Army (PLA) must be ready to 'act at any second' and should remain on 'full-time combat readiness'." He also added, "Frontline frictions must be used to polish troop capabilities and training exercises need to incorporate technology."[29] Vietnam is listening to these cautionary statements.

The Sino-India standoff continued unabated from April 2020 till the disengagement process commenced in early 2021. The situation on India's borders was very fluid in 2020; the Chinese side preparedness was prohibitive with the best of military hardware. India deployed around 50,000 troops in various mountainous locations in Eastern Ladakh. This was despite the apparent bonhomie between the two leaders having met more than 18 times since 2014 and despite the Wuhan and Mamallapuram summit meetings, in 2017 and 2019, respectively. A report claimed that President Xi Jinping had given a go-ahead for the People's Liberation Army (PLA) to test drones and new infantry launchers, upgraded with anti-tank and anti-bunker capacities near the Line of Actual Control (LAC) border it shares with India.[30] China's completion of the strategic Tibet highway close to Arunachal Pradesh as well as its gaining control of the Hambantota port and Colombo City project in 2021 portends that India cannot let her guard down.

---

[28] China's global Navy eyeing sea control by 2030, superiority by 2049, https://www.sundayguardianlive.com/news/chinas-global-navy-eyeing-sea-control-2030-superiority-2049 Captain James E. Fanell (Retd); June 13, 2020, accessed on January 9, 2021.

[29] Xi-Jinping orders Chinese Military to scale up combat readiness, https://www.business-standard.com/article/current-affairs/xi-jinping-orders-chinese-military-to-scale-up-combat-readiness-121010500708_1.html; January 5, 2021; accessed on January 9, 2021.

[30] Mansi Asthana, November 3, 2020; https://eurasiantimes.com/why-indian-t-90-especially-t-72-tanks-are-highly-vulnerable-to-chinese-kamikaze-drones/; accessed on January 9, 2021.

7.3.3.5 A China-Led Asian Global Order

Several American Presidents were keen to see China being mainstreamed in the multilateral system. In fact, the Clinton administration helped China become a member of the WTO. Ever since, China has reaped the gains of free trade, signing several bilateral and multilateral deals. Obama, during his Presidency, desired to anchor America's presence in East and Southeast Asia through the Trans-Pacific Partnership (TPP), which was expected to yield rich, long-term dividends for the American economy. In fact, Trump gifted China a major geopolitical gift by walking away from the TPP. China did not lose much time in bringing ASEAN countries along with Japan, South Korea, Australia, and New Zealand into RCEP in November 2020.

The AIIB is another major initiative by China not only to fund BRI projects in partner countries, but also to be viewed as a benefactor for the developing world. Although during the entire period of the Cold War, America took the lead in building the world's multilateral architecture, which included the Bretton Woods system, the Marshall Plan, and NATO, it is now China, not America, that is taking the lead in edifying a new multilateral architecture. Despite the USA opposing these initiatives, it could not stop the UK, Germany, India, and Vietnam from joining as founding members of AIIB, which is proving itself to be a better-governed institution than the IMF and the World Bank. Its standard of corporate governance is higher and more transparent (Mahbubani, 2020: 45–49).

7.4 Conclusion

There is clear evidence of an alignment of India—ASEAN strategic interests. These alignments and convergences are perceptible particularly with Vietnam, as both countries have common concerns, especially with regard to a China-led Asian/global order. Both countries uphold the importance of safeguarding the freedom of navigation of the seas, the right of overflight and the importance of peaceful settlement of disputes in accordance with the United Nations Convention on the Law of the Seas (UNCLOS). There is an urgency among the maritime ASEAN nations for the Code of Conduct to be signed. This was expressed at the April 2021 Boao Forum, wherein the expectation of this being finalized with China by end 2021 remains elusive as ever. India has reaffirmed its position through joint statements issued with Vietnam and other countries such as Japan and the USA. There is every intent that disputes must be resolved through peaceful means without coercion and the exercise of self-restraint. Several experts believe that India has been shaken out of its erstwhile position of non-alignment and coerced to align with major powers, due to the latter's uncompromising and unpredictable strategizing. Strategists also believe that India's potential of a system shaping capacity seems intertwined with the USA continuing its thesis of propping up India to counter China (Singh, 2021: 40).

Vietnam is a partner of significance for India, not only for its cultural and historical linkages, but also for the strategic rationale. In this context, Ambassador Chau, in an interview to the authors opined, "Vietnam and India are now in preparations for the 50th anniversary of the diplomatic relations and 5th anniversary of the comprehensive strategic partnership. We have been enjoying mutual interests in various fields ranging from political, defence, economic to scientific-technological, cultural and people-to-people exchanges. There remains, however, considerable room for further development.

Given that India and Vietnam are both serving as non-permanent members of the United Nations Security Council in 2021, we should closely work together to contribute to the maintenance of peace, stability and prosperity in the region and the world. You also mentioned the fact that both countries are having territorial tensions with China. It is not about going with one against another, but we have shared interests in defending the status quo and rule of law. We need to articulate our opposition to and coordinate our actions against unlawful claims and coercive behavior. Peace, stability, and rules-based order South China Sea is not only an issue among the concerned parties but also one of regional concerns which could affect the interests of all countries in and outside the region. Therefore, countries should raise their voices to protect peace, stability, security and freedom of navigation and overflight in the area, emphasize the legal framework set out by the UNCLOS. I would emphasize, Vietnam and India share the position that UNCLOS is the basis for determining maritime entitlements, sovereign rights, jurisdiction and legitimate interests over maritime zones." India is also committed to supporting Vietnam with combat aircraft and cruise missiles, as potent capabilities against China.

To manage the China challenge, both countries are expanding their security alliances with USA and Japan. With India, both countries are engaged in the Quadrilateral Security Dialogue with joint naval exercises, exhibiting the potential for subverting any collision on the seas.

The Biden administration's Vietnam policy is fairly lucid, seeking greater engagement; the evidence is palpable that there will be more continuity than change, and bilateral ties will strengthen despite certain setbacks. First, the two countries' strategic interests should continue to converge, especially in the South China Sea. Due to the intensifying US–China strategic competition, the Biden administration will likely maintain a tough stance on China. If China continues to act aggressively in the South China Sea, the two countries may further deepen their strategic engagement. USA should continue to provide Vietnam with maritime capacity building assistance and engage Vietnam in minilateral security arrangements like Quad-based exercises. Vietnam may acquire arms and military equipment from the USA or offer American forces greater access to its military facilities. Second, the issue of America's trade deficit with Vietnam will need to be assessed in the context of the former reducing reliance on imports from China.

It may be too early to predict the extent to which Biden would endeavor to reassert US leadership role in the Comprehensive and Progressive Agreement for Trans-Pacific Partnership (CPTPP).

Third, Biden personally has a positive view of Vietnam. From his experience of a visit to Vietnam in 2015, to the appointment of Blinken, who has a friendly disposition toward Vietnam, expectations of a well-articulated Vietnam policy are in the offing. While there may be apprehensions of his view on issues of human rights, it is expected that Vietnam will improve its record, and this will not be a thorn in the bilateral engagement (Le Hong, 2019).

In fact, the anti-China stance taken by Trump seems to have found favor among the strategic community both in India and Vietnam. The tough posture by the USA has also provided opportunities for an industrialization-led growth thrust in the two countries.

Hence, it is important to interrogate: Will China change? The answer is "highly unlikely." According to Yun Sun, "With the heightened great power competition and a heightened sense of vulnerability, China is likely to grow even more defensive and counterattack any country, any media, or any individual critical of China's behavior and performance in the pandemic. It is also a war of competing narratives, competing for political systems and a war of competing ideologies (Sun, 2020).

The Chinese are the masters of Wei qi, or the game of 'Go', which implies encirclement. In this decade of the 2020s, China is preparing itself for multiple battles and multiple encounters. China's grey zone operations with the maritime militia ships have been spotted operating with the China Coast Guard and People's Liberation Army Navy ships in the SCS. A U.S. carrier strike group and amphibious ready group are also in these waters after their age-old ally Philippines raised the alarm in March 2021, when over 200 Chinese vessels entered their EEZ.

The growth in total military spending in 2019 was largely influenced by expenditure patterns in the United States and China, which together account for over half of the world's military spending. The USA increased its spending to reach $732 billion in 2019. This was 2.7 times larger than the $261 billion spent by China, the world's next highest spender. China's total was 5.1% higher than in 2018 and 85% higher than in 2010. With a 16% decrease in its spending, Saudi Arabia fell from being the third-largest spender in 2018 to fifth position in 2019. India's spending of $71.1 billion ranked it as the third-largest spender for the first time, while Russia's increase of 4.5% moved it up from fifth to fourth (SIPRI Report, 2020).

Countries rise in defense expenditure is evidently to be battle-ready. The turmoil in the global order heightened in 2020 shows no signs of an ebb in 2021 and beyond. Hanoi's and New Delhi's mounting sense of the China threat have been converging for some time, as is evident from the above discussion. However, post the pandemic, this trend has been even more pronounced than anticipated, as evident from Beijing's aggressive postures and muscular positions in the South China Sea and on the Sino-India border. To hedge its bets and in recognition of these similar views, both Vietnam and India have strived to further strengthen diplomatic ties and partnerships with key powers, including the United States, Japan, the EU, and Australia. These powers have improved security collaboration, devoting special attention to maritime issues. It was not without reason that The May 1st, 2021 edition of the Economist had "*Taiwan: The most dangerous place on Earth*," for its cover story: It is in the waters in the vicinity of Vietnam that the complexities are escalating!

The next, i.e., the final chapter of our book provides a futuristic perspective even as this bilateral partnership remains supercharged on the foundations of strategic compulsions.

References

Ahmed, I. (2012). Regionalism in South Asia: A conceptual note. *Millennial Asia, 3*(1), 95–103.

Ali, S. M. (1999). *Cold war in the high Himalayas: The USA, China and South Asia in the 1950s.* Routledge.

Anand, V. (2020). https://www.vifindia.org/article/2020/december/26/yearend-assessment-of-vietnam-s-chairmanship-of-asean-in-2020, December 26, 2020.

Deshpande, G. P. (2010). China and the politics of Southern Asia. *Strategic Analysis, 34*(3), 470–475.

Fickling, D. (2020). Biden, like Trump, will Deepen integration with China. https://www.bloomberg.com/opinion/articles/2020-11-09/biden-like-trump-will-deepen-integration-with-china. Accessed on November 29, 2020.

French, H. W. (2017). *Everything under the Heavens: How the past helps shape China's push for global power* (pp. 17–22). Knopf.

Le Hong, H. (2013). Vietnam's hedging strategy against China since normalization. *Contemporary Southeast Asia, 35*(3), 333–368. http://www.jstor.org/stable/43281263

Le Hong, H. (2019). *Vietnam's position on the South China Sea code of conduct*, issue No. 22 , ISEAS—YUSOF ISHAK INSTITUTE, Singapore

Le Hong, H. (2020). Vietnam–US relations under the Biden Administration. Commentary 2020/191, ISEAS–Yusof Ishak Institute as Fulcrum.

Hoang, P. (2019). Domestic protests and foreign policy: An examination of Anti-China protests in Vietnam and Vietnamese policy towards China regarding the South China Sea. *Journal of Asian Security and International Affairs, 6*(1), 1–29.

Hollihan, T. A., & Zhang, Z. (2016). Media narratives of China's future. *Global Media and China, 1*(1–2), 7–11. https://doi.org/10.1177/2059436416654382

Jaishankar, S. (2020). *The India way: Strategies for an uncertain world.* Harper Collins.

Jorgensen, M. (2020). https://www.lowyinstitute.org/the-interpreter/china-overturning-rules-based-order-within; August 12, 2020. Accessed on January 9, 2021.

Kumar, P. (2021). India balancing China: Exploring soft balancing through Indo-Pacific. *Millennial Asia.* https://doi.org/10.1177/0976399621998274

Lama, M. P. (2017). Renegotiating alternative integration model in the SAARC. *International Studies, 54*(1–4), 82–105.

Madan, T. (2020). https://www.uscc.gov/sites/default/files/2020-09/Madan_Testimony.pdf. September 9, 2020, Accessed on January 9, 2021.

Mahbubani, K. (2020). *Has China won: The Chinese challenge to American primacy.* Public Affairs.

Marwah, R. (2018a). 8: China studies in South and Southeast Asia: A comparative perspective through Sri Lanka and Thailand. *China Studies In South And Southeast Asia: Between Pro-china And Objectivism* (pp. 3–23).

Marwah, R. (2018b). Interview to BBC on March 29, 2018.

Marwah, R., & Ramanayake, S. S. (2021). *China's economic footprint in South and Southeast Asia: A futuristic perspective—Case studies of Pakistan.* World Scientific.

Nguyen, T. T., & Truong, M. V. (2018). The 2014 oil rig crisis and its implications for Vietnam-China relations. In Le & Tsvetov (Eds.), Vietnam's foreign policy under Doi Moi (pp. 72–95). ISEAS Publishing.

Nguyen, Q. H. (2019). Vietnam-China trade relations and the effects of the US-China trade war. *Business and Economic Research, 9*(4), 1. ISSN 2162-4860. http://ber.macrothink.org

Pakhomov, O. (2021). East Asian civilization and the problem of region making. *Millennial Asia, 12*(1), 57–75.

Panda, R. (2017). India-Vietnam relations: Prospects and challenges. *Liberal Studies, 2*(1).

Pant, H. (2018). *India and Vietnam: A "strategic partnership" in the making, Policy brief.* RSIS, NTU

Parameswaran, P. (2018, June 18). India-Vietnam defense relations in the spotlight with bilateral visit. The Diplomat. https://thediplomat.com/2018/06/indiavietnam-defense-relations-in-the-spotlight-with-bilateral-visit

Nguyen. The Phuong|December 17, 2019. https://amti.csis.org/vietnams-2019-defense-white-paper-preparing-for-a-fragile-future. Accessed on January 13, 2021.

SIPRI Report. (2020). https://www.sipri.org/sites/default/files/2020-06/yb20_summary_en_v2.pdf

Sarma, S. (2020). India-Vietnam relations through the prism of the Indo-Pacific concept. *Strategic Analysis, 44*(4), 360–377. https://doi.org/10.1080/09700161.2020.1809213

Scott, D. (2016). Buddhism in current China-India diplomacy. *Journal of Current Chinese Affairs, 45*(3), 139–174. https://journals.sagepub.com/doi/full/10.1177/186810261604500305

Sears, N. A. (June 18, 2020). International politics in the age of existential threats. *Journal of Global Security Studies, ogaa027*. https://doi.org/10.1093/jogss/ogaa027

Singh, S. (2021). The evolving Asian security architecture. In E. Sridharan (Ed.), *Eastward Ho? India in the Indo-Pacific* (p. 40). Orient Blackswan publishers.

Sridharan, E. (2014). The political context of economic cooperation in Asia: The relation between trade integration and security rivalries. *Millennial Asia, 5*(2), 129–136.

Stauch, T. R. (1994). The United States and Vietnam: Overcoming the past and investing in the future. 28 Int'l L 995. https://scholar.smu.edu/til/vol28/iss4/7

Sun. (2020). http://www.theasanforum.org/chinas-wolf-warrior-diplomacy-in-the-covid-19-crisis/. The Asan Forum.

ISEAS Survey. (2020). https://www.iseas.edu.sg/wp-content/uploads/pdfs/TheStateofSEASurveyReport_2020.pdf

Thayer. (2017). Vietnam's foreign policy in an era of rising Sino-US competition and increasing domestic political influence. *Asian Security, 13*(3), 183–199.

Le Thu, H. (2020). Rough waters ahead for Vietnam China relations, Carnegie Endowment, 2020. https://carnegieendowment.org/2020/09/30/rough-waters-ahead-for-vietnam-china-relations-pub-82826. Accessed on January 2, 2021.

Wang, G. (2004). The fourth rise of China: Cultural implications. *China: An International Journal, 2*(2), 311–322. https://doi.org/10.1353/chn.2004.0016

Wong, E. (2010, October 6). Chinese civilian boats roil disputed waters. *The New York Times.* www.nytimes.com/2010/10/06/world/asia/06beijing.html

Chapter 8
Vietnam and India: A Futuristic Perspective

Each period in history comes with its unique set of challenges. The world is in a time of considerable uncertainty, but what is certain is that India and Vietnam's choices will define our future bilateral relations.

As the two countries, Vietnam and India, move toward the next decade of the twenty-first century, their aspirations must be articulated. These emanate from both internal and external motivations. Given that both countries have the world's continuous civilizations, marked by rich histories, the nationalist pride of the people is justified (Maddison, 2001).

8.1 India–Vietnam: Partnering a Vision for the Future

8.1.1 The Political, Strategic, Defense, and Security Vision

India is home to one-sixth of the world's humanity, and its people aspire for a prosperous and safe future in which they can pursue their dreams without fear. India aspires to be a $5 trillion economy in 2025 and become the third world's largest economy in 2030. Her ambitions include assuming a pivotal place in global affairs, achieving a secure neighborhood, peaceful resolution of internal conflicts, protecting people, and strengthening its capacities.[1]

In Vietnam, the Thirteenth Party Congress (25/1–2/2/2021) has outlined specific objectives for the future trajectory of her development: (1) By 2025, when Vietnam celebrates the 50th anniversary of the complete liberation of the South, the reunification of the country: Vietnam is a developing country with modern industry, surpassing the low middle-income level; (2) By 2030, celebrating the 100th anniversary of the Party's establishment: being a developing country with modern industry and high

---

[1] India's National Security Strategy, https://manifesto.inc.in/pdf/national_security_strategy_gen_hooda.pdf.

© The Author(s), under exclusive license to Springer Nature Singapore Pte Ltd. 2021   171
R. Marwah and L. T. Hằng Nga, *India–Vietnam Relations*, Dynamics of Asian Development, https://doi.org/10.1007/978-981-16-7822-6_8

middle income; and (3) By 2045, at the 100th anniversary of establishing the Democratic Republic of Vietnam, now the Socialist Republic of Vietnam: becoming a developed and high-income country. The future trajectory of bilateral relations was articulated to the authors by Ambassador Chau, "In February 2021, Vietnam held the 13th National Congress of the Communist Party of Vietnam, which laid out directions and guidelines for the country in the next five and subsequent periods. The Congress sets out milestones to make Vietnam a developing, upper-middle-income country with modern industry by 2030 and a high-income developed country by 2045. In this regard, I think the major challenge is whether the country could focus on two tasks, (i) maintaining a favourable environment to focus resources on national development; (ii) reform itself domestically to create motivations to grow sustainably. They are very challenging as many factors are beyond its control and many inertias are within the country. Fortunately, these are areas India has advantages and can boldly step in as a partner. First, India is a significant country in the region, which has a vital role in maintaining peace, stability and the rule of law in the region. Through its Act East Policy and Indo-Pacific vision, India can counter any attempts to destabilize the region. Second, India also serves as a critical development partner. Currently, India is one of Vietnam's top ten trading partners and has provided funding for 37 quick-impact projects in 33 provinces in Vietnam. In the longer-run, two countries can help each other grow sustainably through cooperative projects in science and technology, agriculture, manufacturing, among others" (Amb Chau to authors on May 11, 2021).

The joint vision indicates the future pathways for the two countries. The Joint Vision for Peace, Prosperity and People signed by Prime Ministers Narendra Modi and Nguyen Xuan Phuc on December 21, 2020, encapsulates the future of their partnership. Amidst the emerging regional and global geopolitical and geoeconomic landscape, the joint vision elucidates the necessity to enhance their defense and security partnership. Greater engagement is expected in military-to-military exchanges, training, and capacity building programs across the three services and coast guards; intensification of defense industry collaboration building on India's defense credit lines extended to Vietnam; and institutionalization of defense exchanges through mutual logistics support, regular ship visits, joint exercises, exchanges in military science and technology, information sharing, and cooperation in UN peacekeeping.

The joint vision reaffirmed India and Vietnam's convergent views on the importance of maintaining peace, stability, and freedom of navigation and overflight in the South China Sea. Both sides emphasized "the legal framework set out by the UNCLOS within which all activities in the oceans and seas must be carried out, and that UNCLOS is the basis for determining maritime entitlements, sovereign rights, jurisdiction and legitimate interests over maritime zones."[2] The two countries called for the full and effective implementation of the Declaration on the Conduct (DOC) of Parties in the South China Sea in its entirety and early conclusion of a Code of Conduct (COC) in the South China Sea in accordance with international law.

---

[2] India–Vietnam Joint Vision for Peace, Prosperity and People, https://mea.gov.in/bilateral-docume nts.htm?dtl/33324/India__Vietnam_Joint_Vision_for_Peace_Prosperity_and_People; accessed on May 14, 2021.

Prof. DeCastro elucidated the use of such statecraft by China in the South China Sea. China has a unique naval system with two components. One is the People's Liberation Army Navy (PLAN) which operates on major confrontations, and this is backed by the second component which is China's Surging Second and Third Sea Forces. In the latter, it has the People's Liberation Army Maritime Militia and the Coast Guards which function through the local bodies. They work with the local fishing boats which by their overwhelming presence in the South China Sea intimidates their neighbors. Prof. DeCastro highlights his view of the objective of China which is to accomplish its overwhelming presence. Since China is unable to realize it with diplomatic, economic, and naval power, she employs gray zone operations to use with a liberal mix of political, military, and commercial instruments.[3]

As envisioned, India and Vietnam will require closer collaboration in regional and global issues, including the United Nations, ASEAN-led mechanisms, and Mekong subregional cooperation, thereby promoting multilateralism for representative international organizations proficient in addressing global concerns. Collaboration in pandemic-induced health strains will encourage experience-sharing in pandemic management, supporting online training of health professionals, cooperation in vaccine development, promotion of open supply chains, and maintenance of close contact and coordination in multilateral bodies like WHO.

8.1.2 The Economic Vision

8.1.2.1 Vietnam: Reforms and Recovery

It is well known that Vietnam has had a tumultuous history with several wars and devastation. Its per capita GDP grew by only about 0.4% a year between 1820 and 1960, which then declined for more than a decade. It was the Sixth National Party Congress in 1986 that announced the policy of Doi Moi (renovation reforms). The objective was to help the economy in transitioning from central planning to a market-orientated economy, thereby catalyzing growth. The key objectives were: (1) to emerge from economic embargo and diplomatic isolation; (2) to boost the national economy, through trade and investment; and (3) to integrate Vietnam into regional and international organizations. Hence, the post-Đổi Mới period has transformed the country significantly.

Given that Vietnam has demonstrated growing investments in infrastructure development and rising disposable income of its middle class, it was identified by McKinsey research as one of 11 recent global outperformers. The reasons cited include Vietnam's attractiveness as a destination for tourism and foreign direct investment, its increasing focus on investments in education, and the move toward privatization.

---

[3] Prof. Castro delivered a special lecture on April 21, 2021.

A major part of Vietnam's aspirations for 2035 thus derives from its desire to reclaim its place among the community of nations—and not lag behind. That desire is not new, nor is the idea that the desired convergence with the world economy will not crystallize without investments in human capital. In a letter to students on their first day at school in the newly established Democratic Republic of Vietnam in 1945, President Ho Chi Minh wrote, "… whether Vietnam will become glorious or not, the people of Vietnam will be abreast with other strong nations on the continents or not, it is largely attributed to the children's effort in education…." (World Bank Group and Ministry of Planning and Investment of Vietnam, 2016).

While there is continuity in policymaking, as is evident from the policy direction received at the 13th Party Congress, held from January 25 to February 1, 2021, Vietnam will not be free from operational risks. For instance, there is potential for unintended consequences from the government's efforts to maintain international competitiveness. The risk of Vietnam being reprimanded by the USA and other Western countries for limiting the appreciation of its local currency could partially jeopardize the tariff-free access it has to major markets. Moreover, efforts to keep wage costs low for foreign enterprises via modest minimum wage increases and limited mandatory employee benefits could stoke disquiet, which could later develop into labor protests (EIU P. 14).

Likewise, the economy would require annual growth of 7.0–7.5% from 2021 to 2030—a major increase from the 6.3% Vietnam averaged over the ten years before 2018, as per a 2019 joint report from the World Bank and the Vietnam Academy of Social Sciences (McKinsey, 2020).

Given the pandemic-induced disruptions in the global economy and rising protectionism within the developed markets, it is difficult to predict the trajectory of the much-anticipated global resurgence, which must keep countries' levels of optimism relatively muted. India and Vietnam continue to be rewarded with expectations of better-than-average recovery levels and, hence, continue to be upbeat about their economic success.

8.1.2.2 India's Reforms and Growth Trajectory

India also initiated its reforms in the early 1990s, after which it has been steadily growing. The ten years after the 1991 economic crisis, when India was compelled to devalue its currency by 22% against the dollar and borrow from external donors, resulted in major economic reforms of liberalization, privatization, and globalization. The economic turnaround and recovery were hastened with India clocking growth rates of over 8% per annum in the mid-1990s. The progress continued in the first decade of this century. India made progress in reducing absolute poverty, witnessing a decline from 21.6% in 2011 to 13.4% in 2015 (at the international poverty line), lifting more than 90 million people out of extreme poverty. The Modi government, since 2014, has undertaken important reforms to spur economic growth—introducing the bankruptcy code, implementation of the GST to integrate the national market, and launched a series of reforms to ease the conduct of business.

Given that the majority of India's labor force is employed in the informal sector, the pandemic has heightened vulnerabilities. While the government is making efforts to rework its social protection architecture to protect these workers, unemployment is rising. Even before the pandemic, the economy was already decelerating. Real GDP growth had moderated from an average of 7.4% in FY16/19 to 4.2% in FY19/20, due to structural rigidities in key input markets; increased risk aversion among banks and corporates; a decline in rural demand; and a subdued global economy (The World Bank, 2020). This is a tall order for any country, especially for India with infrastructural constraints, limited risk-taking ability, and a dearth of creditworthy proposals in the current, unstable, and uncertain times.

According to PwC, for India to take the Winning Leap as a higher rate of growth of GDP, there must be an investment in human and physical capital (as in the previous two scenarios) as well as focus on investment in R&D and innovation to envision a 9.0% CAGR for GDP between 2021 and 2034 (India spends a mere 0.7% of its GDP on R&D as compared to China, which invests 2.1%). This scenario forecasts aggressive growth and is the only scenario that will generate 240 m new jobs that India's growing population needs over the next 20 years (PWC Report, 2014).

8.1.3 The Cultural Vision

India–Vietnam relations are historical, cultural, and civilizational. Hence, the past will fortify the future trajectory of bilateral relations. As has been demonstrated in previous chapters, the people of these two countries connected not only as a result of economic and commercial motivations, but as friends. The joint vision of December 21, 2020, will revive the two countries' civilizational and cultural linkages by implementing new projects in heritage conservation in Vietnam and an encyclopedia on India–Vietnam civilizational and cultural interactions.

8.1.3.1 Opportunities and Challenges

It is important to identify both opportunities and challenges for effective future cultural exchanges and cooperation. Opportunities can be identified in the positive changes in Vietnam–India relations in the context of a "flat" world. Over the past decade, the Government of India has constantly made adjustments to its Look East Policy (now Act East policy) in a direction that India is increasingly taking part in the affairs of Southeast Asia and East Asia–Pacific. Vietnam is a credible and strong pillar of India's AEP.

Despite the progress and convergences, it is to be seen that Vietnam–India cultural cooperation is not commensurate with the potentials of the two sides, given that India is a cultural power and the bilateral cultural connection goes back to antiquity.

India has not created an "Indian Wave" in Vietnam (unlike by Korea in Vietnam and elsewhere). For example, the screening of movies at the Swami Vivekananda

Cultural Centre cannot attract many people due to the distance and difficulty in commuting. To get access to a larger audience, films and shows should be broadcast on television channels, while a few movies or serials that have reached the Vietnamese audience through TV are not in tune with the preferences of younger generation. Moreover, movies which depict age-old customs and traditions do not resonate well, sending faulty impressions about India's development. According to Mr. Lâm Thiện, Director-General of IMC (interviewed by the Law Newspaper on July 13, 2016), Balika Vadhu or "Eight-Year-Old Bride" is the highest rated film on television in Vietnam (attracting the most significant number of watchers), in which 70% are housewives and elders. With social media choosing to proliferate the negative information of India's outdated attitudes, this inculcates the prejudice of some Vietnamese people about India.

8.1.3.2   Causes of Limited Cultural Cooperation Between India and Vietnam

While India and Vietnam have deep affinities and similarities through Buddhism and Hinduism, the "Indian Wave in Vietnam" is missing, highlighting that cultural differences are equally significant. Vietnamese people believe that Indian culture is more Western-oriented, as historically, India has been strongly influenced by Western cultures: from Aryan to Greek, and later the Islamic and European cultures, particularly British culture. Indian history is full of events involving the West rather than the East: the invasion of the Aryans; the charge of the Greeks (Alexander the Great); the invasion of the Turks; the Mongols; and most recently, the colonization of the British. In contrast, Vietnamese culture is more orientalist, having been under the more powerful influence of East Asian culture; experienced Chinese domination for over 1000 years; and later influenced by the Japanese, French, and American cultures.

Vietnam and India indeed share similarities in Buddhism. However, modern India is a land of a vast majority of Hindus where the presence of Buddhism is miniscule. Though Buddhism originated from India and continues to prosper in Sri Lanka, Myanmar, Thailand, China and even Japan, it is today a minor religion in India. Less than one percent of the Indian people are Buddhists. When Vietnamese people visit India, they are disappointed to learn that not many Indians practice Buddhism. Hence, the special connection toward India in terms of Buddhism is almost a form of one-sided love (a term used by Tadao Umesao in his book titled "History from an ecological perspective," World Publishing House, Hanoi, 2007). Hence, given that Vietnam receives waves of cultural influences from both China and India, evidently, the Chinese wave is forceful and much more potent; the Indian wave is mainly peaceful and benign. Vietnam, an East Asian culture, is strongly influenced by Confucianism; Vietnamese Buddhism too is primarily influenced by Chinese Buddhism, although Buddhism was directly introduced to Vietnam from India during the reign of Emperor Ashoka the Great.

The primary cause of the limited cultural cooperation between Vietnam and India remains the lack of accurate information. Despite the thousand-year friendship, many

Vietnamese people are unaware of India's natural beauty and attraction of its diversity and people, and many Indian people do not know about Vietnam. Apart from this, the protection and conservation of Champa heritage sites have become an important aspect and a challenge of Vietnam–India cultural cooperation. This work requires time, huge budgetary commitments, and technical expertise. There are many Indian cultural and religious traces in Vietnam. However, many relics face the risk of ruin if the governments do not pay due attention to their conservation. This underlines the salience of forging tourism cooperation.

8.1.4 Vision for Tourism Cooperation

Given that the tourism sector occupies a pivotal role in galvanizing and embedding multisectoral cooperation, including people-to-people contacts, business and entrepreneurial opportunities, student exchanges, conferences, events, this sector merits utmost policy attention toward dispelling prejudices and enhancing mutual understanding. This section outlines the potential for expansion of two-way flows of tourists.

8.1.4.1 India: Toward Enhancing Inbound Tourism from the Region

Given the paucity of direct air connectivity between India and Vietnam till 2019, there were only about 30,000 Vietnamese who traveled to India in 2018. Before the pandemic struck, India had made significant strides in projecting itself as a country that welcomes tourists and provides them a safe and memorable experience.

In this context, the specific measures for encouraging tourists from the MGC countries include:

(a) Improving competitiveness in the travel and tourism sector, through additional accommodation capacity, entertainment facilities, and related services.
(b) Development of the Northeast region as a medical and sports tourism hub for people from MGC countries, given that overland route is preferred by about 20% of Vietnamese people who traveled to India in 2019. There are 13 operational airports in the Northeastern provinces and direct flights between Imphal and key cities in MGC countries is on the anvil.
(c) The Buddhist connection is being invigorated. Although there are only 8.4 million Buddhists in India constituting 0.7% of the country's population, seven of the eight most significant Buddhist sites are located in India; this lends her a unique source of legitimacy in promoting Buddhism. In contrast, 16.4% or 15 million of Vietnamese are Buddhists, who desire to travel to India at least once in their lifetime.
(d) There are several circuits in addition to the Buddhist Circuit that are being considered for development for tourists from the region. These include among

others: a Coastal Circuit, Himalayan Circuit, and the North-East Circuit. Other circuits being developed include the Madhya Pradesh Buddhist Circuit Development of Sanchi–Satna–Rewa–Mandsaur–Dhar and the Uttar Pradesh Buddhist Circuit Development of Srawasti, Kushinagar, and Kapilwastu.

(e) Other initiatives include harnessing the potential of the Ramayana Circuit, viz. Uttar Pradesh Ramayana Circuit Development of Chitrakoot and Shringverpur.

(f) Promotion of sustainable rural tourism in India by taking advantage of globally important heritage sites.

(g) Host Country Newsletter: The Embassy of India in Vietnam has initiated the publication of a monthly newsletter "Bản tin Ấn Độ" (India's newsletter) which helped to inform the Vietnamese audience the most update and official information about India's new developments. The latest newsletter (May 2020) informs that the Archeological Survey of India has discovered a sandstone Linga dated ninth century in Vietnam. This could be replicated by the embassies of other countries.

(h) Social Media: Creating social media accounts including Facebook, Twitter, Instagram, etc., for enhancing tourism and providing visibility of cultural festivals is another initiative.

(i) Diasporic Connect: India has also made efforts to reach out to overseas Indians (including Indian diaspora in MGC countries) and organized events to showcase and "nation-brand" India; it has also made use of new social media to reach out to younger, tech-savvy audiences.

8.1.4.2 Vietnam: An Attractive Destination for Indian Tourists

According to the WEF Report 2019, Vietnam has recorded the greatest improvement in air transport infrastructure as well as international openness. This was evidenced by the fact that to meet rising demand for travel between Vietnam and India as well as across the region, Vietjet in 2019 opened three new direct routes connecting Vietnam's three largest hubs, Da Nang, Hanoi, and Ho Chi Minh City, with two of India's largest economic, political, and cultural centers of New Delhi and Mumbai. The country, which saw the least numbers of COVID-19 cases, is optimistic about bringing tourists back.

Specific measures being taken include:

(a) Tourism Center: Vietnam has been moving ahead with a smart tourism operation center to digitize the tourism industry during and after the pandemic.

(b) Communication Campaign: Vietnam will launch a communication campaign "Vietnam NOW—Safety and Smiling"—a tourism stimulus program with preferential packages for domestic and Asian tourists.

(c) Special Travel Offers: Interestingly, even as Vietjet made attractive offers for Indian tourists, as it started direct flights, the period May 2019 to February 2020 saw a substantial increase in the number of tourists traveling both ways.

(d) Promotional Initiatives as Theme-based Road Shows: In 2017, 110,000 Indians travelled to Vietnam. Since 2018, several special initiatives have been taken to promote tourism. Speaking at a Road Show, organized by the Embassy of the S.R. of Vietnam, in association with OM Tourism, on December 8, 2018.

HE Pham Sanh Chau said,

"Vietnam is home to 8 UNESCO world heritages, well-preserved historic relics and beautiful beaches. Indian travelers can find the affluence of Indian culture in Vietnam through Hindu temples in Ho Chi Minh City or at the My Son sanctuary as well as many Indian restaurants. Vietnam has all kinds of services to satisfy the need for foreign tourists, whether for holidays, shopping, leisure, food exploration, wedding, honeymoon or for business and conference." He invited Indians and especially Delhi tour operators and travel agents to take advantage of geographical proximity between India and Vietnam to promote tourism and expand their tourist business with Vietnam.[1]

What are then the inter-country learnings?

8.1.4.3 Environmentally Sustainable Tourism in a Culturally Vibrant Region

Results show that the number of UNESCO cultural and natural sites, as well as intangible cultural heritage listings, keeps growing, indicating greater commitment to preserving some of the key attractions driving people to visit destinations. The MGC countries are home to 58 World Heritage Sites (India—38, Vietnam—8, Thailand—5, Cambodia—3, Myanmar—2, Laos—2).

1. **Initiatives as Road Shows, Special Cultural events in host countries**: Events as the Road Show in 2018 organized by the Embassy of Vietnam in Delhi, festivals depicting country cultures can further promote tourism. India has promoted yoga and wellness through an International Day of Yoga; such initiatives enable cross-cultural understanding.

2. **MGC Special Tours for Youth, Academics, Media persons**: Given that the opportunities for travel will grow within the region, in the post-pandemic phase, even as people prefer travel to less distant locations and undertake shorter journeys by surface, language learning would be a game changer. This would also help create synergies between tour operators and encourage exchange trips of students, academics, and journalists. Safety of young girls and women must be assured through special, sponsored tours. Encouragement for writing of travel blogs and special tie-ups with media houses to generate increasing visibility would be useful. As stated earlier, country newsletters would help provide information for tourists.

3. **Destination for weddings, film shooting, corporate, and social events**: Tourist sites can be continuously developed and promoted in Vietnam. Low-cost flights and competitively priced hotels, along with the continuous promotional offers for corporate events, wedding destinations, film shootings, and group tours have the potential to attract Indian tourists.

4. **Study Centers**: Partnering with academic institutions and think tanks for establishing India Study Centers in Vietnam and Thailand has facilitated tourism, through an enhanced understanding of cultures and peoples. Vietnam too established a Center for Vietnam Studies in India. These can function well, both independently and by organizing special lectures and tours in cooperation with the local embassy/consulate. Publicizing scholarships offered by India is another important requirement; this could be done through university fairs and other initiatives. At present, according to an ICCR official, the number of students applying for ICCR fellowships for ASEAN countries is underutilized.

8.1.5 Vision on Science, Technology, and Innovation Cooperation

Given that strategic competition among major powers has intensified, several countries require multi-alignment. The Indo-Pacific has emerged as a dynamic geospatial development. As the situation in the East Vietnam Sea (South China Sea) becomes more complex, it threatens the fabric of peace and stability in the region (Vu et al., 2021).

Most importantly, the COVID-19 pandemic situation continues to be complicated, causing severe recession and global economic crisis. It will have a lasting impact on the world economy and profoundly change the economic order, global governance modes, economic cooperation, and social organization. The 4th Industrial Revolution has an immediate and far-reaching impact on all aspects of society, culture and the environment. In this context, Vietnam–India cooperation in the field of science, technology, and innovation provides hope for sustainable, tangible outcomes.

8.1.5.1 Opportunities

India's strengths and Vietnam's potential in S&T provide both opportunities and challenges for bilateral cooperation. Despite its limited resources, Vietnam has made encouraging progress and gradually reduced the gap in scientific capacity and innovation in the region. With over 35 years of reforms and innovation (since 1986), Vietnam's national strength and power have scaled new heights. The sociopolitical situation is mainly stable; the national prestige and global stature have resulted in the country being wooed for its geoeconomic and geostrategic weight.

Even as Vietnam's government is vigorously promoting joint research with advanced economies, it is endeavoring to improve capacity and S&T standards to participate in equal and mutually beneficial partnerships. This is reflected in Resolution No. 20-NQ/T.W. of the XI Congress of the Vietnam Communist Party; Science and Technology Law of 2013; and Vietnam's Strategy of Science and Technology Development through 2020.

The Thirteenth (13th) Party Congress (25/1–2/2/2021) also focusing on sciences, technology, and innovation identified six critical tasks and three strategic breakthroughs for the coming term, of which task number 2 states: "Promoting research, transfer and application of science, technology and innovation, especially the achievements of the Fourth Industrial Revolution; implementing national digital transformation; developing the digital economy; improving productivity, quality, efficiency and competitiveness of the economy…" The three strategic breakthroughs emphasize the importance of innovation of national governance; utilizing and attracting talents; promoting research, transfer, application, and innovation; giving special attention to information and telecommunication infrastructure development; and gradually developing the digital economy and digital society (Central Office of the Vietnam Communist Party, 02/2021, pp. 40–44).[4]

The 13th Congress also adopted the ten-year Socio-Economic Development Strategy for 2021–2030 with the strategic theme: "To arouse the aspiration for national development (among the Vietnamese people), to strongly promote the cultural values of the Vietnamese people…; to mobilize all resources, to develop rapidly and stably based on science, technology, innovation and digital transformation; to strive to be a developing country with modern industries, high middle income by 2030 and to become a developed country with high income by 2045" (Central Office of the Vietnam Communist Party, 02/2021, p. 48).

The stance of the development strategy reiterates the primacy of new thinking and action, proactively and timely leveraging of opportunities from the Fourth Industrial Revolution associated with the international integration process, developing the digital economy, and to consider this as a decisive factor to improve productivity, quality, efficiency, and competitiveness (Central Office of the Vietnam Communist Party, p. 49).

The main targets of the ten-year Socio-Economic Development Strategy 2021–2030 include, among others, a gross domestic product (GDP) growth rate of 7%/per year, GDP per capita of $7.500, and contributions of the manufacturing sector and digital economy to each be about 30% of GDP (Central Office of the Vietnam Communist Party, p. 49).

The 13th Congress also passed the Five-Year Plan 2021–2025 with the overall objective as follows: "To ensure rapid and sustainable economic growth based on macro-economic stability, science and technology development and innovation" (Central Office of the Vietnam Communist Party, p. 65). "Actively integrate into the world; improve the efficiency of foreign affairs and enhance Vietnam's position and reputation in the international arena" (Central Office of the Vietnam Communist Party, p. 66). Thus, the documents of the XIII Congress of the Communist Party of Vietnam, including the ten-year Socio-Economic Development Strategy 2021–2030 and the Five-Year Plan 2021–2025, focus on science, technology, and innovation

---

[4] Central Office of the Communist Party of Vietnam [Văn phòng Trung ương Đảng Cộng sản Việt Nam], Results of the XIII National Congress of the Communist Party of Vietnam [Kết quả Đại hội Đại biểu Toàn quốc Lần thứ XIII Đảng Cộng sản Việt Nam], Tài liệu lưu hành nội bộ [Confidential Documents], Hà Nội, 02/2021.

in addition to enhancing research capacity. Given the latent possibilities in these areas, India and Vietnam should encourage diplomacy science for robust bilateral cooperation.

8.1.5.2   Challenges

Although labor productivity has improved significantly and is one of the highest among ASEAN countries, with an increase of 4.87% per year over 2011–2019, the technology absorbing capacity of Vietnam's companies is weak. The spirit of science and culture of innovation/creativity/entrepreneurship has not been deeply ingrained into the community. According to Mr. Nguyen Tuan Anh, Permanent Vice Chairman of the Vietnam Association of Foreign Investment Enterprises (VAFIE), Vietnamese enterprises lack information and do not understand the possibilities and technological levels of Indian enterprises.[5] Hence, there is an imperative to organize communication campaigns and undertake broader promotion of India's potentials and strengths in information technology, innovative city development, Indian start-ups, medicine, and health care among others.

Both countries concur that strategic partnership must be tied to developments in science and technology.[6] However, the gap in the level of scientific and technological development of the two countries is a factor hindering the practical cooperation. India is one of the leading countries in the world in terms of technology. In contrast, the level of science and technology development in Vietnam is relatively low. Therefore, science and technological cooperation between the two countries has been largely one-sided. India has played the role of a supportive government and Vietnam being the supported country. It is mainly to serve political and strategic relations. This has also led to several other limitations such as: small size of the joint research projects, limited state-level budgets for scientific research projects, lack of participation and investment of private sector, weak linkages between research and market demand as well as complicated administrative procedures in implementing research projects. Referring to Indian investors, Mr. Saxena, in an interview to the authors, affirmed this view, when he said, "Indian investors are disinclined to invest in greenfield ventures. They prefer to invest in brownfield projects, where the risks are relatively low."

---

[5] Việt Nam - Ấn Độ tăng cư`ờng hợp tác trong lĩnh vực công nghệ thông tin và phát triển đô thị thông minh [Vietnam-India enhancing partnership in information technology, smart city development], October 8, 2020. https://dangcongsan.vn/doi-ngoai/viet-nam-an-do-tang-cuong-hop-tac-trong-linh-vuc-cong-nghe-thong-tin-va-phat-trien-do-thi-thong-minh-565179.html; accessed on May 14, 2021.

[6] Nguyễn Thị Quế, Quan hệ Việt Nam - Ấn Độ: Quá kh´ư, hiện tại và tương lai", Kỷ yếu hội thảo khoa học quốc tế "Việt Nam - Ấn Độ: 45 Năm Quan hệ Ngoại giao và 10 năm Đối tác Chiến lược, Nxb. Lý luận Chính trị, Hà Nội, pp. 94–108.

8.2 Elucidating the Convergences in Aspirations of India and Vietnam

The World Bank and the Ministry of Planning and Investment of Vietnam (2016) report define Vietnam's aspirations for 2035. India's aspirations in the economic domain have been defined by its vision for becoming a USD 5 trillion economy by 2025, which is now under revision.

A few salient points of convergence in the two countries' aspirations are outlined here:

8.2.1 Economic and Commercial: Pathways and Inter-country Learnings

Vietnam aims to build a prosperous society that will be private sector-led, competitive, and intensively integrated with the global economy. Modern industries and a knowledge-based economy, housed in an efficient and well-connected network of modern cities, will drive growth. Due to its GDP-per-capita growth of more than 5% annually for 20 years, in addition to its successful effort to lift a significant percentage of its people out of poverty, Vietnam has the elements in place to continue as an outperformer—especially with growing disposable income, continued investment in infrastructure programs, and an attractive business environment.

According to the IMF's assessment, despite COVID-19, Vietnam's economy has remained resilient, expanding by 2.9% in 2020—one of the highest growth rates in the world—and growth is projected to be 6.5% in 2021. This is due to the solid economic fundamentals, decisive containment measures, and well-targeted government support (Norris and Zhang, IMF Asia and Pacific, 2021).

Vietnam also has a sizeable informal sector; this sector has been impacted adversely, especially due to limited access to social insurance. This weakness needs to be addressed by enhancing the formalization of labor. Vietnam (according to the IMF) must also improve the business environment, ensuring a level playing field for small and medium-sized enterprises, with reforms geared toward reducing the regulatory burden faced by firms, enhancing their access to resources, enhancing governance and access to technology and innovation, and reducing skills mismatches. Reforms in these areas would also help Vietnam reap greater benefits from participation in global value chains in the post-pandemic world.[7]

India is urbanizing at a fast pace and seeks to modernize its industries, through several initiatives as Skill India, AtmaNirbhar (self-reliant) India, among others. The Modi government has undertaken several reforms to position India as a leading global economy. The prepandemic vision articulated was for India to become a $5 trillion

---

[7] Vietnam successfully navigating the pandemic, https://www.imf.org/en/News/Articles/2021/03/09/na031021-vietnam-successfully-navigating-the-pandemic; accessed on August 12, 2021.

economy by 2025. The economy suffered a major setback in 2020–21, with growth declining by 0.7% in FY2021. However, it is expected that there will be significant recovery in 2021–22 (Reddy & Subash, 2021). The IMF projects an 11.5% growth rate for India in 2021, making her the only major economy of the world to register double-digit growth amidst the coronavirus pandemic. With the latest projections, India regains the tag of the fastest developing economies of the world (Jha, 2021).

Given this brief outlook and overview of the two economies, we assess inter-country learnings and potential collaborations in key sectors. Similar internal challenges and economic pathways can be calibrated through cross-country learnings and initiatives.

8.2.1.1   Reform and Stimulus Packages

The Indian Government's budget for the year 2021–22 does provide a stimulus for infrastructure growth and job creation. Given that tax revenue collection is expected to be low, the government relies on a private sector-led economic recovery in 2021–22. There have been announcements of measures as wholesale privatization of the PSUs, including public sector banks and insurance companies, enhancing FDI cap in the insurance sector, among others. While this has enabled huge inflows of FDI, competitiveness remains a key deficiency and restricts India's export capabilities.

In an interview to the authors on April 15, 2021, former Vietnam's ambassador to India, Tôn Sinh Thành, was instructive when he said, "India can look at Vietnam in terms of competition; we just open the economy but we survive. If India can open up, it will prosper. We are not afraid of competition, but India is always afraid of competition, maybe because of farmers, industrialists, and other groups. However, then competitiveness cannot be improved. In terms of investment, India has succeeded, but the bureaucracy is an obstacle. For the fourth Industrial Revolution, India has to fast-track projects."

As stated above, Vietnam is also relying on private sector-led investment growth, which needs to be further incentivized, so that it will continue to invest in physical infrastructure for improved North–South connectivity.

8.2.1.2   Pandemic Management

In terms of COVID-19 management, both countries were swift to introduce containment measures, combined with aggressive contact tracing, targeted testing, and isolation of suspected cases. Hence, death rates were notably low on a per capita basis. In terms of vaccinating their populations, India commenced its vaccination program for the above 60 age group in March 2021, followed by vaccinating 45–60 from April 1, 2021. Given the upsurge in cases in March 2021, marking a second and more virulent phase of the pandemic, India's vaccination drive seeks to immunize at least 300 million people by August 2021. This scale of immunization is possible for India, as Indian-made doses of the AstraZeneca shot and a homegrown one from Bharat

Biotech. India, a member of the Quad grouping, also comprising the USA, Japan, and Australia, is committed to the group's endeavor to supply one billion doses of the vaccine to Asian countries by the end of 2022 (Business Today, 2021; Reuters, 2021). The second wave of the pandemic that hit India in April–May 2021 was unprecedented. Vietnam responded by helping India with emergency supplies. In separate ceremonies held on May 11 and 12, Vietnam-India Friendship Association (VIFA) and Vietnam Buddhist Sangha (VBS) announced gifting of 200 ventilators and 50 oxygen concentrators as expressions of solidarity toward the people of India in their fight against the pandemic.[8]

Vietnam had kept the total number of infections in the country of 96 million at around 2500 and reported just 35 deaths. It also commenced its vaccination program on March 8, 2021, and acquired 150 million jabs for its COVID-19 vaccination program, including those directly purchased and doses obtained via the COVAX vaccine-sharing scheme. However, the resurgence of the pandemic resulted in a swift response from India in August 2021, when India sent critical supplies of oxygen concentrators and cylinders to Vietnam. Vietnam also hopes to receive doses of the India-made vaccine in 2022, even as the surge in COVID infections in July 2021 in Ho Chi Minh City has resulted in rising distrust of China-made vaccines.[9]

Even as India is being accepted globally as the emerging pharmacy of the world, India, on March 15, 2021, organized a webinar that aimed at connecting the pharma companies virtually and deliberated on the market opportunities as well to meet the medical requirements of the pharmaceutical business houses from Vietnam. Such initiatives must be continued, and Vietnam could also be included in the vaccine initiative of the Quad grouping. Vietnam's Nanogen Pharmaceutical Biotechnology, based in Vietnam's Ho Chi Minh City, is willing to share know-how and technology for developing its COVID-19 vaccine candidate. However, locating manufacturers with the capacity to produce it in low-income countries is a restraint. This presents an opportunity for India's Pune based Serum Institute of India and Bharat Biotech to collaborate (Lei Ravelo, 2021).

8.2.1.3 State to State Initiatives

The Consulate General of India in Ho Chi Minh City coordinated with the People's Committee of Kien Giang Province and Government of Odisha State in organizing a webinar on "Partnership between Odisha State and Kien Giang Province in Agriculture & Fishery" on December 29, 2020. The webinar aimed to explore opportunities for partnership and trade in these sectors by encouraging interactions among the business community. Kien Giang is one of the four provinces of the key economic region of the Mekong Delta that is endowed with a variety of natural terrain, a long

---

[8] Assistance by Vietnam to India in the fight against COVID-19, https://www.indembassyhanoi.gov.in/event_detail/?eventid=453; May 13, 2021; accessed on May 31, 2021.

[9] Was Vietnam's Chinese COVID-19 vaccine debacle just a stunt? https://thediplomat.com/2021/08/was-vietnams-chinese-covid-19-vaccine-debacle-just-a-stunt/; accessed on August 21, 2021.

coastline with many rivers, mountains, islands, and rich and diverse natural resources. The location and natural conditions have created several economic advantages for Kien Giang's development in agriculture—forestry economy, marine economy, agricultural and aquatic processing industry, production of construction materials (CGI, HCMC, 2021).

The State of Odisha, with geographical proximity to Southeast Asian markets including Vietnam, offers various incentives for investors, including a Mega Seafood Park, which is an exclusive industrial park in an area of 152 acres for seafood/marine product industry with fully developed infrastructure, standard facilities, cold storage, packaging units, etc. Moreover, it has a major fishing harbor networked with five little harbors and 28 fish landing centers (InvestOdisha, 2021). More such twin city initiatives can be identified.

8.2.1.4 Smart Cities

Urban areas are expected to house 40% of India's population and contribute 75% to India's GDP by 2030. In India, the Smart Cities Mission, an initiative for urban city planning, was initiated by the Government of India in 2015 to transform the country's urban landscape (IBEF Knowledge Center, 2021). The primary goal is to convert all Indian cities into smart cities by leveraging technologies and promoting local area development. Through its various programs, the government is testing new products and initiatives to implement "smart cities effectively." Initiatives such as the Smart Cities Forum gather collaborative insights from all relevant sectors for effective project planning and implementation. Also, private sector players collaborate with cities to develop new products and services to respond to local needs (IBEF, 2021a, b).

Hanoi shows the way when the city hosted the ASEAN Smart Cities Network High-Level Forum in October 2020. The objective was to promote sharing initiatives, experiences, and cooperation between Vietnamese cities and their urban counterparts throughout the region. Given India's focus on smart urban planning, digital infrastructure for smart cities, smart services within cities as part of the digital transformation process, and smart transportation, similar to that initiated by Vietnam, there could be learnings for both countries.

8.2.1.5 Leveraging the Trade War

Here, we assess the strengths of India and Vietnam concerning policies in two sectors, viz. manufacturing electronics and footwear.

If the Plus One strategy was the catalyst that initiated a wave of electronics manufacturing in Vietnam, then the U.S.–China trade war was the stimulant that charged it. A common refrain in Southeast Asia is that the U.S.–China trade war is over and Vietnam is the winner, and this is apparent in both trade and investment trends. According to the Asian Development Bank (ADB), the U.S.–China hostility caused a redirection in trade, as U.S. imports from the PRC fell by 12% in the first six months of 2019 while U.S. imports from Vietnam increased by 33%, with electronics and machinery accounting for the bulk of this jump. The ADB further reported that in a prolonged and intensified trade conflict, the worst-case scenario would result in Vietnam, Malaysia, and Thailand being the biggest winners, "in that order."

(a) Synergizing the manufacturing of electronics

The Government of India launched the National Policy on Electronics, 2019, which aims to achieve a turnover of US$400 by 2025. It also targets the production of a billion mobile handsets by 2025, valued at US$190 billion, including exports of 600 million handsets valued at US$110 billion. In addition, India is also witnessing a surge in demand for high-end consumer electronics. To reduce its dependence on China and provide a fillip to the industry, several policy measures linked to the production-linked incentive (PLI) scheme, scheme for promotion of manufacturing of electronic components and semiconductors (SPECS) scheme, modified electronics manufacturing clusters (EMC 2.0) scheme, and remission of duties or taxes on export products (RoDTEP) scheme have been initiated. Samsung has been gearing up to move a significant portion of its production line to India. This decision would impact the existing operations in other countries, including Vietnam. Vietnam is another production center of Samsung and the second largest exporter of smartphones after China. Several companies have made commitments to invest in India. These include Foxconn, Apple, Amazon, Nokia, Pegatron, among others. India's Minister for IT among other portfolios, Ravi Shankar Prasad, in a blog post dated February 16, 2021, said, "India is an attractive investment destination and is poised to become a major player in the global supply chain in the electronics and IT products industry. We welcome Amazon's decision to set up a manufacturing line in Chennai, as it will enhance domestic production capacities, and create jobs as well. This will further our mission of creating an *Aatma nirbhar Bharat,* which is digitally empowered" (IBEF, 2021a, b).

On the investment side, a March 2020 Gartner, Inc. survey of global supply chain leaders revealed that 33% had "moved sourcing and manufacturing activities out of China or plan to do so in the next two to three years." While this survey did not mention specific winners, the ADB reported that "newly registered FDI in Vietnam from the PRC and Hong Kong rose by 200% year on year in the first seven months of 2019," indicating the move of Chinese suppliers to Vietnam. Additionally, a review of media reports indicates firms like Apple, Nintendo, and Dell are encouraging suppliers to relocate parts of their supply chains to Vietnam. These suppliers have agreed. Hence, Compal Electronics, GoerTek, HZO, Inventec, Pegatron, USI, and Wistron, to mention a few, have announced plans for new investments in Vietnam.

Within Vietnam, microelectronic facilities are located in a few geographic hubs. In the South, the Saigon High Tech Park in Ho Chi Minh City attracted Intel and Samsung, with firms like Nidec and Jabil soon following. The largest investment capital, however, developed in the Northern provinces that ring Hanoi. Băc Ninh, near Hanoi, was the site of Samsung's first investment and has since attracted Foxconn and Canon. More recently, firms have been drawn to the port city of Hải Phòng, the country's third largest city, which is already home to Samsung and LG. The city's close proximity to other manufacturing clusters, its new deepwater port, and its expressway that provides a 12-h trucking route to China's electronics epicenter in Shenzhen are helping make the city Vietnam's new high-tech production center. Local phone manufacturer VinSmart is also producing the country's first 5G smartphones in Hải Phòng. In November, USI, a subsidiary of Taiwan-based ASE Holding, broke ground on its first production base in Southeast Asia, a $200 million phase-one investment in the production and assembly of chips for wearable electronic devices. USI's investment, which is moving into the DEEP C Industrial Zones (managed by a Belgian) in Hải Phòng, is "intended to move us closer to our overseas customers and accommodate their ever-increasing demand" (Schaag, n.a.).

Given that market leaders in electronics (with LG having closed down its smartphone business in 2021) are increasingly shifting production bases to India and Vietnam for their obvious advantages of low-cost skilled labor and large markets, there could be synergies in logistics and supply chain management, by creating joint manufacturing and distribution hubs. One example is the growing demand for low-cost wearable electronic devices.

The ADB forecasts that Vietnam will be one of the fastest-growing economies in SEA in 2021, with GDP growth rate estimated to increase at about 7% p.a. for the next few years. The Ministry of Industry and Trade also reports that several of the world's largest technology corporations plan to shift their production chains to Vietnam. It is expected that technology firms could accelerate relocation plans in 2021/22. Vietnam's relative success in curbing the pandemic, combined with its strategic location, low wage rates, and foreign trade agreements, will ensure that the region continues to benefit from the shift in supply chains in Asia, making it the new destination for electronics manufacturing (Suneja, 2021).

(b)   Leather and footwear production

India is the second largest consumer of footwear in the world and its leather products, and footwear market is estimated to be about USD 12 billion. Despite the pandemic, the Council for Leather Exports has endeavored to tap the potential available in various markets. For this sector, Vietnam and Korea are important markets. Virtual buyer–seller meets are being proposed with 7 countries, namely Vietnam, Germany, UAE, and the UK, during 2021 (Aqeel Ahmed, IBEF, 2021a).

Vietnamese companies have proved their capacity in research and development (R&D) and design, according to Chairman of the Vietnam Leather, Footwear and Handbag Association (LEFASO), Nguyen Duc Thuan. Signs show that Vietnam is further penetrating into the leather footwear supply chain, he said, as the design and R&D processes rake in high added value for products. The domestic supply of materials for the sector now represents 60%. Local businesses can take the initiative in producing soles and molds, as well as packaging and labeling. According to Thuan, this was possible due to their ability to manufacture the materials locally. This sector will benefit as a result of the FTA with the European Union. Though China still accounts for half of the global footwear production, Vietnam's exports to its Northern neighbor surged 15% for the first time in 2020, he noted (Vietnamplus, 2021).

(c) *Electric vehicles manufacture in Vietnam*

Interestingly, while the Vietnamese consumer would not be perceived as buying new four wheeler models, the Vietnamese corporation VinFast has raised the curtain on three new electric vehicles for the global market. Pham Nhat Vuong, Vietnam's richest man, aims to take the car to the US market and compete directly with Tesla and General Motors.[10] This presents a possibility for a partnership in the electric vehicles (both two wheelers and four wheelers) sector for India and Vietnam. Japan could also be brought in, for both technological competence and investment. Mr. Amit Saxena in an interview to the authors also flagged this sector as suitable for joint ventures.

(d) *Export of Indian textiles to Vietnam*

When in December 2018, Nguyen Hong Giang of the Vietnam Cotton and Spinning Association (VCOSA) said there was plenty of opportunity for cooperation in yarn, cotton, and fabrics between businesses in the two countries, he highlighted the strength of India-made cotton fabrics and textiles. He also referred to the tax incentives that Indian investors would be eligible for. In his words, there was a win–win opportunity for both countries, as he said "You buy more yarn from Vietnam and we will buy more cotton fabric from you."[11]

8.2.1.6 Commercial Interests in SCS

India's commercial interests in the South China Sea are well known. Given that ONGC Videsh Limited (OVL) has applied for a sixth extension to explore Block 128, the license for which was valid till June 15, 2019, there is a renewed interest to expedite further the oil and gas exploration cooperation involving companies such as Petrovietnam and India's ONGC in the exclusive economic zone (EEZ) of Vietnam. This reiterates the bilateral dimension of cooperation in the South China Sea. OVL made a foray into Vietnam as early as 1988, when it bagged the exploration license for Block 6.1. OVL had signed a production sharing contract (PSC) for the 7,058 sq km Block 128 in offshore Phu Khanh Basin, Vietnam, on May 24, 2006. Although the company has not found hydrocarbons in the block, it is continuing to stay invested, given India's strategic interest. The fifth extension for two years was received in 2017. On several occasions, China has dispatched its coast guard ships to deter OVL from continuing with its exploration activities off the coast of Vietnam (PTI, 2019).

---

[10] Vietnam's richest man plans electric vehicle factory in US, to target Tesla; https://auto.hindustan times.com/auto/news/vietnams-richest-man-plans-electric-vehicle-factory-in-us-to-target-tesla-41619761838900.html; April 30, 2021; accessed on May 27, 2021.

[11] Vietnam India eye textile cooperation; https://www.nationthailand.com/international/30359322; November 26, 2018; accessed on May 27, 2021.

However, given that OVL has so far invested USD 50.88 million or 45% stake in Block 6.01 and its share of production was 2.023 billion cubic meters of gas and 0.036 million tons of condensate, it can indeed not be wished away by China. Moreover, if OVL does not continue its activities, it will be liable to pay penalties (PTI, 2019).

Hence, the South China Sea (SCS) is important not just to its littoral countries. It has been a transit point for trade since early medieval times contains abundantly rich fisheries and is a repository of mineral deposits and hydrocarbon reserves (Prasad, 2020).

8.2.2 Cooperation in the Defense Sector

India's Defence Secretary Dr. Ajay Kumar, co-chaired the 13th India-Vietnam Defence Security Dialogue along with his Vietnamese co-chair Sr Lt Gen Nguyen Chi Vinh, Deputy Defence Minister, the Socialist Republic of Vietnam on January 12, 2021. During their virtual interaction, the officials expressed satisfaction at the ongoing defense cooperation despite the limitations imposed by COVID-19. New areas of defense cooperation were also discussed. They reviewed the progress on various bilateral defense cooperation initiatives and expressed commitment to elevate further engagements between the armed forces under the framework of the Comprehensive Strategic Partnership.

"The summit provided an opportunity to handover one High Speed Guard Boat to Vietnam, the launch of two other vessels manufactured in India, and keel-laying seven vessels being manufactured in Vietnam, under the $100 million Defence Line of Credit extended by Government of India for High-Speed Guard Boats Manufacturing Project with Vietnam," said Riva Ganguly Das, Secretary (East), Ministry of External Affairs (MEA), during a press conference (Basu, 2020). The two countries committed to elevating engagements between the two countries' armed forces under the framework of "Comprehensive Strategic Partnership," which was agreed upon in 2016. A decision was also taken to implement the "Joint Vision for Peace, Prosperity and People" through concrete actions proposed to be taken by both sides during 2021–2023.

8.2.3 Cooperation in the Mekong–Ganga Cooperation

There are 26 quick-impact projects funded by India in 22 Vietnamese cities and provinces, 13 of which have been completed while 12 others will be launched during the 2020–2021 fiscal year. Speaking at the event, in September 2020, at Delta's Can Tho City, during which seven memoranda of understanding were signed, for projects each worth 50,000 USD, Indian Ambassador to Vietnam Pranay Verma said the traditional relationship between the two nations is a successful model in terms of institutional support and capacity improvement in various fields. Deputy Head of the

Foreign Ministry's General Economic Department, Pham Thi Anh, said the activity is a symbol of the enduring friendship among member states of the Mekong–Ganga Cooperation (MGC) and between Vietnam and India.

The Mekong Delta has been facing drought and saltwater intrusion at record levels. The level of rainfall in 2020 has been 30–40% lower than previous averages and is forecast to remain low in the future.[12] Launched in 2000, the MGC is one of the longest-standing subregional cooperation mechanisms in the Mekong Delta to enhance solidarity and friendship among nations and promote trade and economic development to improve people's lives in Mekong and Ganga River basins (Thong-tanxa, 2020). Given that lower riparian states have flagged concerns related to dams on the Mekong River and its impact on the livelihoods of local communities, there are plans for cooperation in water resource management among India and Vietnam. All ASEAN countries in the State of SEA Survey seek a particular focus on the river's ecology, which is vital for all ASEAN countries. China's engagement through the Lancang-Mekong Cooperation (LMC) has resulted in a salami-slicing strategy, a challenge for ASEAN unity and centrality (Binh & Thu, 2020).

8.2.4 Cooperation in Science, Technology, and Innovation

8.2.4.1 Development of 5G Technology

Although Vietnam has not officially banned China's telecom giant Huawei, it was the first Southeast Asian country to avoid including the Chinese company's technology in its 5G networks due to security issues. This motivated Vietnam to become one of the first countries in the world to build its own 5G network. Viettel, a telecom company owned by the Vietnamese government, has partnered with Ericsson to create the 5G technology. The technology, passed in early 2020, is now being tested in Ho Chi Minh City, and the plan is for it to be rolled out in 2021. The success of the project could have a larger impact on the region, given Viettel's investments in telecom networks in Myanmar, Laos, and Cambodia. Vietnam's domestic 5G network is also important for the nation to harness cutting-edge technologies and expand high-tech domestic manufacturing, two areas of emphasis for Prime Minister Nguyễn Xuân Phúc. The country has high digital potential, given its young and dynamic demographics. With its 5G and national digitalization plans, Vietnam aims to use this effort as a springboard to further harness its stakes in global technology competition beyond 5G, including e-commerce and online payment systems. In all these areas, cybernorms and standards not only are matters of private and commercial interests but can also be consequential national security issues. It will be interesting to understand how big Chinese tech companies like Alibaba, Tencent, and Baidu make inroads in Vietnam on other technology fronts (Thu, 2020).

---

[12] The MGC is an initiative by six countries: India and the five ASEAN countries of Cambodia, Laos, Myanmar, Thailand, and Vietnam.

India is yet to roll out its 5G technologies. After several months-long eyeball to eyeball confrontation in the Himalayan region among the armies of India and China, India decided to ban over 200 Chinese apps and restrict the entry of Chinese investment into India through the automatic route. Huawei and ZTE, Chinese telecommunication giants, have not been considered in the list of 5G vendors (Sean, 2021). India's Department of Telecom approved applications of telecom companies Reliance Jio, Bharti Airtel, Vodafone Idea, and MTNL to conduct 5G trials, but none of them will be using technologies of Chinese entities.[13] Given the security concerns that several agencies have flagged, India, itself a telecom giant, could consider partnership with the Vietnamese company.

8.2.4.2 Other Significant Agreements Signed in 2020

There are other recent agreements signed for future cooperation.

- Agreement for US$5 million Indian Grant Assistance for Army Software Park at National Telecommunications University, Nha Trang, Vietnam between Embassy of India, Hanoi and Telecommunications University, Ministry of National Defence, Vietnam.
- MOU between India's Atomic Energy Regulatory Board (AERB) and Vietnam Agency for Radiation and Nuclear Safety (VARANS).
- MOU between CSIR-Indian Institute of Petroleum and Vietnam Petroleum Institute.
- MOU between National Solar Federation of India and Vietnam Clean Energy Association. To promote the exchange of knowledge, best practices, and information between Indian and Vietnamese solar power industries and explore new business opportunities to promote solar power in India and Vietnam.
- Completion and handing over of seven development projects with Indian "Grant-in-Aid" Assistance of US$1.5 million for the benefit of the local community in Vietnam's Ninh Thuan Province.
- Enhancing the number of annual quick-impact projects (QIPs) from currently five to ten commencing FY 2021–2022.
- Traditional and non-traditional security issues in India–Vietnam relations.

8.2.4.3 The Way Ahead

The India–Vietnam Joint Vision of December 21, 2020, emphasizes that "the economic and development partnership between India and Vietnam will be increasingly driven by the promise of new technologies, innovation and digitization to deliver

---

[13] PTI, Business Today; https://www.businesstoday.in/current/economy-politics/india-decision-to-allow-5g-trials-without-huawei-zte-a-sovereign-step-us/story/438830.html; May 12, 2021; accessed on May 27, 2021.

good governance, people's empowerments, and sustainable and inclusive development." And to this end, both India and Vietnam will "harness synergies between India's "Digital India" mission and Vietnam's "Digital Society" vision, and deepen cooperation in peaceful uses of nuclear and space technologies, transformative technologies in Information and Communication Technology, ocean sciences, sustainable agriculture, water resource management, holistic healthcare, vaccines and pharmaceuticals, smart cities and startups."[14] India and Vietnam will also partner in new and renewable energy resources, energy conservation, and other climate-resilient technologies. Vietnam should seriously consider participating in the International Solar Alliance, bringing new opportunities for cooperation in the large-scale deployment of solar energy.

To further promote bilateral cooperation in science, technology, and innovation, more efforts should be made from both sides, including:

Firstly, training of staff in science, technology, and innovation should be given priority. From the Indian side, despite signed agreements, implementation is tardy and inefficient in several fields including education and social science collaboration. From the Vietnam side, the major challenge for the Vietnamese scientists is not only the level of expertise in S&T but also proficiency in the English language. A suggestion to surmount this void is the initiation of an Eminent Persons Group who have a good command of English, a deep understanding of strengths, and limitations in forging bilateral cooperation. To achieve tangible outcomes, educational cooperation in science and technology needs to be prioritized (Mukhopadhyay, 2021). The authors believe that achievements of recent years are largely due to the educational cooperation. Many Vietnamese students learning information technology from India have returned to Vietnam and contribute to the S&T collaboration between the two countries.

Secondly, the two sides should consider strengthening existing educational institutions and opening more joint universities in science and technology and innovation in Vietnam such as Hoa Sen University, APTECH, NIIT An Giang, Hanoi-Arena. APTECH has helped train more than 100,000 engineers and programmers (high-quality human resources) in Vietnam over the past few years.[15] APTECH has helped bring India's leading technology to support Vietnam, collaborating with Vietnamese universities, assisting Vietnamese students to get access to the opportunities provided by the Fourth Industrial Revolution. It has also helped train more than 1000 engineers and programmers in Vietnam over the past years.[16] Such outcomes should be multiplied.

Thirdly, research in social sciences and organizing exchange programs and conferences should be encouraged in enhancing mutual understanding. India Foundation

---

[14] India–Vietnam Joint Vision for Peace, Prosperity and People, December 21, 2020. https://www.mea.gov.in/; accessed on June 10, 2021.

[15] Nguyễn Thị Mai Liên, Đẩy mạnh hợp tác giáo dục và đào tạo Việt Nam - Ấn Độ, Kỷ yếu hội thảo khoa học quốc tế, *Việt Nam - Ấn Độ: 45 năm quan hệ ngoại giao và 10 năm đối tác chiến lược*, Nxb. Lý luận chính trị,tr.630.

[16] see Footnote 15.

should support scholars' exchange programs and research projects on Indian studies (like Korea Foundation and Japan Foundation).

8.2.5   Cooperation in the Cultural Domain

Given that India and Vietnam established early cultural linkages and there has been a prolonged cultural interaction between the two countries, there are important elements of convergence in our cultures. In fact, it was the ancient and early medieval periods which are the golden periods of India–Vietnam cultural and civilizational links. According to Dhar, a comparative analysis of select architectural types from ancient India and Vietnam and other SEA countries underlines the importance of examining the processes of sharing and transference of architectural concepts and forms that appear to have transpired during the period before the seventh century CE. Of particular importance is the need for a closer investigation of material that could shed greater light on the largely missing links in wood and brick. It is also equally necessary to investigate the intra-Southeast Asian exchanges more closely and the filter of intermediate cultures in the dynamics of cross-cultural architectural exchange. It is believed that Hinduism and Buddhism became the mainstream religion of the Chams living in the central and Southern parts of Vietnam. The architectural style of My Son relics and the ancient archaeological remnants (scattered in the coastal areas of Vietnam from Da Nang to Binh Thuan), speak about these historical legacies (Trivedi, 2018).

The role of portable architectural models in the transmission of architectural ideas and forms is another important aspect that needs further attention. New research is unfolding newer horizons, and more than ever before, it is now becoming possible to track at least some routes and channels of contact with greater precision. This opens up newer frontiers of research and calls for greater collaboration between archaeologists and art historians to interpret the newly emerging evidence (Dhar, 2018).

Equally crucial and potentially rewarding is the task of fine-tuning the methods and frameworks employed for interpreting intercultural exchange through the lens of the region's rich architectural remains from about the middle centuries of the first millennium onward. The modern period saw a revivalism of these cultural and civilizational linkages: Hindu temples were built in Southern Vietnam; visit to Vietnam by Rabindranath Tagore brought a new wind to the bilateral cultural and civilizational relations.

Renewed interests in cultural diplomacy have conferred a new and conspicuous aspect to India–Vietnam relations. With the resumption of Hinduism/Buddhism in Communist Vietnam, the country has imbibed an insightful connection with India, the cradle of Hinduism/Buddhism and Odisha, the home to several world-renowned Hindu/Buddhist monuments. In India's thriving partnership with Vietnam, Odisha has the prospective to seize the highest importance. India needs to reassess the ancient links of Odisha with Vietnam to improve the present-day collaboration in the spheres of academia, culture, trade, tourism, and commerce. Hence, these civilizational acquaintances should be used well to develop partnerships between the two countries and their people to higher zeniths (Mohanty, 2021).

Recognizing the significance of forging stronger linkages through people-to-people contacts, the two countries' leaders made significant announcements in the domain of culture, during the bilateral Virtual Summit on December 21, 2020. These include three new development partnership projects in heritage conservation in Vietnam (F-block of Temple at My Son; Dong Duong Buddhist Monastery in Quang Nam Province; and Nhan Cham Tower in Phu Yen Province). Another bilateral project for preparing an encyclopedia on India–Vietnam civilizational and cultural relations has been announced. There is also interest in Vietnam about India's films and festivals. Additionally, sports events can be organized to encourage the young generation of Vietnamese and support them with scholarships, improving public relations and religious tourism in Vietnam, and finally, people-to-people relations and city to city cooperation.

To promote India–Vietnam cultural cooperation in the coming years so that culture can be used as a tool to strengthen bilateral Comprehensive Strategic Partnership, a few suggestions include:

Firstly, leaders and governments of the two countries should continue to give weight to the cultural aspect in bilateral ties both at the level of leaders and among the people. The two countries' governments should promote Indian studies in Vietnam and Vietnamese studies in India by approving research projects on India/Vietnam in each country and opportunities for travel. This is also the solution to the issue of lack of accurate information about each other's culture and ideology.

Secondly, research institutions and universities should take the initiative in strengthening research exchange programs and organizing academic conferences to promote mutual understanding. In this context, institutions such as the Institute for Indian and Southwest Asian Studies; Vietnam Academy of Social Sciences, Vietnam; Centre for Vietnam Studies, and various think tanks in India and Vietnam have vital roles.

Thirdly, the two sides should also advertise about each other's culture through media such as TV and Web sites. More Indian films should be selected to show in Vietnam to help Vietnamese audiences better understand Indian culture. Vietnam should also select good Vietnamese movies to showcase in India. In recent years, the situation has improved as more Indian films are screened on Vietnamese television channels, yet more can be done!

8.3 Conclusion

Given that the world order is in a state of flux, the United States is declining "relatively," and China is not yet in a position to emerge as the leader multipolarity will prevail. Hence, in the near to medium term, the international situation will be characterized by the chaos of "no polarity," "Warring States," and "transition," with cooperation between major countries becoming more complex. This presents an opportunity for India and Vietnam to come together through trilaterals or mini-laterals, to engage through political, strategic, security, defense, cultural, economic, education, science, technological, and strategic pursuits. Speaking at a webinar, Prof. DeCastro underlined China's gray zone operations in the SCS with multiple layers of vessels to intimidate the littoral states; hence, Vietnam could work together with its friends and major powers of the region—Japan, South Korea, Australia, and India—along with the US. He also mentioned that China is following the game of *GO* rather than chess which implies that China intends to win without a war. Evidently, China follows Sun Tzu's Art of War and the notion of *Chi*. It follows the maxim of Sun Tzu that states, "The supreme art of war is to subdue the enemy without fighting" and the statecraft based on power through the water. With the notion of Chi, China believes that there is a constant change in the dynamics of state relations. Chinese would rather capture the resources, the army, and the kingdom of the enemy intact, instead of destroying resources as in a war. This can only be achieved through the incremental slow moves designed to improve its diplomatic and strategic position. Hence, the bilateral engagement of India and Vietnam will be tethered to minilateral and multilateral alignments.[17]

At the bilateral level, opportunities and challenges exist in all areas of bilateral cooperation. India has had several achievements in the S&T sector, such as in space and IT. Cooperation in these fields would help capacity building in Vietnam. There are significant learning opportunities for India as well, especially in areas such as agriculture, health governance, construction of smart cities, manufacturing of electronics, electric vehicles, and production and export of textiles. Moreover, bilateral investment and trade present significant opportunities. India and Vietnam should establish a bilateral trade agreement that helps overcome current trade barriers and bring about more effective economic cooperation. Even as the two countries rely on FDI, trade, and tourism as key drivers for growth, political stability and security are equally important (Marwah & Ramanayake, 2019: 414). Vietnam must be embedded in India's Act East Policy as a strategic partner; enhancing people-to-people exchanges through joint research, military cooperation, and joint initiatives for the capacity building would result in a more enhanced Indian presence in the region. India must become a true Comprehensive Strategic Partner in Vietnam's vision to become a high middle-income country by 2030 and a developed economy by 2045.

It is pertinent to conclude here with remarks by Ambassador Chau regarding future cooperation during the times of the pandemic, "To the moment we must admit that the pandemic has deeply affected all countries and the whole world. It forced us to think, to live, to work, and to interact differently. Economically, trade flow was disrupted, and the implementation of many investment projects has been delayed or prolonged. The two prime ministers worked out a Joint Vision for the future development and

---

[17] Prof Renato Cruz De Castro, International Studies Department, De La Salle University, Manila. Spoke on Rising Powers in Global Governance at the Association of Asia Scholars webinar on April 21, 2021.

our foreign ministers agree on the plan of action for 2021–2023. We will implement it with vigor, and I do believe that our partnership will continue to grow" (H.E. Chau interview). In the last week of August 2021, Vietnam received supplies of oxygen cylinders and concentrators for COVID relief. Vietnam also expects to receive India-made vaccines in the near future. This was mentioned by H.E. Chau. On the occasion of the National Day of Vietnam (September 2, 2021), a bust of the late President Ho Chi Minh was erected in New Delhi on September 1, 2021. The Ambassador H.E. Pham Sanh Chau also gave awards to people who had contributed to the strengthening of relations between both countries. He also spoke of the forthcoming visit of Prime Minister Pham Minh Chinh's visit to India in late 2021 to celebrate 50 years of the establishment of bilateral relations.

The bilateral relationship will witness key partnerships in defense, maritime, energy, and cybersecurity cooperation, even as the China factor will continue to require India to demonstrate greater calibration with Vietnam especially in the fields of maritime and offshore oil and gas cooperation.

Note

1. E-boarding passes (44%), touchless lavatories (43%), contactless journeys from airports to hotels (40%), no more middle seats in transportation (36%), and digital health passports (35%) are some of the new ideas which global travelers hope to see implemented in the near future, https://travelmail.in/roa dshow-in-delhi-vietnam-a-charming-destination-for-indian-tourists/; accessed on September 19, 2020. Blackbox Research, data provider Dynata, and language partner Language Connect, *Unravel Travel: Fear & Possibilities in a Post Coronavirus (COVID-19) World,* examine the sentiments, preferences, and expectations of 10,195 people across 17 countries regarding travel in a post-COVID-19 world. For details, see http://travelspan.in/unravel-travel-global-survey-finds-asians-most-confident-towards-travelling-in-the-new-normal/.

References

Basu, N. (2020, December 21). https://theprint.in/diplomacy/south-china-sea-defence-cooperation-what-india-vietnam-discussed-at-virtual-summit/571352/

Binh, L. H., & Thu, T. M. (2020). ISSUE: 2020 No. 77; Why the Mekong Matters to ASEAN: A perspective from Vietnam. https://www.iseas.edu.sg/wp-content/uploads/2020/06/ISEAS_Perspective 2020_77.pdf

CGI, HCMC. (2021). https://www.cgihcmc.gov.in/news_detail/?newsid=104. Accessed on March 31, 2021.

Dabla-Norris, E., & Zhang, Y. S. (2021). Vietnam: Successfully navigating the pandemic, IMF Asia and Pacific Department, March 10, 2021. https://www.imf.org/en/News/Articles/2021/03/09/na0 31021-vietnam-successfully-navigating-the-pandemic

Dhar, P. P. (2018). Monuments, motifs, myths: Architecture and its transformations in early India and Southeast Asia. In P. P. Dhar (Ed.), *Cultural and civilisational links between India and Southeast Asia* (Chapter 19) (pp. 325–345). Palgrave Macmillan. (Vol. 10.1007/97).

EIU. (2021). Rising star: Vietnam's role in Asia's shifting supply chains. https://www.thestar.com.my/aseanplus/aseanplus-news/2020/10/24/vietnam-asean-smart-cities-is-the-way-forward-to-the-future

IBEF. (2021a). https://www.ibef.org/blogs/leather-and-footwear-industry-huge-potential-for-growth. Shri P.R. Aqeel Ahmed, Chairman, CLE; February 25, 2021. Accessed on March 31, 2021.

IBEF. (2021b). https://www.ibef.org/blogs/india-is-set-to-become-an-alternative-investment-des tination-for-electronics-manufacturers-replacing-china. IBEF Knowledge Center, March 24, 2021. Accessed on March 31, 2021.

IBEF Knowledge Center. (2021). https://www.ibef.org/blogs/revitalising-india-s-smart-city-mis sion. March 31, 2021. Accessed on March 31, 2021.

India–Vietnam Joint Vision for Peace, Prosperity and People. https://mea.gov.in/bilateral-docume nts.htm?dtl/33324/India__Vietnam_Joint_Vision_for_Peace_Prosperity_and_People

India's National Security Strategy. (2019). https://manifesto.inc.in/pdf/national_security_strategy_gen_hooda.pdf

InvestOdisha. (2021). Odisha Fisheries Policy, 2015, Government of Odisha. https://investodisha.gov.in/sea-food-processing/. Accessed on April 7, 2021.

Jha, L. K. (2021). The print. https://theprint.in/economy/imf-projects-11-5-growth-rate-for-india-in-2021-only-country-with-double-digit-growth/592698/. Accessed on March 22, 2021.

Lei Ravelo, J. (2021, March 18). https://www.devex.com/news/covid-19-vaccine-developer-in-vie tnam-willing-to-share-data-99413. Accessed on April 7, 2021.

Le Thu, H. (2020). September 30, 2020. https://carnegieendowment.org/2020/09/30/rough-waters-ahead-for-vietnam-china-relations-pub-82826

Maddison, A. (2001). World economy, Development Centre of the Organisation for Economic Co-operation and Development, Paris, France.

Marwah, R., & Ramanayake, S. S. (2019). The development trajectories of Thailand and Sri Lanka: A comparative analysis. *Millennial Asia, 10*(3), 395–416.

McKinsey. (2020). September 9, 2020. https://www.mckinsey.com/featured-insights/asia-pacific/what-will-it-take-to-achieve-vietnams-long-term-growth-aspirations

Mohanty, A. (2021). https://www.indiavietnam.com/html/articles6.html; accessed on April 2, 2021

Mukhopadhyay, A. (2021). Post-pandemic economic recovery: Seven priorities for India. *ORF Occasional Paper No. 295*, January 2021, Observer Research Foundation.

Prasad, J. (2020, July 6). https://www.thehindu.com/opinion/op-ed/more-expansion-further-isolat ion/article32015849.ece

PTI. (2019). https://www.business-standard.com/article/pti-stories/ovl-seeks-2-year-extension-for-exploring-vietnamese-oil-block-119090200384_1.html. September 2, 2019. Accessed on April 4, 2021.

PWC Report. (2014). p. 13. https://www.pwc.in/assets/pdfs/future-of-india/future-of-india-invest ors.pdf

Reddy, K., & Subash, S. (2021, January 13). Building a $5-trillion economy. https://indianexp ress.com/article/opinion/columns/india-economy-5-trillion-covid-china-jobs-unemployment-7145152/

Reuters. (2021, March 13). https://www.businesstoday.in/current/world/quad-leaders-agree-to-send-1-billion-vaccines-across-asia-by-end-2022/story/433713.html. Accessed on April 7, 2021.

Schaag, S. (n.d.). https://www.semi.org/en/about/Vietnam%E2%80%99s_Growing_Electronics_I ndustry. Accessed on March 31, 2021.

Sean. (2021, March 22). https://www.gizmochina.com/2021/03/22/huawei-zte-qualify-india-tru sted-5g-gear-vendors/

Source: Vietnamplus.vn. http://asemconnectvietnam.gov.vn/default.aspx?ID1=2&ZID1=8&ID8= 104329. January 28, 2021. Accessed on March 31, 2021.

Suneja, K. (2021, March 29). https://economictimes.indiatimes.com/news/economy/foreign-trade/india-against-asean-in-supply-chain-trilateral/articleshow/81739784.cms?utm_source=conten tofinterest&utm_medium=text&utm_campaign=cppst

The World Bank. (2020). https://www.worldbank.org/en/country/india/overview. October 8, 2020.

Thongtanxa. (2020). https://moc.gov.vn/en/news/64356/india-funds-seven-water-projects-in-mek ong-delta-.aspx. Accessed on April 8, 2021.

Trivedi, S. (2018). The Pioneer, 2018; Why Vietnam matters? Sonu Trivedi. https://www.dailypion eer.com/2018/columnists/why-vietnam-matters.html

Vu, V.-H., Soong, J.-J., & Nguyen, K.-N. (2021). Vietnam's perceptions and strategies toward China's belt and road initiative expansion: Hedging with resisting. *The Chinese Economy, 54*(1), 56–68. https://doi.org/10.1080/10971475.2020.1809818

World Bank Group and Ministry of Planning and Investment of Vietnam. (2016). Vietnam 2035: Toward Prosperity, Creativity, Equity, and Democracy, Washington, DC.

Lightning Source UK Ltd.
Milton Keynes UK
UKHW021041120123
415164UK00001B/11

9 789811 678240